Unofficial Guide to
FamilySearch.org

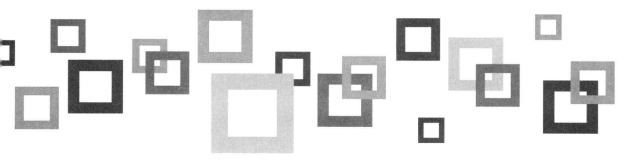

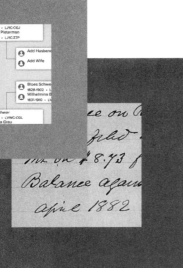

Unofficial Guide to
FamilySearch.org

How to Find Your Family History on the World's Largest Free Genealogy Website

Dana McCullough

**FAMILY
TREE
BOOKS**

Cincinnati, Ohio
shopfamilytree.com

CONTENTS

Since I was a young girl, I've always believed that family is important. I was first exposed to genealogy research in the fifth grade during a school assignment to research my family history. I put together a video presentation I called "Ancestral Journal" that showcased what little I knew then about my family history. The video showed me playing the role of a news anchor, reading stories I learned from interviewing relatives about their childhood memories, sifting through family photographs, and gathering family heirlooms and old letters from relatives.

Today, I believe this early experience was a foreshadowing of what was to come in my life. I graduated from college with a degree in journalism (the print kind, not the broadcast kind) and started working at *Family Tree Magazine*. While at the magazine, my interest in researching my family history blossomed. It was also where I was first introduced to FamilySearch.org **<www.familysearch.org>**.

Over the years, FamilySearch.org has become my go-to genealogy research website. It's usually the first place I turn to research records for a specific ancestor for two reasons: It's free, and it has an extensive (and continually growing) digital records collection.

FamilySearch.org is where I've found federal and state census records and transcriptions for both my ancestors and my husband's. It's where I found the naturalization record for my great-grandfather, who immigrated to America from Italy in the early 1900s. It's also where I've found birth, death, and marriage records for several ancestors. In addition, because of FamilySearch.org, I learned that my grandmother worked as a maid before she got married, and I learned the year that some of the relatives on my dad's side of the family came to America. All of the records and information I have found have provided clues to my ancestors' lives and given me a deeper sense of who my ancestors were, as well as when and where they lived.

Through my work with *Family Tree Magazine* as an assistant editor and later as a freelance writer and editor, I learned that many genealogists (especially beginners) don't know about FamilySearch.org—or their knowledge only scratches the surface. Although it's got billions of records, FamilySearch.org is a hidden gem, an underutilized resource. I've come to find this online resource extremely valuable, and because of that, I want to share my knowledge and experience of this website with other genealogy enthusiasts. It's a website I think every genealogist should know about and use.

As you research your own family, I hope the tips and insights in this book help you fine-tune your searches to locate a genealogy gold mine of records for your ancestors. Of course, any technology or website can change rapidly, and FamilySearch.org is no exception. From my research conducted for this book, I know that FamilySearch.org is continually working to enhance its website and the search features it offers. Although certain features, search options, and record collections may change after publication, the strategies included should be adaptable to new iterations of the site and search forms. Further, the insights and success stories provided by genealogists throughout the book can serve as inspiration to start (or continue) your ancestor search on FamilySearch.org.

I hope you enjoy the book and find it useful. Happy searching!

Dana McCullough
<www.danamccullough.com>
Milwaukee, Wisconsin
April 2015

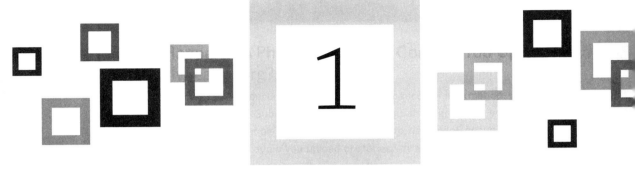

Getting Started

former president Jimmy Carter was once quoted as saying, "We've uncovered some embarrassing ancestors in the not-too-distant past. Some horse thieves, and some people killed on Saturday nights. One of my relatives, unfortunately, was even in the newspaper business."

As this quote illustrates, you never know where your genealogy research journey will take you or whom you'll find in your family tree. That said, FamilySearch.org is a great place to start your journey. This free website, operated by The Church of Jesus Christ of Latter-day Saints (LDS), has more than 3.5 billion names in searchable collections. Each month, it adds another thirty-five million records. This amazing amount of online records is largely thanks to FamilySearch, the genealogy arm of the LDS church, and its volunteer indexers and digitizers around the world.

WHAT'S ON FAMILYSEARCH.ORG?

FamilySearch.org's main treasures are its family trees, historical records, genealogies, and digitized books. It also has user-submitted "Memories," which are photos, stories, and documents posted to the website by registered users. Here's a quick overview of the most important categories and features of FamilySearch.org.

Family Tree

Under the Family Tree tab on the home page (and after registering with the website), you can create an online family tree. For each person on your tree, you can add vital information such as birth date and place, christening date and place, death date and place, and burial date and place. You also can add other details about the person's life.

Historical Records

These are the gold mine for genealogists on FamilySearch.org. The website offers thousands of historical records collections (and growing) covering more than ninety countries. Records here cover everything from censuses and vital records to probate, court, immigration, and military records, as well as some miscellaneous school records, church records, and city directories. The earliest records date primarily from the 1300s, but some village records for Japan date as far back as 709 and church records from Switzerland date back to 1277. Some records are searchable, while others have not yet been indexed. Similarly, some records have transcriptions only, while others have digital images on FamilySearch.org or link to digital images on partner websites.

User-Submitted Genealogies

The original searchable data on FamilySearch.org came from information collected from the Ancestral File, International Genealogical Index (IGI), and Pedigree Resource File (see "The Roots of FamilySearch.org" box). Today you can search user-submitted genealogies from the Ancestral File and Pedigree Resource File under the Search tab, then the Genealogies link (or go to **<www.familysearch.org/family-trees>**). The information contained in user-submitted genealogies is considered a secondary source, so be sure to confirm the information you find in primary sources (such as an official record or record copy).

Family History Books

You can search more than 150 thousand digitized genealogies, family histories, county and local histories, genealogy periodicals, gazetteers, and more. This collection contains digitized publications from ten libraries, including such major genealogy libraries as FamilySearch's Salt Lake City-based Family History Library; the Allen County Public Library in Fort Wayne, Indiana; Houston Public Library's Clayton Library Center for Genealogical Research in Texas; and the Mid-Continent Public Library's Midwest Genealogy Center in Independence, Missouri.

The Roots of FamilySearch.org

FamilySearch.org didn't always have billions of online records. The website started out in 1999 with a database containing the Ancestral File, the IGI, and Pedigree Resource File. You could search the website, which had roughly four hundred million names at the time, by name and an event and year range. Most of the information came from user-submitted genealogies. These legacy resources are still available on the site.

- The **Ancestral File** contains millions of births, deaths, and marriages submitted by LDS members. These records are known for containing pre-1500s "research" without source citations. No more records are being added to this source.

- The **Pedigree Resource File**, formerly available only on CD or DVD, contains two hundred million records submitted by users. Entries typically include source notes and citations, but FamilySearch does not verify the accuracy of the information in the Pedigree Resource File, and when many files were created, corrections were not accepted. Thus, people may have submitted information multiple times, creating duplicate files. You can still submit pedigree files to be added to the Pedigree Resource File, which is now searchable on FamilySearch.org (see more about this in chapters 2 and 4).

- The **IGI** was originally created on microfiche in 1973. The index contains entries of vital events such as births, baptisms, marriages, and deaths. Throughout the years, people from the genealogical community extracted and contributed vital-records information from vital records and church records, and LDS members submitted information about their ancestors to the index. Duplicates of records in the index are common. The index grew until it was discontinued at the end of 2008.

FamilySearch Wiki

This is the destination for genealogy newbies on FamilySearch.org. It has genealogy how-to articles so you can learn more about available records for certain locations. You can search more than eighty thousand articles in the wiki by location or topic.

FamilySearch Catalog

The FamilySearch Catalog allows you to search the holdings of the Family History Library. If you can't find the records you want online, you may be able to locate the genealogical records you seek on microfilm or other publications held at the library. If you find a microfilm you want to look at, you can order it to view at a local FamilySearch Center near you; FamilySearch operates thousands of these centers around the world.

Memories

Under this tab on the site, you can submit your own photos, stories, documents, and audio recordings. You also can search the "Memories" that others have posted.

Indexing

You'll use this portion of the website only if you decide to become a volunteer indexer for FamilySearch. Under the Indexing tab, you can read an overview about how indexing for FamilySearch works and find indexing projects to get involved with. More than 450 record-indexing projects are ongoing. In 2014, indexers completed more than 160 million records.

GENEALOGY BASICS

Before jumping onto FamilySearch.org to research ancestors, you'll need to do a little groundwork. After all, you need an idea of whom you're looking for. It's also helpful to know (or have an educated guess about) roughly when and where your ancestors lived.

Start With What You Know

Building your family tree is sort of like building a house. First, you need a foundation so you can build the frame. Once the foundation and frame are there, you can go to the next step, until ultimately you get to the nitty-gritty finishing details.

When you build your family tree, you need to set the foundation by pulling together the information you already know. Write down the names and birth dates of your parents, grandparents, and other relatives you know. If you know their birthplaces, marriage dates, or any other details about their lives, write those down, too. As you figure out what you already know, fill out a pedigree chart (image **A**, also called an ancestor chart) with the information you have. Use the blank Five-Generation Ancestor Chart in appendix C or download one for free from *Family Tree Magazine* **<www.familytreemagazine.com/ info/basicforms>**. Your personal knowledge is the foundation, and the pedigree chart is like the frame of a house.

As you research your family tree, you'll be able to add more and more details for each ancestor, sort of like adding the finishing touches on a house—drywall, then paint, then trim. But unlike a house, most genealogies are never "finished": There's always something more family historians want to discover, whether it's tracing the family line back yet another generation or understanding more about the time and place their ancestors lived in.

Once you've written down everything you know, start gathering documents to confirm what you know. Start with documents you have in your home, such as

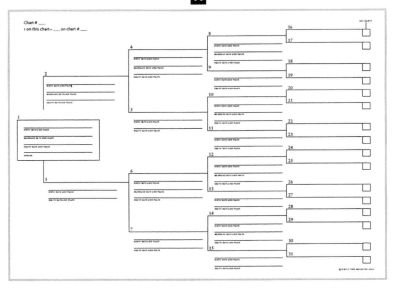

A

- baptism and confirmation certificates
- birth, marriage, and death certificates
- diaries and journals
- family Bibles
- heirlooms and artifacts
- newspaper clippings
- old family photographs
- school report cards and yearbooks
- scrapbooks and wedding albums

Next, talk to your relatives—parents, grandparents, aunts, uncles, and first cousins. Find out if any of them have researched any of the family lines already. It's amazing what some relatives may have collected over the years. For example, my great-aunt Elgene (on my dad's side) kept genealogy records on the entire family line. She was thrilled when I asked her about it and was pleased to share it with "the next generation." Elgene let me photocopy everything she had—it filled a two-inch-thick three-ring binder. She had information about at least six generations, with all the family groups, as well as photos and marriage and death announcements from local newspapers. She also had made notes on family group sheets about family stories she had heard over the years. It was a wealth of information that would have taken me years to uncover on my own. It also has helped me focus my research because she'd marked down some vital-records dates that I didn't have. Knowing those dates has helped me narrow my search for official vital-records documents on FamilySearch.org and other websites.

If any of your relatives have home sources (think vital-records certificates, baptismal certificates, yearbooks, diaries, tombstone photos, old family photographs, etc.) or have conducted genealogy research, ask them if they will send you a copy of the materials they have. You never know what gems they'll share with you.

Interview Relatives

After you've gathered all the documents and materials you can, interview your relatives to gain more clues for records and stories to research. Start with your eldest relatives first. I once made the mistake of intending to interview my great-aunt Ann (on my mom's side), but kept procrastinating because my busy work and personal life got in the way. I had a lot of questions for her about what it was like to grow up with my grandfather (her brother). Unfortunately, before I could ask her any questions, she passed away. So make it a priority to interview your relatives. First, ask your relatives about their own lives, with questions such as

- What are your favorite childhood memories?
- What were your parents like growing up?
- What was it like growing up with your brothers/sisters?
- What was school like?
- Did you have any special family traditions?
- How did you meet your spouse?
- What was it like to live through _____ ? (insert a historic event in the blank, such as the Great Depression, World War II, etc.)

Next, ask them what they know about others in the family. Some good questions for gleaning helpful family history include

- What do you know about the different generations of the family?
- What do you know about Grandma or Grandpa's childhood?
- What stories did your parents tell you?
- Do you know when the family immigrated to America?
- Do you know where the family has lived throughout the generations?
- What did your parents do for work?

Take notes as you interview relatives or record the interviews you conduct in person or via the phone. The app Saving Memories Forever **<www.savingmemoriesforever.com>** can help you get started. It suggests interview questions to ask about different times in your relative's life, and it has an audio recorder you can use to record the interview.

Genealogy and The Church of Jesus Christ of Latter-day Saints

The world's largest free genealogy website is part of an even bigger storehouse of family history: the massive genealogical archive of The Church of Jesus Christ of Latter-day Saints. On top of the billions of online records at FamilySearch.org, the church maintains a family history research collection encompassing 2.4 million film reels, one million microfiche, 356 thousand books, and 4,500 periodicals documenting ancestors from around the world. You might call it the "great-grandmother lode." And it's all accessible to the public free of charge through the church's Salt Lake City-based Family History Library and more than 4,600 local branch FamilySearch Centers worldwide.

So how did the church get all these materials? Its genealogy arm, FamilySearch—formerly called the Genealogical Society of Utah—has been traveling the world since 1938 to microfilm genealogical records in archives, courthouses, churches, and libraries (today, records are imaged digitally). FamilySearch has filmed in 132 countries, territories, and possessions to date. The original reels of microfilm and sheets of microfiche are stored in the secure, climate-controlled Granite Mountain Records Vault near Salt Lake City (shown); copies of most are in the Family History Library.

In 1998, FamilySearch began digitizing the microfilm and microfiche in the vault. Partnerships with genealogical and historical societies have sped up the acquisition of new records, and volunteer indexers are making many of them searchable online in FamilySearch.org's free Historical Records collection (see appendix B for more on FamilySearch Indexing).

For those who aren't LDS, you might wonder why the church does all this. To understand the motivations, it helps to know a little about the church's roots. The story begins in 1827 near Palmyra, New York, when a young man named Joseph Smith, acting on a vision of the angel Moroni, claimed he'd dug up golden plates engraved with mysterious writings. He published a translation as the Book of Mormon in 1830, and his followers organized into what became The Church of Jesus Christ of Latter-day Saints. In search of an American "New Jerusalem," the group moved to Ohio, Missouri, and then Illinois, picking up members and being run off by locals along the way.

In Nauvoo, Illinois, Smith espoused the practice of "plural marriage" if commanded by God; he might have had up to thirty wives, though he publicly denied it. (The church officially renounced polygamy in 1890.) After a rift led several former members to establish a competing church and newspaper, Smith was charged with inciting riots and other crimes. He and his brother were killed while awaiting trial in a Carthage, Illinois, jail in 1844. Smith's successor, Brigham Young, led the remaining followers to Utah Territory and incorporated the church.

Smith's theology of family relations is the source of Mormons' intense interest in genealogy. Church doctrine states that "saving ordinances"—which include baptism, confirmation, endowment, and marriage—be made available to everyone who's ever lived. Latter-day Saints, also called Mormons, do genealogy research to identify their ancestors and arrange for ordinances to be performed in a temple by proxy, with a living person standing in for the deceased person. They believe souls are free to accept or reject these ordinances. Souls who accept are sealed to their families for eternity. The church began creating its collection of genealogical resources to facilitate that process.

Because family history is so central to its core beliefs, the church aims to promote genealogy beyond the ranks of its members. Non-Mormons are welcome to use the church's genealogy resources and facilities no matter their motivation or religion. Proselytizing is prohibited, and the staff and volunteers are always ready with helpful research advice. It's possible that a Mormon with whom you share an ancestor might research that ancestor and submit him or her for ordinances or "temple work," but your relatives won't be posthumously baptized simply by virtue of your using FamilySearch resources.

—*Diane Haddad*

Organize Your Records

As any genealogist knows, as you start delving further and further into the past, you'll start to accumulate piles of paper and countless digital files. Before the piles and files overwhelm you, it's good to get an organization plan in place.

PAPER RECORDS

There are many ways to organize your paper files. I use binders to hold all my printed copies of records, pedigree charts, and family group sheets. My binders are organized by divider tabs labeled with each family surname. I find family group sheets are particularly helpful to jot down important notes in an ancestral couple's life. They also help me keep all the members of a family straight, since a family group sheet includes a place to list a couple and their children, plus vital events in their lives. You can download a free family group sheet at **<www.familytreemagazine.com/info/basicforms>**, or make copies of the blank family group sheet in appendix C.

Other genealogists use color-coded file folders to organize each family line according to surname and store these folders in a file cabinet. For more ideas on how to organize your paper files, see *The Organized Family Historian* by Ann Carter Fleming (Thomas Nelson) or the free e-book *Family Tree Tips: 23 Secrets to Organize Your Genealogy* **<www.familytreemagazine.com/family-tree-tips-23-secrets-to-organize-your-genealogy>**.

DIGITAL RECORDS

Organizing digital files is becoming increasingly complicated as we conduct genealogy research on multiple devices such as laptops, tablets, and smartphones. I organize my digital genealogy records—census record images and transcriptions, PDFs of vital records, heirloom family photos, images of military draft registration records, and more—in a designated Genealogy folder on my computer. Within the Genealogy folder, I have folders for each surname I'm researching, along with a folder for Record Requests (copies of letters or completed forms used for requesting official records). Within each surname folder, I have a folder for each record type such as censuses, deaths/obituaries, immigration, marriages, naturalizations, maps, and military. I put photos of ancestors I'm researching within surname folders as well. I back up my files periodically on an external hard drive.

Other genealogists have different digital record-organization strategies, and you may find that a different organization method than the one I use works best for you. The key when organizing your digital files is to keep your organization scheme consistent. Name your folders similarly, and give each file a consistent name. For example, a file name might be *schmidt_harold_WWII_draftregistration.jpg*. This file name uses the last name, first name, and a description of the record. Some genealogists like to include the record date

FamilySearch-Compatible Products and Services

FamilySearch collaborates and partners with several external products and services to enhance the website users' experience, including apps for searching records, creating charts, using genealogy software, and posting photos and stories. Below is a list of some of its current partners. For a complete list of more than fifty apps that work with FamilySearch.org, you can search the FamilySearch App Gallery **<www.familysearch.org/apps>**.

- **Web:** FamilySearch.org is compatible with websites such as AllMyCousins, BillionGraves, Puzzilla, RootsMapper, and TreeSeek among other tools for accessing family trees and records sources.

- **Windows software:** Among the family tree software programs for Windows PCs that are compatible with FamilySearch.org are RootsMagic, RootsMagic Essentials, Ancestral Quest, and Charting Companion. In addition, the Kodak Web uploader for FamilySearch, a picture saving and document scanning tool, is compatible on Windows computers.

- **Mac OS X software:** Only two Mac software applications are compatible with FamilySearch.org: MacFamilyTree and Evidentia.

- **Mobile applications:** Android and iOS apps are compatible with FamilySearch.org. For example, RootsMagic (for iOS and for Android), BillionGraves for iOS, Legacy Mobile for iOS, FamilyMap for iOS, LegacyMobile for iOS, and Are We Related? for Android are all compatible.

For a full list of products and services, see **<www.familysearch.org/products>**.

and/or location of the record in the file name as well. Again, the key to file names is to be consistent and use the same file-naming scheme for all files so they will be easy to find again later.

GENEALOGY SOFTWARE

Many genealogists use family history-specific software to organize and track their research and build their family trees. Popular genealogy programs include Family Tree Maker, RootsMagic, Legacy Family Tree, and MacFamilyTree. Some software is compatible with FamilySearch.org (see the sidebar for details).

For more tips on organizing your genealogy records, see the FamilySearch Wiki at **<www.familysearch.org/learn/wiki/en/Organize_your_genealogy>** or my *Family Tree Magazine* article "9 Habits of Highly Organized Genealogists" at **<www.familytreemagazine. com/article/9-habits-of-highly-organized-genealogists>**. To learn more about organizing ancestor photos, consult *How to Archive Family Photos* by Denise May Levenick (Family Tree Books).

Create a Research Plan

Now that you've gathered information and documents from your home collection and from relatives and have set up your organization method, it's time to start creating your plan of attack. After all, it's impossible to research everything at once.

Choose one family line to research—perhaps the one you know the most about. Identify which relative(s) you want to research first, and make a list of the records about that person you want to search for. As you make the list, think about the time period in which the person lived to determine what records might be available. For example, if you choose to research an ancestor born in the United States in 1780, you'll likely find that no official birth record exists because most US states did not begin official vital-record keeping until the mid-1800s or early 1900s. Or if your ancestor was born in 1905, she would appear only in 1910 and later US censuses.

Keeping the person's birth and death dates in mind can help you narrow the window for the records you'll want to search for on FamilySearch.org. It also will help you determine if a specific historical records collection is worth your time to search, because many of the collections list the years the records cover. For example, if your ancestor is from Virginia, you may notice that FamilySearch.org has a searchable collection of nearly two million records called Virginia, Births and Christenings, 1853–1917. If your Virginia ancestor was born in 1825, he won't be in this collection. In contrast, if your ancestor was born in Virginia in 1870, it would be a great collection to search.

Track Your Searches

When I first started researching my family history, I didn't track my Internet searches for ancestors. What a mistake! Eventually, I found myself on FamilySearch.org having déjà vu as I saw the same search results again and again. I had electronic copies of record images and transcriptions from FamilySearch.org in my genealogy folders on my computer, but I didn't have an easy way to track what searches I had already done and what records I had already found.

I decided to get organized. I started using a records checklist for records available during each ancestor's lifetime. I started with the *Family Tree Magazine* Records Checklist (see appendix C), then created my own checklist for each state I was researching. Many of my ancestors lived in Iowa and Illinois, so I created a checklist for Iowa ancestors' records (image **B**). The checklist includes state censuses, types of vital records that might be available, federal censuses available, and a list of miscellaneous records I could check

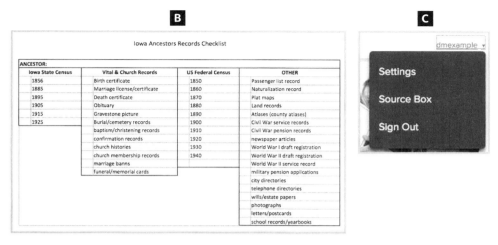

B

Iowa Ancestors Records Checklist			
ANCESTOR:			
Iowa State Census	**Vital & Church Records**	**US Federal Census**	**OTHER**
1856	Birth certificate	1850	Passenger list record
1885	Marriage license/certificate	1860	Naturalization record
1895	Death certificate	1870	Plat maps
1905	Obituary	1880	Land records
1915	Gravestone picture	1890	Atlases (county atlases)
1925	Burial/cemetery records	1900	Civil War service records
	baptism/christening records	1910	Civil War pension records
	confirmation records	1920	newspaper articles
	church histories	1930	World War I draft registration
	church membership records	1940	World War II draft registration
	marriage banns		World War II service record
	funeral/memorial cards		military pension applications
			city directories
			telephone directories
			wills/estate papers
			photographs
			letters/postcards
			school records/yearbooks

C

(such as passenger lists, naturalization records, property maps, land records, military service and pension records, newspaper articles, city directories, school yearbooks, etc.). I started the years listed for census records based on the dates my ancestors lived.

I also started tracking the collections and search terms I used each time I spent a few minutes (or hours) searching for an ancestor on FamilySearch.org. I print off a form and use it each time I search. Before I search for an ancestor, I check to see if the search has already been completed and look at the notes on what I found. (The FamilySearch.org Research Tracking Worksheet in appendix C can help you track your searches.)

Cite Your Sources

This is another area where I lacked skill and interest when I first started my genealogy research. Later, however, I began to wonder: Where did I get this census record? On what website did I find this vital-record transcription or World War II draft registration card?

I realized that citing my sources was as important as tracking my online searches. In fact, citing sources is another way to avoid repeating the same searches: When I look at a record I already have, I know where it's from and don't need to search that source again. Alternatively, if I want to dig a little deeper and research other ancestors listed on a particular record (such as a parent or spouse listed on a marriage certificate), I can go back to the website where I found the original record to begin my search for that relative.

FamilySearch.org has a great built-in tool to help you cite the sources you find. It's called the Source Box. After you log in to your account, you can find the Source Box in the upper right corner. Just click on the down arrow next to your display name, then select the Source Box link from the drop-down menu (image **C**).

Within your Source Box, you'll see options for organizing sources into folders and creating new sources. When you view search results and find a record you want to

Saving Sources From Other Websites to FamilySearch.org

If you use other websites in addition to FamilySearch.org to research your family history, you can keep your source citations all in one spot by using the Tree Connect bookmarklet at **<recordsseek.com>**. Tree Connect lets you save website URLs as well as images or other media. The tool works on your computer, tablet, or smartphone so you can use it no matter where you're researching—from home or on the go.

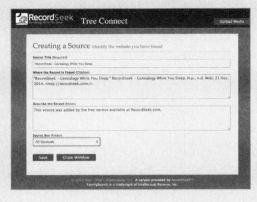

To get started, simply drag and drop the Tree Connect button to your web browser's Bookmarks Bar. Sign in with your FamilySearch.org account credentials. When you're on other websites, click the Tree Source bookmark and enter the source title, the source citation information (where you found the record), and a description of the record. In the drop-down box, select the folder in your FamilySearch.org Source Box where you would like the source saved. Later, you can attach the source to your FamilySearch Family Tree (see chapter 2).

save, you can choose to save it to your Source Box or attach it to your family tree on FamilySearch.org. Either option will save the record to your Source Box and allow you to easily access the record again later if you want to view it or print it for your paper files. We'll cover this in more depth in chapter 2.

SETTING UP YOUR
FAMILYSEARCH.ORG ACCOUNT

To take advantage of many convenient tools on FamilySearch.org, such as saving records to a Source Box, attaching records and source citations to individuals in your online family tree, and adding photos and other memories, you'll need to register for a free account.

Step-by-Step Instructions: Creating Your Account

Signing up for a free account is easy. Follow these steps.

1 LOCATE THE SIGN IN PAGE. On the home page **<www.familysearch.org>**, click the Free Account button.

2 **FILL IN THE REGISTRATION FORM.** You'll need to enter your name, a username, password, e-mail address (or phone number), your gender, your country, your birth date, and whether or not you're an LDS church member. You'll also need to enter a contact name, which is a public name that everyone can see and is displayed with any information you contribute to the site.

3 **READ THE SITE'S FINE PRINT.** Before you submit your registration information, read the website's Rights and Use Information (aka the Terms of Use) and Privacy Policy. If you agree to these terms, check the box at the bottom of the registration form and then click the Create an Account button.

4 **VERIFY YOUR ACCOUNT.** FamilySearch.org will send you an e-mail to verify your account, so check your e-mail and click the Complete Registration button in the e-mail. A thank-you web page should appear in your Web browser to indicate your account setup is complete.

1

2

3

4

Strong Passwords

When choosing a password for your account, use a strong password to protect your personal information. Strong passwords should have numbers and letters, uppercase and lowercase letters, and should not be a common name (especially your mother's maiden name—this is a genealogy site after all!). For tips on setting strong passwords, see the *PCMag* article "Password Protection: How to Create Strong Passwords" **<www.pcmag.com/article2/0,2817,2368484,00. asp>**, Boston University's "How to Choose a Strong Password" **<www.bu.edu/infosec/how-tos/how-to-choose-a-password>**, or Microsoft's advice **<windows.microsoft.com/en-us/ windows-vista/tips-for-creating-a-strong-password>**.

Privacy and Other Account Settings

After you set up your FamilySearch.org account, you'll want to check that the account settings are what you want them to be. You can adjust some privacy-related settings, contact settings, notifications from FamilySearch.org, connected accounts, and other preferences.

To view and/or set your account setting preferences, sign in to your FamilySearch.org account. Your username should appear in the top right-hand corner of the page. Click the username and select Settings from the drop-down menu.

GENERAL ACCOUNT SETTINGS

The first page you'll see when you select Settings is a general Account page. This page shows you the name you entered, your username, your contact/display name, birth date, gender, LDS member status, and a Helper Number. Next to your birth date, there's a check box to make this information public. If you want to keep your birth date private (which I would recommend for privacy reasons), do not check this box. The five-digit Helper Number you'll see is a number FamilySearch.org automatically assigned to you upon registering for the site. According to the website, "a helper number is an identification number that allows someone to use FamilySearch.org on behalf of someone else." In the general account settings, you also have the option to reset your password. If you make any changes to the settings here, click the Save Changes button at the bottom of the page before moving to a different page.

CONTACT

If desired, you can add your mobile phone number and street address to your account. This page has check boxes next to each piece of your contact information (e-mail, phone number, address, etc.). If you want to share your contact information publicly, check the box. If you want your contact information to remain private, do not check the box. If you make any changes to the Contact settings, click the Save Changes button at the bottom of the page before moving to a different page.

NOTIFICATIONS

This is where you can select what information you'd like FamilySearch.org to send you via e-mail. You can choose from five different communications: FamilySearch General Newsletter, Family History Consultants and Leaders, Weekly Updates to Ancestors I'm Watching, Family Tree Announcements, and the Indexing Newsletter. If you make any changes to selections here, click the Save Changes button before moving on to another page.

PREFERENCES

Under this tab, you can select the starting person for your family tree on FamilySearch.org. You are the starting person by default; however, you can change that by typing in the Person ID Number of the person you want to be the starting person of your tree. The Person ID Number is a seven-digit number with a hyphen in it, for example: KWCR-3JE. You also can set the preferred language for e-mails you receive from FamilySearch.org. As with the other settings tabs, click the Save Changes button if you make changes to any of the default settings here.

CONNECTED ACCOUNTS

This section shows any other accounts you have connected, such as FamilySearch partner services. For example, a benefit to LDS church members is that they get free access to Ancestry.com and other large subscription genealogy websites. Connections to those sites will appear under the Connected Accounts tab. For non-LDS church members, any tools from FamilySearch partner services you use may show up in this section (for example, if you use the Tree Connect bookmarklet mentioned earlier, it will appear under this tab in your account).

KEYS TO SUCCESS

★ Identify ancestors to research on FamilySearch.org by starting with what you know, gathering home sources, and interviewing relatives.

★ Set up a free FamilySearch.org account to take advantage of all the website's features and benefits. Create a strong password to protect your personal information.

★ Track your searches on FamilySearch.org and other websites so you don't duplicate efforts.

★ Use the Source Box to document and organize your FamilySearch.org finds.

GETTING STARTED CHECKLIST

Before You Begin
☐ Gather home sources (see list below).
☐ Talk to relatives and ask for home sources or genealogy information they have.
☐ Interview relatives (see list below).
☐ Fill out a five-generation ancestor chart (see appendix C).
☐ Fill out a family group sheet for each couple/family (see appendix C).
☐ Organize paper and digital file folders.
☐ Choose a genealogy software (if you plan to use one).
☐ Create your research plan.
☐ Create or download a record checklist.
☐ Track online searches (see appendix C for forms).
☐ Cite your sources when you find records.

Home Sources Gathered
☐ baptism and confirmation certificates
☐ birth certificates
☐ death certificates
☐ diaries and journals
☐ family Bibles
☐ heirlooms and artifacts
☐ marriage certificates
☐ newspaper clippings
☐ old family photographs
☐ school report cards and yearbooks
☐ scrapbooks and wedding albums
☐ wills
☐ _____
☐ _____
☐ _____

Relatives to Interview
Grandparents, parents, siblings, aunts, uncles, cousins
☐ _____
☐ _____
☐ _____
☐ _____
☐ _____
☐ _____
☐ _____
☐ _____
☐ _____
☐ _____
☐ _____
☐ _____
☐ _____

Questions to Ask Relatives
_____
_____
_____

The FamilySearch Family Tree

Family trees have always been a big part of FamilySearch.org. The first iteration of the website had searchable pedigrees submitted by LDS members and indexed from various vital records sources. In 2001, the "New FamilySearch" website allowed users to edit their family tree data, but this feature was only available to church members until 2009. In early 2013, this transitioned into what's now called the FamilySearch Family Tree—an online tool for anyone to put a family tree online along with other memorabilia, including photos, audio recordings, and stories.

In this chapter, we'll explore the ways you can create your free family tree on Family-Search.org, the items you can add to your family tree, how to search for ancestors in other family trees, and more.

WHAT'S IN THE FAMILYSEARCH FAMILY TREE?

Family trees on FamilySearch.org may contain a great deal of vital information on your ancestors. The amount of information varies depending on how much detail researchers have input in the tree listings. The credibility of the information varies as well, with some entries containing excellent source citations and others containing no source information at all.

When you log in to your FamilySearch.org account, you can view your own family tree (if you've created one), view individuals in your family tree and on other family trees, search for ancestors on others' family trees, and even "watch" people in your tree so you know when another user makes changes. Whether you're viewing a family tree you created or one someone else posted, the information you can view on each person remains consistent across all family trees. Let's explore what you can see for each person.

Person Details

Each person listed in a family tree has a Person page, with a Details tab that provides the basics on the ancestor. Each Person Details tab has several sections of information and tools (image **A**). Note that certain fields and features, namely Watch/Unwatch, Sources, Discussions, and Record Hints, do not appear for living people.

1 PHOTO

If a photo of the ancestor has been uploaded to FamilySearch.org, it will appear in the upper left, next to the ancestor's name and ID number.

2 WATCH/UNWATCH

At the top of the Person page, there's a link to Watch this person. By clicking on this link, the person will be added to your watch list, and you'll get notifications when updates to the person's entry are made. Once you click the Watch link, the Person page will show an Unwatch link you can click on to remove the individual from your watch list. To view your list of all the ancestors you are "watching," click the Family Tree tab, then select Lists, and a list will appear. You can sort the list by clicking on the Name or Vitals column heading. At the top of the page, click the Changes to People I'm Watching link to see what others have changed. You can hide any changes you made by clicking the Hide Changes I've Made check box.

3 ID NUMBER

Each person entered into a family tree on FamilySearch.org is automatically assigned a unique ID number. You'll find each ancestor's ID number under the ancestor's name.

4 LIFE SKETCH

This field, which can hold up to ten thousand characters (about fifteen hundred words), is not meant to hold your ancestor's entire life story. It's a place to provide a brief narrative overview about the person. You can write just about anything you want in this field, but keep in mind that you can add longer stories to the Memories tab of the person's record.

FamilySearch.org recommends writing in the third-person to describe the ancestor or the information on the page, including important facts that other relatives may not know

A

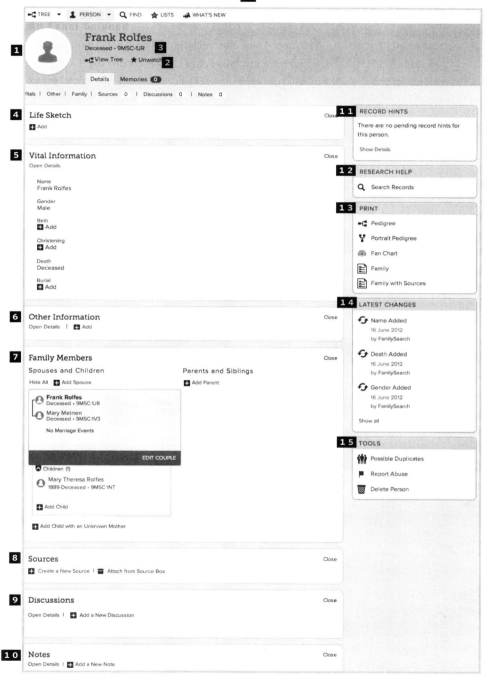

1 Frank Rolfes
Deceased • 9M5C-1JR **3**
⊷⊏ View Tree   ★ Unwatch **2**

Details   Memories **0**

Vitals | Other | Family | Sources **0** | Discussions **0** | Notes **0**

4 Life Sketch   Close
➕ Add

11 RECORD HINTS
There are no pending record hints for this person.
Show Details

5 Vital Information   Close
Open Details

Name
Frank Rolfes

Gender
Male

Birth
➕ Add

Christening
➕ Add

Death
Deceased

Burial
➕ Add

12 RESEARCH HELP
🔍 Search Records

13 PRINT
⊷⊏ Pedigree
🏺 Portrait Pedigree
🧠 Fan Chart
📄 Family
📄 Family with Sources

6 Other Information   Close
Open Details | ➕ Add

14 LATEST CHANGES
🔁 Name Added
16 June 2012
by FamilySearch

🔁 Death Added
16 June 2012
by FamilySearch

7 Family Members   Close

Spouses and Children   Parents and Siblings
Hide All ➕ Add Spouse   ➕ Add Parent

Frank Rolfes
Deceased • 9M5C-1JR
Mary Meinen
Deceased • 9M5C-1V3

No Marriage Events

EDIT COUPLE

Children (1)
Mary Theresa Rolfes
1889-Deceased • 9M5C-1NT

➕ Add Child

➕ Add Child with an Unknown Mother

🔁 Gender Added
16 June 2012
by FamilySearch

Show all

15 TOOLS
👥 Possible Duplicates
🚩 Report Abuse
🗑 Delete Person

8 Sources   Close
➕ Create a New Source | 📦 Attach from Source Box

9 Discussions   Close
Open Details | ➕ Add a New Discussion

10 Notes   Close
Open Details | ➕ Add a New Note

(for example, she was blind, or her husband died while fighting in the Civil War and she remarried several years later). To add a Life Sketch, click the Add link and type in the information you want.

5 VITAL INFORMATION

This section is probably the part of the Person Details page you'll refer to most often. It contains the ancestor's name, gender, birth, christening, death, and burial information. For each life event, it may include the date and location of the event.

6 OTHER INFORMATION

In this section, researchers can add non-vital-event information such as an alternate name. It also has options for adding the date and place for the following:

- Stillborn
- Bar Mitzvah/Bat Mitzvah
- Military Service
- Naturalization
- Residence
- Affiliation
- Religious Affiliation
- Title of Nobility
- Occupation
- Cremation
- Caste Name
- Clan Name
- National Identification
- National Origin
- Physical Description
- Race
- Tribe Name

You can create your own custom event or custom fact if a piece of information you want to enter is not on the list of options.

7 FAMILY MEMBERS

This section provides information on spouses and children, as well as on parents and siblings, of the person whose record you are viewing. In this box you can view and add spouses, parents, or children. By clicking a link to a family member's name listed here, a summary card for that person will pop up. Additionally, the Edit Couple link lets you update information about the couple, such as marriage date and source information.

LDS Members-Only Family Tree Icons

LDS members have additional tabs when they log in to FamilySearch.org, including one for Temple work. When logged into the Family Tree, LDS members will see icons that indicate whether or not a family's Temple Ordinances are done. In the Details tab of a Person page, you'll see a link to Ordinances as well.

8 SOURCES

View the sources cited for this person in this section. You can add a new source by clicking the Create a New Source link or the Attach From Source Box link. If you choose the Create a New Source option, you'll need to enter a source title, a Web URL (or add a memory—a document, photo, or story you have in your own records), the source citation, and a description of the record.

9 DISCUSSIONS

This is the place on the Person Details page to bring up concerns about included information or ask for additional research help. It's a collaboration tool that works similarly to posting comments on social media sites. To see comments in a discussion, click on the discussion's title. If a comment or discussion is lengthy, you'll see a More link to click to continue reading. To comment on an existing discussion, simply click the Add Comment link and type in your comment. To add a new discussion topic or question, click on the Add a New Discussion link and then enter a title and description for your discussion item. You can delete a discussion you began, but that also will delete any comments for that discussion item.

10 NOTES

This section is exactly what it sounds like: a place to input miscellaneous notes. To add a note, simply click the Add a New Note link and enter a title and the content for your note. To view notes others have added, click the Open Details link in the Notes box.

11 RECORD HINTS

FamilySearch.org updated how its system handles hints in family trees in late 2014. In the Record Hints box, you'll find suggested indexed records that may pertain to a specific ancestor. According to the FamilySearch blog, "These hints are identified by comparing the ancestor's vital information, relatives, and the relative's vital information against all historical records published on [the] FamilySearch database." The records matched could be any record that names your ancestor, such as his own birth record or his daughter's birth record listing him as the father. If there's a corresponding document image to go with the indexed listing, FamilySearch.org provides a link so you can view the image.

When you see Record Hints, you can click on the name link to preview the record that may mention your ancestor. If you agree it's a match, you can hit the Review and Attach button to attach it to your family tree. To get pertinent hints, it's important to have correct vital information listed in records for your ancestors that you create.

1 2 RESEARCH HELP

This box contains a Search Records link. When you click this link, it will automatically search for the person in FamilySearch.org's Historical Records collection. Depending on the amount of detail you enter for the person, you may need to refine the search. The search results here allow some filtering to refine your search, but not as many filtering options as when you go to the Historical Records search form directly and type in your own criteria to search. You may get lucky and find several new records for your ancestor, but if you don't, try your own searches in the Historical Records collection.

1 3 PRINT

The Print box provides five printing options: Pedigree, Portrait Pedigree, Fan Chart, Family, and Family With Sources.

- **Pedigree** generates a two-page pedigree chart that includes spaces for each person's birth, marriage, and death date and place, as well as a section to put contributor information and notes. You can enter information in additional fields on this chart before printing.
- **Portrait Pedigree** creates a simple pedigree chart that includes the photos of ancestors who have been submitted to the FamilySearch Family Tree, as well as the name of the ancestor and birth and death dates (if available).
- **Fan Chart** creates a half-circular fan chart with the person at the center.
- **Family** generates a family group sheet for the person. It includes a space for the spouse and children, along with each family member's birth, christening, death, and burial date and place. It also has spaces for the person's and the spouse's parents names, as well as the children's spouses' information. Similar to the Pedigree option, you can enter information in the fields on this chart before printing.
- **Family With Sources** is exactly what it sounds like: It's a family group sheet that also has a space for sources and notes, as well as contributor contact information.

1 4 LATEST CHANGES

This box provides a history of updates to each person's family tree listing. It lists the type of change (such as Name Added or Death Added), the date the update was made, and the Display Name of the person who made the update. If you click on the Display Name link, it will launch a pop-up box showing the submitter's full name, contact name, address, phone number, and mailing address. The amount of contact information will vary, depending on what information the submitter has opted to keep private vs. share publicly in her user account settings. If you click on the type of change, it will take you to a page that displays the specific information added.

1 5 TOOLS

The Tools box gives you three options: Possible Duplicates, Report Abuse, and Delete Person. The **Possible Duplicates** link takes you to a page that lists potential duplicate family tree records for a single person (this does not apply to living people). After carefully reviewing possible duplicate individuals, you can decide whether or not to merge the records, which includes choosing which information should be kept.

If you find something entered into a family tree that is considered offensive, could harm living relatives, links to inappropriate content online, or solicits business or research services, you can report it by clicking the **Report Abuse** link.

If you make a mistake when adding an ancestor (such as you added one person twice), you could use the **Delete Person** link here to remove the person's record. After you click the Delete Person link, you'll get several warning statements encouraging you to review the person and her relationships and letting you know what could happen to any attached sources, discussions, or notes if you continue. There's also a box to type in a reason statement for why you are deleting the person. If you choose not to delete a person, you can always select the Cancel link.

Person Memories

Each Person page also has a Memories tab (image **B**). Under this tab, you can add photos, documents, stories, and audio for this ancestor. The accepted file formats vary depending on the Memories category. For example, you can upload

- photos in JPG or PNG format
- documents in JPG, PNG, or PDF format
- audio files in MP3 or M4A format

For stories, a form allows you to type in your story in an online text box; currently there's no option to upload a story, but you can attach a photo to the story you type online.

SEARCHING FAMILY TREES

Before you search for historical records on FamilySearch.org, and even before you post your own family tree, why not see if someone else has already done the heavy lifting?

When you and others create a family tree on FamilySearch.org, your tree becomes searchable in the Family Trees section only (not in any historical records collection or in user-submitted genealogies sections of the website). You can search for family trees others have posted on the website by going to the Family Tree tab and selecting Find from

B

C

D

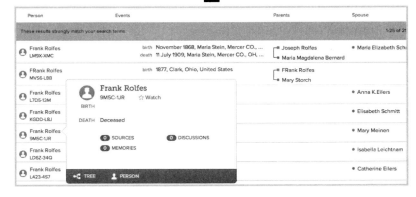

the drop-down menu. This brings up a search form where you can search for deceased ancestors by name or ID number. Note: There's an Advanced Search form for family trees, but the only apparent difference from the Basic Search form is check boxes to search for exact matches only. The Basic Search form (image **C**) has fields for

- your ancestor's first and last names
- gender
- an event (birth, christening, marriage, death, or burial), year range, and place
- father's first and last name
- mother's first and last name
- spouse's first and last name

Start your family tree search by doing a broad search. For example, enter just the first and last name for your ancestor, then hit the Find button. If you get too many results to sift through, you can narrow your results by clicking the Refine button in the search results window. This will take you back to the search form where you can enter additional search criteria, such as a life event or the name of a parent or spouse.

Interestingly, when I did a search for my ancestor Frank H. Rolfes, he came up in the top four results when I searched on just his name. When I tried a narrower search using his name and death place (Iowa), he came up several results lower, in a section of results that "do not strongly match what you searched for." How did I know the listing was my ancestor? The search results window shows columns for Events, Parents, and Spouse. Frank's wife, Mary Meinen, was listed in the Spouse column. If you find an ancestor who could be a match to your family tree, you can click on the Person name to see a summary card with more information about the person. The summary card (image **D**) displays

- the person's photo (if one has been uploaded)
- the person's ID number on FamilySearch Family Tree
- any birth and death information listed in the FamilySearch Family Tree
- the number of sources, memories, or discussion that exist for this person
- a Watch option
- a Tree link (to view the person within the pedigree chart he or she is listed in)
- a Person link (to view the complete listing for the particular person listed)

CREATING YOUR FAMILY TREE

You can post your family tree for free on FamilySearch.org. As you create your tree, keep in mind that anyone can change anything in any family tree on this website. So if you create an ancestor listing in your tree, someone else researching the same family could go in and update or change the information for each ancestor. This can be good if you have missing information, but if you want this to be a tree managed solely by you, choosing another service to host your online family tree may be a better option for you.

FamilySearch.org has two ways you can begin posting your family tree: manually and importing data from a GEDCOM (the universal genealogy computer file format).

Step-by-Step Instructions:
Manually Adding People to Your Family Tree

Before you begin creating your family tree online, decide whom you want to start with: yourself, your parents, or another ancestor. Your decision may be influenced by whether or not you want to start with a living person. Anyone identified as a living person in your

The Difference Between FamilySearch Family Tree and the Pedigree Resource File

To beginning users and even to the more experienced, it can be confusing to grasp the differences between the various types of user-submitted pedigree information on FamilySearch. org. FamilySearch Family Tree is a separate feature from the user-submitted genealogies that contain the Pedigree Resource File, a searchable database with more than two hundred million records submitted by FamilySearch.org website users and LDS members.

Think of FamilySearch Family Tree **<www.familysearch.org/tree>** as your evolving family tree. It's a living, breathing organism. You can add to it as you find new records. You can make changes to the information if the documents you find indicate a different place or time than you originally had entered for a life event. To search the information you and others have posted online to FamilySearch Family Trees, you must use the Family Tree Find tool (under the Family Tree tab, select the Find option from the drop-down menu).

In contrast, the Pedigree Resource File is sort of like a final resting place for your family tree. When you submit a GEDCOM file (the universal genealogy computer file format) of your family tree to the Pedigree Resource File **<www.familysearch.org/upload>**, it is preserved forever by FamilySearch. You can't change any of the information you submitted in your GEDCOM file. It's an archival copy. But you can submit a new, updated GEDCOM file in the future. After you submit your GEDCOM file, it becomes searchable in the Genealogies section of FamilySearch.org at **<www.familysearch.org/family-trees>**.

FamilySearch Family Tree and the Pedigree Resource File are connected in only one way: After you submit your GEDCOM file to the Pedigree Resource File, you have the option of importing that information to your FamilySearch Family Tree.

family tree will remain private and viewable only by you. Anyone identified as a deceased person in your family tree will be publicly viewable for anyone on the Internet to see. Manually inputting your tree has three steps.

1 SIGN IN AND GO TO FAMILY TREE. Log in to FamilySearch.org and select the Family Tree tab, then click Tree from the drop-down menu. If it's the first time you've visited the Family Tree page, your name will appear in a family tree chart, and you'll see a Start Here button pop up. Clicking this button will "retrieve" your tree, but the process could take a long time. Instead, click on the page (anywhere but on the Start Here button) to remove the pop-up window.

Adding Dates

FamilySearch.org automatically converts any dates you enter (such as a birth or death date) into a standardized date format used worldwide by genealogists that starts with the day, then the month, and the full year: DD Month YYYY. So even if you typed in January 15, 1801 as a birth date, a standardized 15 January 1801 will appear. Be sure to select this standardized date as the date in your family tree.

1

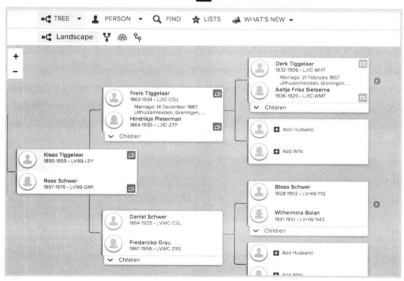

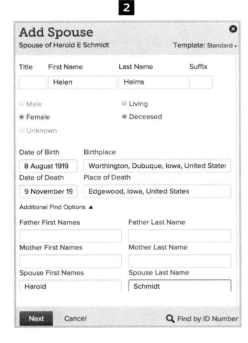

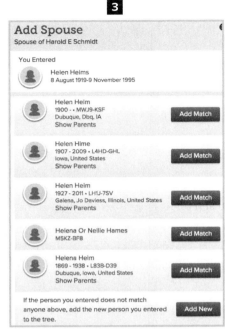

2 **ADD OR FIND ANCESTORS.** In the upper left corner, choose the Landscape view to see a standard-looking pedigree chart. Click the Add link (such as Add Husband or Add Wife) to add an ancestor. This automatically takes you to an Add Parents or Add Spouse form. Type the individual's name, as well as his/her birth date and place and spouse's name. If the person is deceased, input a Date of Death and Place of Death. Hit the Next button. This will check to see if this person already exists on the Family Tree.

3 **CHOOSE A MATCH OR ADD A NEW ANCESTOR.** If there's a person who is a match, hit the Add Match button. It will automatically add info for that person (or couple) into your tree. If you've reviewed possible matches and determined none of them are a match, scroll to the bottom of the window and click the Add New button. The person will now appear in your family tree chart.

Continue to add ancestors going back as many generations as you have information for. After you have added each ancestor's birth and death information, you can go back and enter additional details on their Person page.

Importing a GEDCOM to Create Your Family Tree

If you already have created a family tree in other genealogy software, you can import a GEDCOM file to FamilySearch.org, but there's a catch: You must first submit the GEDCOM to FamilySearch.org as a user-submitted genealogy. To do this, go to the Search

Upload Your GEDCOM

Choose File

Choose File | Dana_s Family Tree.ged

Tree Name

Name your tree to make it easy to identify.

Description

Tell others about where this tree came from and the research behind it.

Upload   Cancel

tab and select Genealogies. Scroll to the bottom of the user-submitted genealogies page, and click Submit Tree (or go to **<www.familysearch.org/upload/trees>**). Click the Add GEDCOM button. From there you can select a GEDCOM file (up to 100MB) to upload, create a Tree Name, and add a Description (image). Within about fifteen minutes, your tree will become searchable in the user-submitted trees portion of FamilySearch.org and a copy of your tree will be preserved by FamilySearch indefinitely.

After the file is finished uploading and processing, you can click the Compare button in a chart called My Uploaded Files to compare the GEDCOM file you submitted to your current Family Tree listings. When the comparing process is complete, you'll see a View button. Here, you can see a summary of the results, including numbers of potential matches and numbers of people already in Family Tree.

You'll need to review potential matches and determine if you want to add any to Family Tree. The system will ask you if two people who appear to be matches are the same person. If it is the same person, you can review the information listed for vital life events and choose whether or not to replace the existing information so that the most accurate information is used in Family Tree. If it's not the same person, you can click the Not a Match button and click Add (a plus sign icon) to add the person to your Family Tree. For highly detailed instructions on uploading a GEDCOM and importing the data into Family Tree, visit **<help.familysearch.org/kb/UserGuide/en/tree/t_tree_upload_gedcom.html>**.

MANAGING YOUR FAMILY TREE

A family tree is never finished. There are always more generations or family members you can research, newfound details about a person's life to incorporate, and newly digitized records you could add. After you initially set up your FamilySearch Family Tree, you'll need to get acquainted with the ways you can view the tree, as well as how you can add, delete, and manage the information for each ancestor as you learn more about each ancestor and find new records.

Family Tree Viewing Options

You can view your family tree on FamilySearch.org four ways: as Landscape, Portrait, Fan Chart, and Descendancy charts. To choose how you want to view your tree, select one of the icons from the bar beneath the Tree button. When you hover over or click on an icon, the name for that view displays.

LANDSCAPE

This view (image **F**) is similar to most five-generation pedigree charts. It lists a person's ancestors to the right and the person's children to the left. Each entry displays the ancestor's name, birth and death years, and the ID number FamilySearch.org assigned to the person. Clicking on the name brings up an ancestor's summary card, from which you can watch or unwatch ancestors or go to the Person Details page.

PORTRAIT

This pedigree-chart-style view includes photos of each ancestor (if photos have been uploaded to FamilySearch.org), as well as the ancestor's name and birth and death years (image **G**). Click a portrait to bring up the summary card for that ancestor; you can then go to the Person Details page if you want to change or add to the ancestor's entry.

FAN CHART

This shows your ancestors in a format exactly like it sounds (image **H**). The default is for you to be at the center of the chart, but you can make other ancestors the focal point. Simply hover your mouse over the inside portion of the box with your ancestor's name in it. A gray fan chart icon will appear. Click the icon to make that ancestor the center of the chart. This will show you that person's ancestors and descendants. Each box displays an ancestor's name and birth and death years.

DESCENDANCY

This view (image **I**) shows a flow chart of sorts, with the selected ancestor, his or her spouse, and their children. This view includes the ancestor name, birth and death dates (if known), and a photo (if one has been uploaded). At the top of the screen, you can select the number of generations for the chart to display. Click on an ancestor's name to bring up his or her summary card. Note that the children shown are the ones you have linked to your family tree. So if only three children are listed and the couple had six, the others won't appear until you add them. Also, to the right side of the screen, you may see icons for Research Hints, Research Suggestions, and Data Problems. Clicking on an icon reveals details about the hint, suggestion, or problem.

F

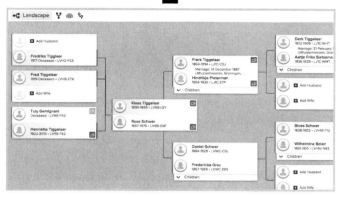

G

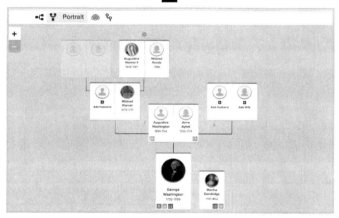

H

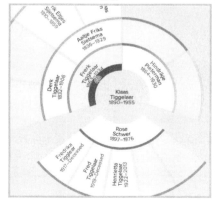

I

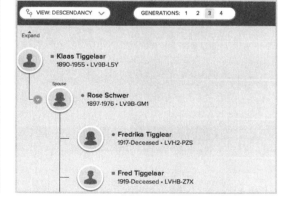

What Happens to Photos and Other Content You Upload to FamilySearch.org?

When you upload a photo, document, story, audio file, or ancestor information, you agree to FamilySearch's Content Submission Agreement. You also agree that you have the appropriate copyright and/or permission to submit a photo, document, or audio recording. Any photos, documents, or audio you upload or stories you add are made publicly viewable by *anyone* online. FamilySearch does allow you to remove photos or documents you've contributed, but others could have already copied and posted your photos in their trees or for their own use, and FamilySearch is not obligated to remove links or references to your deleted content.

In addition, by submitting content to the website, you grant FamilySearch "an unrestricted, fully paid-up, royalty-free, worldwide, and perpetual license to use any and all information, content, and other materials ... for any and all purposes in any and all manners, and in any and all forms of media that we, in our sole discretion, deem appropriate for the furtherance of our mission to promote family history and genealogical research." Essentially, you are giving FamilySearch the materials to use in any way it wants, without limitation. That means the photos, stories, documents, and other information you provide could become part of an advertisement or brochure, or part of a product that FamilySearch may sell at a later date, or it may remain linked on the site forever.

Read the full Content Submission Agreement **<www.familysearch.org/legal/familysearch-content-submission-agreement>** before you submit information or other materials. And heed the advice in the agreement, which says, "Do not submit any content which you do not want to be accessed or used by others."

Editing Vital Information

If you make a typo when you enter a person on your family tree, don't worry. You can edit the information later. How? Go to the Person Details page within your tree (click on the person's name to get to this page, or go to the Person tab and select the down arrow to select a person from the list). Then click on the information you want to edit. For example, if you typed a name in all lowercase letters and want to capitalize it, go to the Vital Information box and click on the person's name. Next, click on the Edit link in the upper right corner of the Name box. Type in the correct information, then add a note to explain why you changed what you did (your justification for why the change is correct). Then click the Save button.

Adding Details

When you initially create an entry for a person in your FamilySearch Family Tree, a standard form allows you to enter the person's name, gender, date and place of birth, date and place of death, and whether the person is living or deceased. If you want to add a Life Sketch, a Discussion, Notes, or other information, such as a marriage date and place, immigration date and port of entry, naturalization details, occupation, a nickname, or other information you have confirmed, you'll need to open the Person Details page.

You can get to the Person Details page in a couple of different ways:

- Under the Family Tree tab, click the down arrow next to the Person navigation and select the person's name from the list.
- Under the Family Tree tab, click Tree. In the Landscape view, click the name of the person in the pedigree chart, and in the summary card, click the Person link or click on the name again.

Once you're on the Person Details page, scroll to the section where you want to add information and click the Add link (usually displayed next to a plus sign icon). Input information by following the prompts or typing information in the form that pops up.

Adding Sources

You can add sources to each ancestor's Family Tree Person page at several different times:

- while working directly on the Person page in the Family Tree
- while reviewing Record Hints and adding relevant source information
- while searching Historical Records collections and adding relevant source information

DIRECTLY ON A PERSON PAGE

When you're on a Person page for an ancestor, you can add a source in the Sources box. It gives you two options: Create a New Source or Attach From Source Box. The Create a New Source option (image **J**) lets you add a source that's not on FamilySearch.org. You have the option to input a URL for the record or Add a Memory (such as adding a copy of a death certificate or photo of a tombstone). You'll also need to fill in fields for the Source Title, Where the Record Is Found (the source citation), and Describe the Record (Notes). The Attach From Source Box option (image **K**) will take you to your Source Box. Locate the source you want and click on the Attach link in the Attach column of the Source Box. A box will pop up with a field for you to enter your reason for attaching this source. The pop-up box also will show which ancestor's record you are connecting the record to. Click the Attach button to finish attaching the source to the ancestor's Family Tree Person page. A Paper Clip icon will appear in the Attach column in your Source Box once a source is attached to a person.

Create a Source

Identify the record you have found. This will be called a "Source."

Source Title (Required)

Example: England, Death Certificate of Hugh S. Smith - (1832-1912)

Web Page (Link to the Record)

○ WEB PAGE URL   ○ ADD A MEMORY

Example: http://www.uk1841census.com/census_online.htm

Where the Record Is Found (Citation)

Example: UK Census, 1841, Arbroath, Perth, Scotland. Population schedule. Dwelling address. Federal archive. Digital Image

Describe the Record (Notes)

Example: Hugh S. Smith Family Page 7. Lines 23-27. Arbroath, Scotland. UK Census 1841 Father: Robert Smith. Mother: Helen Strachen. Children: Hugh Sidley Smith, Robert Smith.

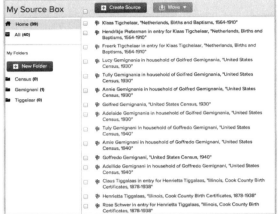

My Source Box

+ Create Source   Move ▼

🏠 Home (39)
📋 All (40)

My Folders

+ New Folder

📁 Census (0)
📁 Gemignani (1)
📁 Tiggelaar (0)

- Klaas Tigchelaar, "Netherlands, Births and Baptisms, 1564-1910"
- Hendrikje Pieterman in entry for Klaas Tigchelaar, "Netherlands, Births and Baptisms, 1564-1910"
- Freerk Tigchelaar in entry for Klaas Tigchelaar, "Netherlands, Births and Baptisms, 1564-1910"
- Lucy Gemignania in household of Golfred Gemignania, "United States Census, 1930"
- Tully Gemignania in household of Golfred Gemignania, "United States Census, 1930"
- Annie Gemignania in household of Golfred Gemignania, "United States Census, 1930"
- Golfred Gemignania, "United States Census, 1930"
- Adelaide Gemignania in household of Golfred Gemignania, "United States Census, 1930"
- Tuly Gemignani in household of Goffredo Gemignania, "United States Census, 1940"
- Amie Gemignani in household of Goffredo Gemignania, "United States Census, 1940"
- Goffredo Gemignani, "United States Census, 1940"
- Adellide Gemignani in household of Goffredo Gemignania, "United States Census, 1940"
- Claus Tiggalaas in entry for Henrietta Tiggalaas, "Illinois, Cook County Birth Certificates, 1878-1938"
- Henrietta Tiggalaas, "Illinois, Cook County Birth Certificates, 1878-1938"
- Rose Schwer in entry for Henrietta Tiggalaas, "Illinois, Cook County Birth Certificates, 1878-1938"

Rose Schwer
mentioned in the record of Fred Tiggelaar

Name:	Rose Schwer
Age:	21
Birthplace:	Chicago, Illinois
Gender:	Female
Husband:	Nick Tiggelaar
Child:	Fred Tiggelaar

Other information in the record of Fred Tiggelaar
from Illinois, Cook County Birth Certificates

Name:	Fred Tiggelaar
Event Type:	Birth
Event Date:	13 Feb 1919
Event Place:	Chicago, Cook, Illinois, United States
Registration Place:	, Cook, Illinois
Gender:	Male
Father's Name:	Nick Tiggelaar
Father's Age:	28
Mother's Name:	Rose Schwer
Mother's Birthplace:	Chicago, Illinois

Review and Attach

RECORD HINTS

Rose Schwer
Illinois, Cook County Birth Certificates, 1878-1922

Rose Schwer
Illinois, Cook County Birth Certificates, 1878-1922

Rose Schwer
Illinois, Cook County Birth Certificates, 1878-1922

Rose Schwer
Illinois, Cook County Birth Certificates, 1878-1922

Rose Schwer
Illinois, Cook County Birth Certificates, 1878-1922

Show Details

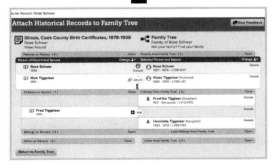

Go for Record | Rose Schwer

Attach Historical Records to Family Tree

Give Feedback

Illinois, Cook County Birth Certificates, 1878-1938
Rose Schwer
View: Record

Family Tree
Family of Rose Schwer
Not your family? Find your family

POWER-USER TIP

Seeing the Whole Picture

While in Landscape or Portrait views, your entire pedigree chart may not appear in your web browser window. If you hover your mouse over the blank gray area of the page, you'll see a Move icon (a plus sign with arrows on each end) appear. Click your mouse on a gray area of the screen, then drag the window left or right to view additional individuals on your family tree. Also, you can click the arrows next to an ancestor couple's box to expand the number of generations displayed.

FROM RECORD HINTS

In the Record Hints box, click on the hint you want to view. A preview box will appear. You can scroll through the information listed to confirm whether the record matches your ancestor or not (image **L**). If it does match your ancestor, hit the Review and Attach button. This takes you to an Attach Historical Records to Family Tree page (image **M**). It lists the record collection and ancestor at the top and shows a family group sheet. The record shows where it will attach and you can enter a reason for attaching the source. Once you attach it to one ancestor, it will give you the option to attach it to other ancestors listed on the record, such as the father and child in addition to the mother on a birth record. You also can move children or others on the record into the appropriate sections on this screen by clicking the Add button or dragging and dropping the info from the left side (such as Children on Record) to the right category/person (such as Children From Family Tree). Click the Return to Family Tree button when you're finished attaching it to the appropriate individuals.

FROM HISTORICAL RECORDS COLLECTION SEARCHES

When you search for records in the Historical Records collection on FamilySearch.org, each record results page has an Attach to Family Tree button. Click that button to add the source to your Family Tree. It will take you to the same Attach Historical Records to Family Tree page that the Record Hints take you to. You can attach it to whoever is listed in the record, as well as add any children to the Children From Family Tree category. Click the Return to Record link once you're finished attaching the record to the appropriate individuals. (Note: If you have already added the source to your family tree, you will not see the Attach to Family Tree button on the record results page; instead, you'll see a View in Family Tree link and a Review Attachments link.)

Switching People When Attaching Sources

When you're in the Attach Historical Records to Family Tree screen, notice the Change button. Robert Kehrer, FamilySearch's senior product manager for search technologies, explains that some records (such as marriage records) contain relatives from both sides of the family. If the record you found is for the groom, attach the bride and the groom's parents to the record. Then use the Change button to switch the focus to the bride. (Click the Change button, and other people listed on the record will appear; select the bride's name.) Lastly, attach records to appropriate people in the bride's family tree.

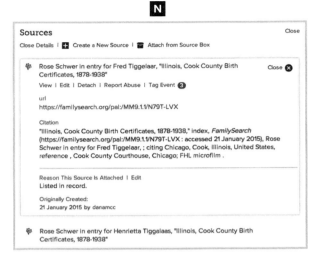

Detaching a Source

If you later discover you attached an incorrect record, you can detach a source. One of the easiest ways to detach a record is to go to the Person page for a particular ancestor and scroll down to the Source box. Click on the link for the source, and a box with additional details will appear (image N). It provides links to View, Edit, Detach, Report Abuse, or Tag Event, as well as the URL for the record on FamilySearch.org. Click the Detach link. A Detach Source Form will appear, with a field for you to enter the reason to detach the source. Hit the Detach button to finish removing the source from the person's Family Tree page.

Removing a Person From Your Family Tree

If you add a person to your family tree and later discover the person isn't the ancestor you were searching for, you can remove that person from your tree. FamilySearch.org calls this "deleting relationships." To delete a relationship, go to the Person Details page and scroll down to the Family Member section. Click the Edit Couple, Edit Parents, or Edit Relationship link, depending on whether you want to remove a spouse or parent-child relationship. Review the information listed, including the sources for the information. If you still want to proceed, click the Delete Relationship link in the Tools box in the upper right corner of the page.

If you have entered a person in error and want to delete that person, you can do so by going to the Person Details page for the ancestor. On the right side of your ancestor's information, scroll down to the Tools box and click the Delete a Person link. This page will ask you a series of questions to confirm whether you really want to delete the person and all the information and relationships she is connected to. Type in the reason for deleting the person, then hit the Delete button to complete the process.

COLLABORATING ON YOUR FAMILY TREE

Keep in mind that anyone can edit any person in a FamilySearch Family Tree. If you see that someone else changed a family tree entry you created, you can collaborate with that person by posting research questions in the Discussions section of the Person Details page or by e-mailing the person (if he has made his e-mail public under his account settings). A recently introduced internal messaging feature allows users to communicate with each other within in the FamilySearch.org system. This provides some level of privacy, but you still can write messages to other researchers without having to publicly list your e-mail address or know the other person's e-mail address.

Additionally, LDS members can help any FamilySearch.org user with his or her family tree, using a Helper Number. To find your Helper Number, click on the down arrow next to your user name, select Settings, then the Account Tab. The "helper" (an LDS member) can sign in to view your family tree as you would see it and can assist with the research. For more information on how this works, see **<www.familysearch.org/blog/en/ signing-family-tree>**.

The Family Tree Mobile App

FamilySearch Family Tree's mobile app for iOS and Android allows you to work on your family tree on the go. Specifically, the Family Tree app lets you view your family tree and add memories to ancestors already in your tree. The app doesn't allow you to find, add, or update ancestor details such as names, dates, and relationships.

On an iOS device, the Quick Start section allows you to quickly sync the information you've entered into your tree online. The pedigree is shown in the Portrait view. You can click each ancestor's Portrait icon to bring up the Person Details page. (Alternatively, you could select the History icon in the upper right and select a person from the list to view.) The Details page allows you to enter or edit vital information, spouse and parent information, sources, photos, stories, or audio. The Charts tab pulls up a pedigree chart in the format you select.

Under the Settings of the app, you can download a six-generation pedigree chart to view offline. This can be helpful to have during research trips, such as visiting a remote cemetery where there's no Wi-Fi or sparse cellular service.

PRIVACY AND YOUR ONLINE TREE

Privacy is always a concern for any information we post online today. From the high-profile hacks of department store computer systems to smaller-scale compromising of Facebook accounts, information breaches have become a fact of life. There's always a chance that any information you post online could become public, even if you don't want it to.

When you submit or post information to a Family Tree or to the Memories tab, that information automatically becomes public on FamilySearch.org, with one exception: FamilySearch.org doesn't display details about living people. In other words, you should

The Memories Tab

On FamilySearch.org, you can add Memories. Memories can be standalone photos, stories, documents, or audio recordings, or they can be connected to an ancestor in your Family-Search Family Tree. You also can search the website to see what memories other researchers have posted.

Adding Memories

How you add Memories depends on whether you want them to be standalone items or added to your family tree.

- **To add a standalone item:** Click the Memories tab, then scroll down to the type of material you want to add (Photos, Stories, Documents, Audio, People, Albums) in the drop-down menu. From there, click the Plus Sign icon and upload a file or enter the information you want to add by following the prompts provided. For most items (photos, audio recordings, and documents), you'll need to upload a file. To add a story, you'll need to type in your story into the online form provided, which includes fields for the story title and the story text, as well as an option to attach a photo.

- **To add an item to an ancestor in your family tree:** Open the Person Details page for an ancestor. Next to the Details tab, click the Memories tab. An area with a Photos, Documents, Stories, and Audio section will appear. Click the Add link (next to the Plus Sign icon) to add a particular item.

- **Using the mobile Memories app:** FamilySearch.org has a Memories app available for iOS devices only. After you download and install the app from the iTunes App Store, you can easily add photos, stories, or audio from your smartphone or tablet. On an iPhone, click the icon for the type of memory you want to add, and click the Plus Sign in the upper right to expect that any information you post to a FamilySearch Family Tree can be seen by *any-one* online. Anyone on FamilySearch.org can also edit or change family tree listings for anyone, even people you added or created pages for in the FamilySearch Family Tree.

This makes it extremely important to indicate whether a person is living or deceased when you initially add an ancestor or relative to a tree. Note that if you enter any text into the death or burial fields, it may automatically consider the person deceased.

Strategies to Protect Privacy

Before you post any family tree information on FamilySearch.org, consider these approaches to help protect your and your family's privacy.

add your content. For ancestor photos, you can snap a photo of an old photograph and then add it. For stories, you can enter a story title and story content, as well as attach a photo. For audio, you can create an audio recording using your device, then upload it. The app recommends keeping the recording under five minutes (and it has a maximum of fifteen minutes for each recording).

Before you add a Memory, you'll be asked to read and agree to the FamilySearch Content Submission Agreement. By submitting any content—photos, stories, documents, audio, albums, or ancestor information—to FamilySearch.org (including to the Family Trees and Memories sections), you are agreeing to the FamilySearch Content Submission Agreement at **<www.familysearch.org/legal/familysearch-content-submission-agreement>**. See the "What Happens to Photos and Other Content You Upload to FamilySearch.org?" box earlier in this chapter for more details on what permission you are giving to FamilySearch when you upload or submit content to its website.

Finding Memories

You can search the Memories (photos, stories, and documents) other people have submitted. To do so, click on the Memories tab, and then select Find from the drop-down menu. Type in your search terms in the box provided and click the Find button. Try inputting a surname and record type in the search box. Results will show items such as marriage announcements, vital records, family photos, obituaries, and more.

At this time, there's no way to refine Memories search results, so if an initial search doesn't return relevant results, add more details to the search box. Also try to narrow results by selecting to search only Photos, Stories, or Documents (click the button next to each option to search only those materials). Note that using wildcards is not beneficial to searching the Memories section of the website.

GET PERMISSION

Talk to living family members you want to add to your online family tree. Ask if they are okay with you listing them in your tree online, even though they shouldn't appear publicly on the website.

EXERCISE DISCRETION

Before you post information, consider carefully whether you want it to be publicly available—to anyone. Posting your family tree online can provide great opportunities for collaboration with other researchers and the possibility of finding long-lost relatives who are researching the same ancestors. But if you're not comfortable with posting family information online, you may not want to post your tree on FamilySearch.org. The same goes for any photos, documents, stories, or audio recordings you add to the Memories section of the website.

USE A STRONG PASSWORD

If you do post living people's information in your tree, even though it's not displayed on the website, it's still present in your online account. Be sure to create a strong password so your account and the information in it have less chance of being compromised.

KEYS TO SUCCESS

⭐ Search the FamilySearch Family Tree to find leads on new ancestors and distant cousins you can collaborate or swap information with.

⭐ Build your own family tree on FamilySearch.org as a tool to manage your research (linking records to people) and potentially have others add to your work. After you've created your initial family tree entries, return to the Person Details pages to add more life events, occupations, immigration dates, and so on.

⭐ Look at the Research Hints box when viewing a Person Details page. Hints provide possible leads to historical records on FamilySearch.org that may list your ancestor.

⭐ Try out each of the FamilySearch Family Tree chart views—Landscape, Portrait, Fan Chart, Descendancy—and select the view you prefer.

⭐ Understand the Family Tree's anyone-can-edit-anything approach and the website's terms and conditions before posting content or personal information into a family tree. Know what rights you're granting and/or giving up. Respect living relatives' privacy.

ONLINE FAMILY TREE CHECKLIST

Use this checklist to ensure you have the information you need at your fingertips when you want to post your family tree information on the FamilySearch Family Tree.

Before Creating Your Online Family Tree

☐ Read the FamilySearch Content Submissions Agreement **<www.familysearch.org/legal/familysearch-content-submission-agreement>**.

☐ Enter family tree information on a hard-copy five-generation ancestor chart (in appendix C and available for free at **<www.familytreemagazine.com/info/basicforms>**) or print a hard copy from your genealogy software for reference.

☐ Confirm vital information (such as dates and places) in official documents such as birth certificates, marriage certificates, death records, and burial records.

☐ Prepare a GEDCOM file to submit and import (if you use genealogy software and also want to submit your information to the Pedigree Resource File, which is searchable on FamilySearch.org).

☐ Ask any living people you plan to include in your tree for permission to post their information in FamilySearch Family Tree.

While Creating Your Family Tree Manually

☐ Analyze matches before adding a new person. If your ancestor is not already listed in the FamilySearch Family Tree, add the new person.

☐ Remember to add details. If you have sources that provide additional details, such as marriage dates and places, burial dates and places, occupations, immigration and naturalization dates, and more, add this information to the Person Details page as desired.

☐ Attach sources. Remember to attach sources to each person's family tree entry as you find records on FamilySearch.org.

☐ Use Research Hints to add more sources you may not have found or added yet.

☐ Add photos, documents, stories, and audio (as desired) under the Memories tab on the Person page.

Searching and Browsing Historical Records

Now we get to the genealogy gold on FamilySearch.org: mining the website's billions of records.

Although searching on FamilySearch.org may seem straightforward at first, don't let the simplicity of the search fool you: There's much more under the hood to help you ferret out your ancestors' records. In addition, the site has many unindexed (translation: unsearchable) records. Using those records is a matter of browsing page by page, like scrolling through a roll of microfilm—but it's well worth the effort, especially when you employ tactics that make the job less tedious. In this chapter, I'll introduce you to the basics for searching historical records on FamilySearch.org and arm you with strategies for finding records relevant to your own family history research.

SEARCHING HISTORICAL RECORDS

There are many ways to search genealogy records on FamilySearch.org, but all of them start with going to the Search tab and selecting Records from the drop-down menu (or go directly to **<www.familysearch.org/search>**). This takes you to a landing page containing the main Historical Records search form, as well as a Research by Location section and a Browse All Published Collections link. From this landing page, we'll explore three options to search the site's genealogy records.

The Historical Records Search Form

The main Historical Records search form appears when you go to the Records search page on FamilySearch.org. This form allows you to do a global search of the website's indexed records. These include census records, immigration and naturalization records, military records, vital records, and other historical documents that record your ancestors. This search form doesn't yet cover digitized books, the FamilySearch Family Tree, or unindexed records on FamilySearch.org. You'll use separate search forms for those resources (see chapters 2 and 4).

The main search form is the key place to start all of your record searches. Once you've utilized this form and its filters, you can move on to searching individual collections.

Let's take a closer look at the search fields. Each option described below is labeled on the search screen (image **A**) for easy reference.

A

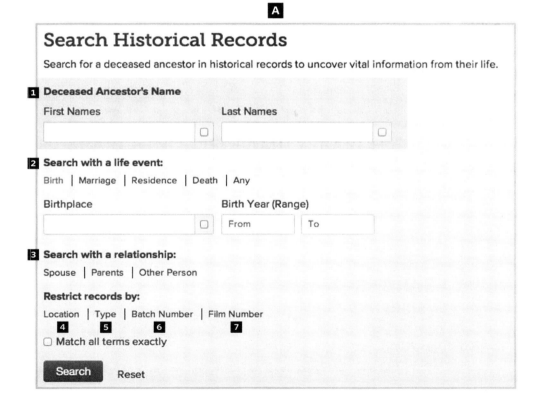

1 ANCESTOR'S FIRST AND LAST NAMES

The form has separate boxes for the first name and last name of your ancestor. Next to each name is a check box. When you click this check box, it restricts your search to the exact name only. This means your search results won't display a record with a spelling variation or nickname, just the precise name you entered. This will help narrow your results to sift through, but it could potentially leave out some relevant results.

For example, when I searched for my ancestor Blasius Schwer, a search on only his name returned more than three thousand results. When I checked the exact name check box for his last name, the search returned 384 results. When I checked the exact name check box for both his last and first name, it returned just six results. Start your search broad, and narrow as needed.

2 LIFE EVENT DATE AND PLACE

Under the Search With a Life Event heading, you can choose to enter a date range and place where a record was created or where an ancestor lived. Click on the Birth, Marriage, Residence, Death, or Any link to bring up additional search fields. Under the Birth link, you can enter the birthplace and birth year range. Under the Marriage link, you can enter a marriage place and marriage year range. Under the Residence link, you can enter a specific location (such as a county and state) where your ancestor lived and also enter the date range for the time period he lived in that place of residence. Under the Death link, you can enter a death place and death year range. Under the Any link, you can add any place (for a record location of non-vital records or place your ancestor lived) and a date range.

You can add as many life events as you want to your search, but keep in mind that adding a lot of detail here could restrict the matches you find. In most instances, it's best to begin your search by entering just one of these life events, such as a birthplace and year range or a place of residence and year range. If you click on a life event but want to remove it later, simply hover your mouse over the category and click on the X in the upper right corner of the highlighted box that appears.

As with names, when you enter a place for any life event, you have the option to restrict your search to the exact place name entered.

▣ RELATIONSHIP

If your ancestor has a particularly common name, such as John Smith, it could be beneficial to add family relationships to your record searches. You can add up to four family relationships in your search: a spouse's name, mother's name, father's name, or one other person's name. To do so, click the corresponding link: Spouse, Parents, or Other Person. In the Other Person category, you could list a sibling's name. Each name field has a check box next to it. Again, checking this box means only names that match exactly will be included in your search results.

▣ LOCATION

In the Restrict Records By section of the main search form, you can enter a specific location for your ancestor. The location field allows you to enter a country and a state or province. After you click the Location link, additional search fields will appear for Country and State or Province.

▣ RECORD TYPE

In the Restrict Records By section of the main search form, you can enter a specific record type you want to search. This is helpful if you are looking for just census records or just birth records. When you click the Type link, it will bring up a list of record types with check boxes:

- Births, Baptisms, and Christenings
- Marriage
- Death
- Census, Residence, and Lists
- Immigration and Naturalization
- Military
- Probate
- Other

Check the box for the record types you want your searches to include. You can select as many as you want.

▣ BATCH NUMBER

You can search records by batch number in the Restrict Records By section of the main search form. A batch number indicates a source type (such as records from a single church). Batch numbers were given to each batch of records when they originally were microfilmed. You can use batch numbers to find other relatives who may appear in records from the same batch.

7 FILM NUMBER

The Restrict Records By section of the main search form lets you search by microfilm number, too. This is helpful if you've already searched the FamilySearch Catalog and found a microfilm you want to view. You can enter the film number to see if the data from that microfilm is available online. For example, suppose you wanted to know whether the Family History Library microfilm #1992052, which has Illinois births from 1842 and from 1849 to 1872, is viewable online. You would enter *1992052* in the Film Number search box. This advanced feature benefits experienced genealogists, as well as genealogy hobbyists who had previously identified microfilm to search, but who hadn't yet gotten around to renting it to view at a local FamilySearch Center.

POWER-USER TIP

Start Broad, Then Narrow

Entering information in too many search fields will limit the search results you'll get, so when you first start looking for records on Family-Search.org, leave most of the search fields blank. The search results page will show a suggestion banner at the top if you need to add more filters to get better results.

Filtering Search Results

After you've entered your search criteria and hit the Search button, a search results window will appear. Search results include the ancestor's name, database name, dates and places of life events in the record, and spouses and children (or other people) listed in the record, as well as a link and icon for more details and a Camera icon and link if a record image is available. The default view shows twenty results per page, but you can change the number of results shown in a single page to fifty or seventy-five. The most relevant results will automatically appear toward the top of the results page. A colored bar will separate least relevant results (such as results for a person with the same last name, but a different first name) from the results the FamilySearch.org search tool deems most relevant.

If after reviewing the results list you want to broaden or narrow your search, you can do so by adding or removing search criteria in the field in the Refine Your Search column on the left side of the page. Additionally, you can filter results by a specific records collection on FamilySearch.org. To do this, click the Collections tab in the search results window. Relevant collections will appear. If you're looking for census records, for instance, you can choose to search only census collections by selecting the check box next to relevant census collections (see image **B**). Once you've chosen all the collections you want to search, you can click the Filter These Results button at the top of the page.

When you want to change gears and search for a different ancestor, clear the search form criteria you had previously entered by clicking the Reset link in the column on the left side of the page.

Farther down on the search results page, there's yet another way to filter your results in a box with the heading Filter Your Results By. This offers an alternate way to filter results using the same categories and tabs mentioned above, with one addition: an option to filter results by Gender (see image **C**). This is extremely helpful if results show gender-neutral first names or only initials for the first name.

Step-by-Step Example: Using the Historical Records Search

Now it's time to put the Historical Records search form to work. For the following step-by-step example, I'm using my ancestor Blasius Schwer. You can follow along by entering

1

FamilySearch   Family Tree   Memories   Search   Indexing

Records
Genealogies
Catalog
Books
Wiki

See Your Roots

Create a beautiful genealogy fan chart that you can share with family in person or via email.

Create now

Fan Chart   Photos   Family Tree   Search   Indexing

2

Search Historical Records

Search for a deceased ancestor in historical records to uncover vital infor

Deceased Ancestor's Name

First Names

blasius

Last Names

schwer

Search with a life event:

Birth | Marriage | Residence | Death | Any

Birthplace

Birth Year (Range)

From   To

Search with a relationship:

Spouse | Parents | Other Person

3

Restrict records by:

Location | Type | Batch Number | Film Number

Country

United States

State or Province

Idaho
Illinois
Indiana
Iowa
Rhode Island

☐ Match all terms exactly

Search   Reset

Browse All Published Collections

4

Records   Collections

Search Results from Historical Records

1-20 of 101 results for Name: **blasius schwer**, Country:**United States**, State or Province:**Illinois**

Number of results to show: 20 50 75

Export Results 1-20

Preview	Name	Events			Relationships		Details	Image
▶	Blasius Schwer Father Illinois Births and Christenings, 1824-1940				spouse: child:	Minnie Boettcher Fred Henry Schwer	📄	
▶	Blias Schwer Head United States Census, 1880	birth: residence:	1829 1880	Germany Worth, Cook, Illinois, United States	spouse: children:	Meena Schwer John Schwer, Margaret Schwer, Bertie Schwer, Annie Schwer, Daniel	📄	📷

5

Search Results from Historical Records

1-20 of 101 results for Name: **blasius schwer**, Country:**United States**, State or Province:**Illinois**

Number of results to show: 20 50 75

Ex

Preview	Name	Events	Relationships	
▼	Blasius Schwer Father Illinois Births and Christenings, 1824-1940		spouse: child:	Minnie Boettcher Fred Henry Schwer

📋 COPY | 🖨 PRINT | 📦 SOURCE BOX ▾ | 📤 SHARE ▾

📇 **Blasius Schwer**
mentioned in the record of Fred Henry Schwer

▶ View
📄 Revie

Name:	Blasius Schwer
Gender:	Male
Wife:	Minnie Boettcher
Child:	Fred Henry Schwer

No ima

Other information in the record of Fred Henry Schwer
from Illinois Births and Christenings

Illinois Bi
Christeni

Name:	Fred Henry Schwer
Gender:	Male
Event Type:	Birth
Event Date:	25 Jan 1866
Event Place:	Worth, Cook, Illinois

6

Refine your search   ▾

Records   Collections

Search Results from Historical Records

Deceased Ancestor's Name

First Names

blasius

Last Names

schwer

Search with a life event:

Birth

Marriage

Residence Place

cook county, illinois

Residence Year (Range)

From   To

Death

Any

Search with a relationship:

Spouse

Parents

Other Person

Restrict records by:

Country

United States

State or Province

1-20 of 70 results for Name: **blasius schwer**, Event: **Resi** or Province:**Illinois**

Number of results to show: 20 50 75

Preview	Name	Events		
▶	Blasius Schwer Father Illinois Births and Christenings, 1824-1940			
▶	Blias Schwer Head United States Census, 1880	birth: residence:	1829 1880	Germa Worth, Illinois, States
▶	Blasius Schwer Father Illinois Deaths and Stillbirths, 1916-1947	birth:	Germany	
▶	Blases Schwer Father Illinois Deaths and Stillbirths, 1916-	birth:	Germany	

Blasius' information, or you can input one of your own ancestor's names and adjust the settings or fields as appropriate to your ancestor. I recommend inputting information in multiple search fields on this form in order to get better quality search results.

1 **GO TO THE SEARCH FORM.** Log on to FamilySearch.org. Under the Search tab, select Records from the drop-down menu or go right to **<www.familysearch.org/search>**.

2 **ENTER YOUR ANCESTOR'S NAME.** On the main Historical Records search form, input your ancestor's first name and last name. In this case, I have entered my ancestor's name: *Blasius Schwer*. I recommend leaving the match exactly check boxes next to the names unchecked for your initial search to find as many record matches as possible. If you need to narrow results later, you can check the exact box in the left column of your search results.

3 **INPUT A LOCATION.** Scroll down to the Restrict Records By heading on the main Historical Records search form, and click on the Location link. In this example, I know Blasius Schwer lived in Illinois, so I have input *United States* in the Country field and *Illinois* in the State or Province field. Click the Search button.

4 **VIEW ALL SEARCH RESULTS.** FamilySearch.org returns 101 search results for Blasius Schwer in Illinois using the criteria from steps 2 and 3. The most relevant results automatically appear toward the top of the search results page.

5 **VIEW DETAILS ABOUT YOUR RESULTS.** Go individually through each result shown to determine if the record truly does include your ancestor. There are two ways to do this: In the Preview column, click on the arrow for a detailed summary of the record to appear on the same page. Or in the Details column, click on the Paper icon to go to a new page within the same browser tab with a detailed record summary. From both locations, you can choose to copy, print, or share the record via social media or e-mail, as well as choose to put the record in your Source Box. In this example, the first search result shows my Blasius Schwer mentioned in the birth record for his son Fred. After viewing the detail, I add it to my Source Box.

6 **NARROW SEARCH RESULTS.** If you get too many results to review, filter your results using the options on the left of the search results page. These options are the same as on the main page (life events, relationships, record types, etc.). The specific terms you'll enter will vary depending on your situation. For example, if search results are bringing up people by the same name, but who live in a different county than your ancestor, you may need to click the Residence link under the Search With a Life Event category to add a county name to the location and/or add a date range.

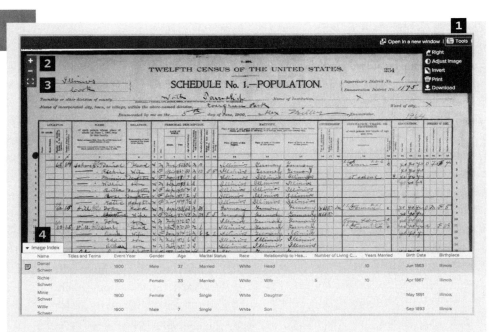

Viewing Indexed Record Images

If the image for a record you find is available directly on FamilySearch.org (not through a partner website), you'll have a few options for viewing the record:

1 Tools: Under this heading, you can rotate the image (Right), change the brightness and/or contrast (Adjust Image), or invert the image so the text is white and the background is black (Invert). These tools allow you to better view difficult-to-read images. You can also print the record (Print) or download the record to your computer (Download).

2 Zoom: To the left of the image are Plus Sign (+) and Minus Sign (-) icons. Click the plus sign to zoom in or the minus sign to zoom out.

3 View full screen: Under the Zoom tools is an icon displaying four corners of a square. Click this icon to view the record image in full screen mode. To exit full screen mode, simply press the Esc button on your keyboard.

4 Indexed Records: An index of individuals in the record appears below the image. Click the image index tab to close the index.

Additionally, in the upper right of the record results page, an Attach to Family Tree button indicates that the record has not already been connected to your family tree. A View in Family Tree link and a Review Attachments link in the same spot means the record is attached to your family tree already.

An Exact Science

At the bottom of the main Historical Records search form, there's a Match All Terms Exactly check box. If you check this box, FamilySearch.org will return results that are an exact match for the information you entered in *all* search boxes you filled in. If you're trying to narrow your results, this could be beneficial, but it's often wiser to use the check boxes next to the desired individual search fields. If you do select Match All Terms Exactly and you get zero search results, uncheck the box and try your search again.

Researching by Location

The second way to search FamilySearch.org is to use its Research by Location search option. To do this, scroll to the Research by Location map on the Records page under the Search tab. When you select a country (in North America only) or continent (all areas outside of North America), a window will pop up with smaller jurisdictions (such as states/provinces or countries). Select the US state or the country you wish to research in, and the pop-up box will show you the number of collections, indexed records, and record images it has for that country or state, as well as the years the records cover. For example, the pop-up box for Hawaii (image **D**) says it has fifty-nine collections of records that cover the years 1500 to 2014. There are more than 7.8 million indexed records and more than 232 million record images for Hawaii.

To continue, click the Start Researching In link. This will take you to a landing page for researching records in the country or state you select (see image **E**). The landing page connects you to a search form for records, learning center courses, FamilySearch Catalog results, and FamilySearch Wiki articles for that location. There's also an Image Only Historical Records section, which lists all of the databases for that location that include unindexed record images.

THE SEARCH FORM

The search form on the location landing page is similar to the main Historical Records search form. You can enter your ancestor's first and last names, as well as enter information on a life event (Birth, Marriage, Residence, Death, Any), family relationships (Spouse, Parents, Other Person), or restrict records by record type, batch number, or film number.

SEARCH FORM DIFFERENCES

One item on this form that's different from the main Historical Records search form is the lack of a global Match All Terms Exactly option at the bottom of the form, above the Search button. Instead, if you want FamilySearch.org to search for only the exact information (dates, location, names, etc.) you enter, you'll need to check the box next to the corresponding search field.

Additionally, this search form has a Filter by Collection option. When you click the Show All Collections link (right above the Search button), you can see all of the individual collections available. For the United States, it lists all the searchable state and federal records collections on the website. To limit your search to one specific collection or multiple collections (perhaps all of the censuses for one state), click on the check box next to the collections you want to limit the search to.

Searching Individual Collections

If you've already done some genealogy research, a more targeted search may be beneficial to your efforts. This is a great search strategy when you have a specific goal in mind, such as looking for an ancestor in a certain census or in a particular state or country's vital-records collections.

The easiest way to access specific collections is to go to **<www.familysearch.org/ search/collection/list>**. This pulls up a list of all the Historical Records collections on FamilySearch.org (image **F**).

VIEWING OPTIONS

You can organize the way you view the full list of collections by clicking on a column heading. For example, clicking on the Title column sorts the collections alphabetically. Clicking on the Records column heading will sort the list so that you see the collections with the highest number of records first, down to the smallest number of records. The Last Updated column lets you see how recently the collection was updated. This notation is particularly helpful to tell at a glance if any records have been added since the last time you searched that collection.

How to Use Wildcards in Searches

Decades or centuries ago, when many of the historical records on FamilySearch.org were originally created, the clerks and record keepers weren't perfect. The volunteer indexers who transcribe records for FamilySearch.org aren't infallible, either. That means spelling errors will almost certainly appear in your ancestors' records. For example, I've seen my ancestor Blasius Schwer's first name appear in records as Bliss, Bloes, and Blassius.

To account for spelling errors or other variations of names, you can use wildcards. Wildcards are special characters you enter in a search box in place of certain letters. On FamilySearch.org, you can use a question mark (?) to represent one missing letter. An asterisk (*) can replace zero or more characters. You can use both wildcards in the same search if desired. You must have at least one letter in the search box, and you can place the wildcard at the beginning, middle, or end of a search field.

For example, if I want to account for all of the different first name spellings I've seen for Blasius, I might enter his name as *Bl*s Schwer*. This pulls up results for people with the last name Schwer who have the first name spellings I've seen, plus several more, including Blazius and Blausis. Apparently he had a difficult name to spell!

Even if your ancestors had easy-to-spell names, expect spelling discrepancies. For example, if your ancestor's last name was Henderson, it could appear in records as Hendersen. To account for this difference, you could enter *Henders?n* in the Last Names search box.

Many search engines, including Google **<www.google.com>**, support Boolean search techniques to help you focus searches, such as enclosing terms in quotation marks or using the word *and* between terms. Unfortunately, FamilySearch.org does not support Boolean techniques, so don't worry about using quotation marks or operators (*and*, *or*) in your Family-Search.org searches.

If a collection contains images of actual records, a Camera icon will appear to the left of the collection title. If a collection is unindexed (meaning you can't search it), it will have a Browse Images link in the Records column. If a collection is indexed and searchable, it will show the total number of records you can search in the Records column. Recently added or updated collections will have an asterisk next to the date in the Last Updated column.

When a collection title piques your interest, click on the collection name to find a brief description of the records the collection contains. If the records are searchable, you'll also see a search form, plus an option at the bottom of the page to browse the images. If the

F

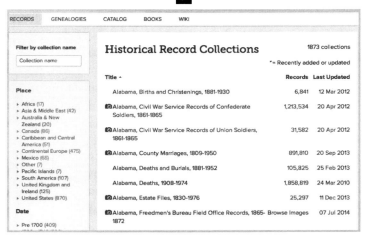

Title ▲	Records	Last Updated
Alabama, Births and Christenings, 1881-1930	6,841	12 Mar 2012
Alabama, Civil War Service Records of Confederate Soldiers, 1861-1865	1,213,534	20 Apr 2012
Alabama, Civil War Service Records of Union Soldiers, 1861-1865	31,582	20 Apr 2012
Alabama, County Marriages, 1809-1950	891,810	20 Sep 2013
Alabama, Deaths and Burials, 1881-1952	105,825	25 Feb 2013
Alabama, Deaths, 1908-1974	1,858,819	24 Mar 2010
Alabama, Estate Files, 1830-1976	25,297	11 Dec 2013
Alabama, Freedmen's Bureau Field Office Records, 1865-1872	Browse Images	07 Jul 2014

G

H

I

POWER-USER TIP

Unfiltering Collections

If you find that you've narrowed the collections too much, you can remove a collection filter by clicking the X next to the item or by click on the down arrows to the left of the filter you chose.

records are not indexed, you'll see only a link to browse the images. To learn more about the record collection, click the Learn More link.

Several filters help you home in on the collections most relevant to your research. The first is use the Filter By Collection Name search box. Enter a term in that search box, such as a location, record type, or date—basically any word that might be in the collection title. The site will narrow results in the Historical Records collections list to ones that match the terms you enter. Keep your filters simple. For example, if you enter *New York* in the Filter By Collection Name search box, it will show only collections with New York in the name. If you enter *New York census*, it will show the seven New York state census collections (image G).

The second way to filter collections is by using the options in the column to the left of the collections listings. This column lets you filter for Place, Date, Collections (aka record type), and Availability (of record images). You can select just one filter or combine filters from each category. Simply click the down arrow next to the item you want to select. For example, if you wanted to find the 1911 England and Wales census collection, you first would select United Kingdom and Ireland. Under Place, choose England; then under Date, pick 1900–1949. When results are sorted by collection Title, the 1911 census now appears fifth on the list of Historical Records collections (image H). Alternatively, instead of selecting the Date, you could have selected Census & Lists for all available England and Wales censuses to appear in the list.

The third way to filter collections is to use a combination of options on the left-hand column and the Filter By Collection Name search box. For example, let's say you want to see whether FamilySearch.org has a city directory for the location you're researching. Select Miscellaneous under the Collections category. Then enter *city directory* (or *city directories*) in the Filter By Collection Name search box. This shows that FamilySearch.org had city directories for only one location—the *Halberstadt Kreisarchiv* in Saxony-Anhalt, Germany—at the time of the search (image I).

BROWSING HISTORICAL RECORDS

Surprise! Not all records available on FamilySearch.org are indexed. That means you can only browse certain records, and not search them instantly via a handy online search form. "Ugh," you say. "How long will that take me to wade through?" Well, that all depends on how many records are available and whether or not years or other categories can help you narrow the search.

Where Are All These Browsable Records?

When you view the list of Historical Records collections on FamilySearch.org **<www.familysearch.org/search/collection/list>**, you'll see that unindexed collections have a link to Browse Images under the Records column. If you want to see what non-indexed records are available for the state or country where your ancestors lived, use the collection filters. For example, if your ancestor lived in Alabama, type *Alabama* into the Filter By Collection Name search box. It will pull up all of the records collections for Alabama, and you can clearly see which collections have the Browse Images link in the Records column.

In addition, you can browse some indexed records. This works only with record images directly on FamilySearch.org (not on third-party partner websites). To do this, click on a record from the search results window, then click on the Camera icon to view the document. At the top of the page, click Open in a new window, and you'll be taken to an image of the record with a toolbar showing the collection name and Image page number. For example, it might show that the record you're viewing is Image 21 of 31. To browse the record, hit the back arrow or forward arrow next to the page number. This could be especially helpful if you suspect other family members are listed on records in the same collection.

Strategies for Browsing Record Collections

Here are a few strategies to help you find and most efficiently browse through unindexed online records on FamilySearch.org.

CHECK THE DATE

Before you begin browsing through a record collection, look at the collection description. Specifically, look at the dates of the collection. If it has death records from 1700 to 1800, but your ancestor died in 1820, stop right there and don't waste your time. If your ancestor died in 1791, go ahead and start browsing. Under the View Images in This Collection heading, click the Browse Through [Number] Images link (FamilySearch.org will display the specific number of records in the link).

CHECK THE LOCATION COVERAGE

Once you're on the landing page for a browsable collection, click the Learn More link. This typically takes you to a page in the FamilySearch Wiki that provides more details on the collection, which may include how the records are organized or what cities or towns for a specific region are included. Checking this information was especially helpful to me when researching unindexed Italian civil registrations. After checking the locations covered by a particular record set, I discovered my ancestors' town wasn't included, so I saved hours of time by not paging through records that wouldn't list them.

PICK A STARTING POINT

After you click the Browse Through [Number] Images link, you'll see more links to drill down further into the collection. The options you get depend upon how the records were organized: You might see locations, dates, or more record categories. To start browsing, keep picking the appropriate links for the ancestor you're looking for. This will take you to the right section of records to browse.

MAKE A GUESS

Now take a closer look at how many records there are, how the records are organized, and how many pages each record appears to be. You might luck out and have only fifty-three pages to go through, with each record taking up one page. On the other hand, you might end up with five thousand pages to examine, with each record taking up two pages. Where should you start? Make an educated guess, based on how the records appear to be arranged. For example, if you're looking for a McCullough ancestor in a set of fifteen hundred alphabetized records, you might choose to start browsing in the middle on page 750, rather than on page 1.

GO PAGE BY PAGE

There's really no way around this when browsing records. In fact, no matter where you start browsing, you'll need to use the right (forward) and left (back) arrows in the record viewing toolbar to move from one record to another. You'll have to move forward or backward depending on whether your starting-point guess was hot or cold. In some cases, you may be comfortable jumping a few pages at a time. You can do this by entering a number in the Image number box at the top of the page and hitting Enter (or clicking the Go button that appears). This can save you time after you figure out how the records are organized, especially if an index is included among the record images.

Step-by-Step Example: Browsing Historical Records

Next, let's see how these strategies actually work in real-life genealogy research. After following this example, apply the same steps to a different collection you'd like to browse.

1 CHOOSE A COLLECTION TO BROWSE. Go to the list of unindexed collections at <**www. familysearch.org/search/collection/list**>. For this example, let's choose the Arkansas Confederate Pensions, 1901–1929 collection. Click Browse Images under the Records column to take you to the collection's summary page. Click the Browse Through 159,626 Images link.

2 FOLLOW THE LINKS. For the Arkansas Confederate Pensions, 1901–1929 collection, the list of browsing categories for the collection's images has an alphabetical listing of the records. Choose the appropriate alphabetical category for your family. Some collections

1

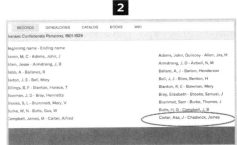

2

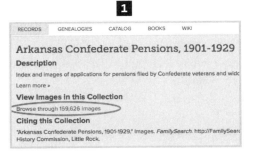

3

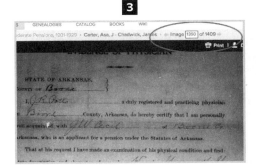

4

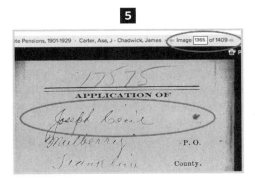

5

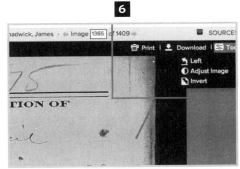

6

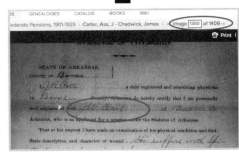

could have more than one link to click to get to the records you seek. In this example, we'll look for Joseph Cecil, so click on the Carter, Asa, J.–Chadwick, James link.

3 SELECT A PAGE TO START WITH. Evaluate the records you've opened and acquaint yourself with how they are organized and how many records there are. Then determine your strategy for browsing them. In this example, records appear to be in alphabetical order, and each record per person appears to take several pages, but there are 1,409 pages to browse. Let's look for Joseph Cecil. The first page starts with the surname Carter and the last page ends with Chadwick, so enter a page number where you think the Cecil application may appear, possibly near the end of the batch on page 1,350.

4 NAVIGATE FORWARD AND BACK. If the record you jumped to was correct, congratulations! If you can't read it, use the forward and back arrows to move one page at a time until you find a record you can easily read. Look at the name of the record. Is it before or after your ancestor's in the alphabet? Use the forward and back arrows to move up or down in the alphabet, or if you're way off, enter a new page number guess. In this case, we've landed on a record on page 1,350 for J.W. Cecil. Is this Joseph? Click the right arrow to move forward a few pages.

5 KEEP CLICKING FORWARD AND BACK. Continue to click through the records page by page until you either find the record you're looking for or determine your ancestor isn't listed. When we get to page 1,358 in our example, we see it lists James Cecil. We're getting close, so keep clicking forward a few more pages. Joseph Cecil's record starts on page 1,365.

6 ANALYZE AND SAVE THE RECORD. Look over the records you find and compare the information listed with the information you know about your ancestor. If something is difficult to read, use the Tools options in the toolbar or the Zoom tools to adjust the image. If all the information checks out, you know you've found a record for *your* ancestor. Now you can save it. Click the Print icon to print a copy, click the Download icon to download the image, or click the Sources (file box) icon to add the record to your Source Box or attach it to your family tree. Keep in mind you'll need to print, save, attach, or download each page image if the record is multiple pages.

ANALYZING HISTORICAL RECORDS RESULTS

When search results appear, it's so exciting. *There's my ancestor!* you might think. But is he really listed there? Before you add a record to your Source Box, attach it to your online family tree, or print or download a copy of the record, stop and take a breath. Then confirm it's really your ancestor. How? After finding a match for a person of the same name as your ancestor, look at several other fields of information.

- Does the date on the record match (within a couple of days, months, or years) the ancestor you're researching?
- Does the location on the record match?
- Are the other family members listed on the record (if applicable) the same family members you know you're related to?

If the dates are way off—perhaps the record indicates this John Schmidt was born in 1832 when you're looking for John Schmidt born in 1871, or the marriage date listed is in 1912, the year before your ancestor was born—it's likely not your ancestor. If your ancestor was born in Virginia, was married in Virginia, and died and was buried in Virginia, and you find a record for a person of the same name in Wisconsin, it's probably not him. If the date and location match your ancestor, but the rest of the members of the household listed don't match his wife, children, spouse, or siblings' names, it may not be him (unless he had been married twice, in which case it could be him, but you'd need to do more digging to be sure).

Errors do happen, however. A record keeper could have written incorrect information on a document. A transcriptionist could have confused an 8 for a 5 and entered it incorrectly. Just be cautious, and do a little analysis before you assume the record you found is the one you've been searching for all night.

You've Found a Record—Now What?

After you've determined a record truly is for your ancestor, you've got several options for what to do with that record in FamilySearch.org and in your personal family history record files (image **J**).

J

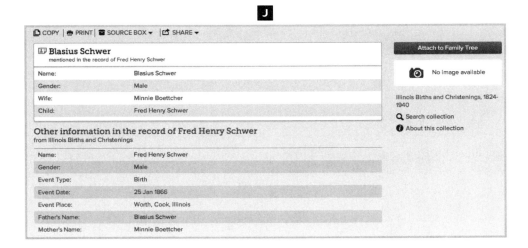

SAVE IT TO YOUR SOURCE BOX

FamilySearch.org's Source Box is a great tool that lets you keep all the records you find in one place. It provides citation information so you can always remember where you found the record—and that you even found the record in the first place. If you think a record might be for your ancestor, but it requires more investigating to be 100 percent sure, you could create a Maybe folder or a Needs Investigating folder in your Source Box. This way you have one place to save all the records you want to take a closer look at later.

ATTACH IT TO YOUR TREE

Add this source to a person in your FamilySearch Family Tree by clicking the Attach to Family Tree button (you'll see this on the records window when you view your search results). FamilySearch.org will automatically match the record to a relative in your tree. (Note: You must have already created a family tree on FamilySearch.org in order to use this feature. If you have trouble getting the image to attach, save it to your Source Box first, then open the person's page on your family tree. Next, scroll down to the Sources section and click the Attach from Source Box link.)

PRINT A HARD COPY

If you keep hard-copy files of your ancestor finds, you can click on the Print icon at the top of the record detail window to print a copy.

COPY THE DATA

The Copy icon at the top of the record detail window copies the text from the record result page and allows you to paste it in a document. For example, you would click the Copy icon, open a new word processor document or Evernote note, then paste the text. This is helpful when no record image is available or you want the record contents to be searchable in your research notes.

DOWNLOAD THE IMAGE

If your record result includes a record image, you'll want to download a copy for your personal files. Record images may be directly on FamilySearch.org or may be accessible through a partner site such as Ancestry.com **<www.ancestry.com>**. If it's on FamilySearch.org, simply click on the Camera icon in the search results, then click the Download link to download the current record shown on your screen. A JPG image of the record will download to your computer; you can move it to the appropriate folder where you keep genealogy record images.

If a record image is on a partner site, viewing and downloading the image usually requires a paid subscription to that third-party website. Alternatively, you could visit a FamilySearch Center in your area to view the record for free.

SHARE YOUR FIND

You can share your record finds via social media on Facebook, Twitter, and Google+, as well as via e-mail. To access these sharing options on FamilySearch.org, click the down arrow next to the Share icon on the record results page.

EXAMINE THE RECORD FOR CLUES

After you download, copy, or add a record to your Source Box, take a closer look at the information provided in the record. Does a death record list the street address of your ancestor or of the person providing information for the record? Does a census record include the year your ancestor immigrated to America? Does a marriage license include the religious affiliation or church name where the wedding ceremony occurred? These bits of information could be valuable clues as you continue your research.

LOG YOUR RESULTS

On your FamilySearch.org Research Tracking Worksheet (see appendix C), be sure to record information on what you searched, when you searched, and what you found. On your family group sheets or five-generation ancestor charts, add any important dates or other information you found. If you use genealogy software, be sure to add information and source citations for new records you've found.

No Luck? Try These Strategies

As genealogists, we all do it at some point: hit a brick wall in our research. If you're not succeeding with your initial searches for your ancestors, consider these strategies to enhance your searches:

- Search for a woman's maiden name as well as her married name, because she will appear in records prior to her marriage with that surname.
- Put only one name at a time in each names search box.
- If your ancestor has a common name, add a middle initial to the First Names field.
- Remove filters to broaden your search, such as date or family relationships.
- Increase or remove date ranges.
- Skip the exact check boxes in your search. Selecting the check box tells FamilySearch.org that not only must the spelling match, but the record results also must contain that field—so checking exact for a marriage date, for example, will eliminate any records that don't list marriage information.

- Try spelling variations of first and last names by using wildcards, as well as by typing in different name spellings (or misspellings) in the search boxes.
- For searchable/indexed collections that have record images, go old school and try browsing through the record collection. From the search results page, click on a record of interest, then click the View the Document link. On the record image page, use the forward and back arrow, next to the Image box. Note: Browsing only works on images that are directly on FamilySearch.org, not on partner sites.
- If you still can't find the record for your ancestor that you're looking for, it's possible that the record may not exist or that it's just not available online (yet).

KEYS TO SUCCESS

★ Begin with broad ancestor searches and narrow your results as needed using FamilySearch. org's filters.

★ Eliminate irrelevant search results from the get-go by limiting your search to a specific location or collection.

★ Check for unindexed collections likely to contain records of your ancestors, and browse them strategically to save time.

★ Save what you find to your FamilySearch.org Source Box and your digital and/or paper genealogy files.

★ Remember that FamilySearch.org adds new records regularly, so keep checking periodically for previously unindexed or unavailable records.

Searching Genealogies, the Catalog, and Books

Historical records aren't the only boon for genealogy researchers on FamilySearch.org. You also can access user-submitted genealogies, digitized family history books, and the FamilySearch Catalog. Each section of the site has its own idiosyncrasies for searching it, including different search forms. In this chapter, I'll walk you through what you need to know to access these special sections of the website and offer strategies for making the most of your searches.

SEARCHING GENEALOGIES

When you searched the Historical Records collections, you might have noticed a result for user-submitted genealogies at the bottom of the search results pages. The genealogies results come from pedigree information people have submitted over the years via the Ancestral File and Pedigree Resource File. Both the Ancestral File and Pedigree Resource File are separate from FamilySearch Family Tree, which we covered in chapter 2.

The Ancestral File contains about forty million records of births, deaths, and marriages submitted by members of The Church of Jesus Christ of Latter-day Saints. These genealogies are known for including pre-1500s "research" of questionable reliability (it predates vital-record keeping). Ancestral File records do not contain notes or source citations, so it's important to double-check the accuracy of what you find. FamilySearch.org stopped accepting new submissions to the Ancestral File in 2003, so no new information is being added to this database.

The Pedigree Resource File, which used to be available only on CD or DVD, contains two hundred million user-submitted records. FamilySearch stores a copy of the Pedigree Resource File entries in its Granite Mountain Vault (along with all the microfilmed and digitized records the organization has captured). Entries typically include source notes and citations, but FamilySearch.org does not check the accuracy of the information in the Pedigree Resource File. Further, corrections were not accepted when many files were created, so duplicate files exist where users resubmitted information. The Pedigree Resource File contains individual names and family relationships, along with vital-records information. This database is still open and continues to grow as users submit more information; however, the information you submit cannot be edited. It does not include information on living people.

The International Genealogical Index (IGI) is also now searchable along with other user-submitted genealogies on FamilySearch.org. We'll cover the IGI in more detail later.

Community Trees are another collection of user-submitted genealogies you can search. These genealogies were mostly compiled by FamilySearch staff genealogists as part of an effort to publish the genealogy for a whole town or community. Sources are included, and some of these genealogies may date back to medieval times.

The Genealogies Search Form

To search user-submitted genealogies, click on the Search tab, then select Genealogies from the drop-down menu (or go to <www.familysearch.org/family-trees>). The search form for user-submitted genealogies (image **A**) offers two main options for searching: by Relationship or by AF Number (the Ancestral File number). When you search by relationship, you can enter the following information into search fields:

- first and last names
- spouse's first and last names
- father's first and last names
- mother's first and last names
- birthplace and year range
- marriage place and year range
- residence place and year range
- death place and year range
- any place and year range
- submission ID number

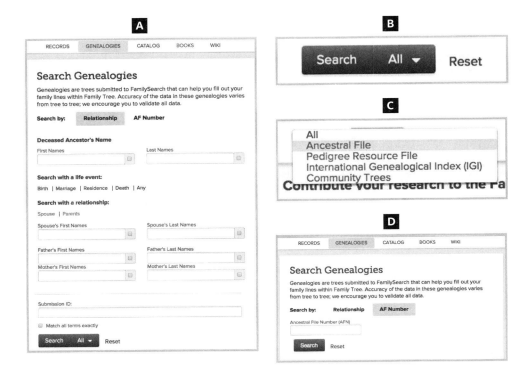

Before you hit the Search button, notice that you can choose to search all of the genealogies collections on FamilySearch.org (image **B**); these include Ancestral File, Pedigree Resource File, IGI, and Community Trees, or you can choose to search just one of those collections (image **C**).

If you search by AF Number, that's the only available search field (image **D**). The AF Number is an ID that was assigned to each published record. It typically has six or seven characters with a combination of consonants and numbers, such as 20V4-RND. To search using this number, you likely would have had to be the submitter of the information or have found the information previously. Note: This only works for Ancestral File entries.

Strategies for Searching Genealogies

Because most researchers, especially beginners, will use the Relationship search option most often, let's focus on strategies for searching user-submitted genealogies that way.

ENTER A NAME AND LOCATION

It's important to start your search broadly, then narrow your results. But I recommend including at least your ancestor's name and a Residence Place when you begin searching unless your ancestor had a really uncommon name. This should help you get more relevant results.

REFINE YOUR SEARCH

If you still get too many results by entering a name and location, try adding information in the Spouse's First Names field or adding dates or places of the person's birth and/or death. The search results page has a Refine Your Search column to the left of the results. If you get too many results to wade through, click the Refine Your Search button (adding life events, searching with a relationship, etc.) to narrow your results. You can also narrow your search by using the list of filters, such as marriage year, birthplace, and gender. In addition, you can check the box next to the genealogies collection name to filter by one or more of the collections. Try different combinations of search terms and filters until you find a combination that produces the results you seek.

AVOID EXACT MATCH

The search form has a Match All Terms Exactly check box that applies to the entire form. In addition, the name and place fields each have exact match check boxes next to them. Because misspellings can occur and spellings of places and surnames can change over time, you may miss out on potential matches by selecting exact match. Furthermore, your search will come up empty if certain information you marked exact on the search form isn't included in the file.

Submitting to Pedigree Resource File

FamilySearch.org continues to accept user-submitted entries to add to its Pedigree Resource File. To submit your entry, go to **<www.familysearch.org/upload>** (or under the Search tab, click on Genealogies from the drop-down menu, then scroll down to the Submit Tree button). You'll need to upload a GEDCOM to make your contribution. Keep in mind that when you submit a GEDCOM, it becomes searchable on FamilySearch.org within about fifteen minutes, and it will be preserved on FamilySearch.org. After you submit your GEDCOM, you can import it into your FamilySearch Family Tree. You cannot make edits to the file you submit, but in some cases you may be able to delete an incorrect file and submit a new file with correct information.

USE WILDCARDS

Just as with the Historical Records collection search form, you can use wildcard characters to search genealogies. As a reminder, an asterisk (*) replaces multiple characters and a question mark (?) replaces one character.

USE THE SUBMISSION ID

Some search results have a submission ID number. Click this ID number to find all names submitted in the same file.

User-Submitted Genealogies Timeline

Ancestral File. Pedigree Resource File. The IGI. FamilySearch Family Trees. With so many different resources with similar types of information, it can be confusing to figure out just where your ancestor could be listed in a user-submitted genealogy. Here's a timeline of how these different user-submitted genealogy files and databases began and have changed over time.

1973 The IGI is published on microfiche with twenty million entries.

1979 The church begins accepting submissions by LDS members for the Ancestral File.

1988 The Ancestral File, with four million names, becomes available at the Family History Library; the IGI is published on CD with 147 million names.

1990 The Ancestral File becomes available on a CD containing seven million names.

1999 With the launch of the FamilySearch.org website, the Ancestral File goes online with thirty-five million names; the IGI goes online, to which 285 million names will be added over time; and the Pedigree Resource File is introduced, allowing users to submit genealogies on FamilySearch.org and view the submission on a CD.

2003 Submissions for the Ancestral File are no longer accepted; users can submit genealogies to the Pedigree Resource File only.

2007 The Pedigree Resource File, now containing 150 million names, becomes viewable online.

2011 A new edition of the Ancestral File with forty million names is made available on the redesigned FamilySearch.org.

2012 FamilySearch discontinues the creation of Pedigree Resource File CDs and DVDs.

2015 The user-submitted genealogies search at <www.familysearch.org/family-trees> adds options to search the IGI and Community Trees (in addition to the Ancestral File and Pedigree Resource File).

Genealogies and Source Boxes

The FamilySearch.org system doesn't currently allow entries from genealogies to be saved to a Source Box or attached to a family tree, like you can do for historical records you find elsewhere on the site. But here's a workaround: Copy the URL for the record, then go to your Source Box and select the Create a New Source button. Paste the URL in the Web page field and add a source title, citation, and description, then click Save.

NARROW BY COLLECTION

When you hit the Search button for genealogies, it automatically searches all collections of genealogies on FamilySearch.org. If you get too many results, or if you just want to search a specific genealogies collection, you can click on the All button (with a down arrow) and select just one of these collections to search: Ancestral File, Pedigree Resource File, IGI, or Community Trees.

Viewing Genealogies Search Results

Search results for user-submitted genealogies contain a category for the person's name (which also includes the file the name it appears in: Ancestral File, Pedigree Resource File, IGI, or Community Trees), events (a listing of birth, death, marriage, and residence information for the person), and relationships (spouse and parents).

To see the full record, click the person's name on the search results page (image **E**). This will bring up a pedigree-chart looking entry on the right and a summary of the information in the record on the left (which may include vital event information and parents' names), plus a citation for the record (image **F**). Collection-specific information is also included:

- If the record comes from the Ancestral File, the Ancestral File number will be listed.
- If the record is from the Pedigree Resource File, FamilySearch.org shows the Pedigree Resource File submission ID number and the "person count" of unique individuals in that particular submission.
- If the record is from the IGI, you'll see an IGI batch number and IGI microfilm number. IGI entries also typically list source information.
- At the top of right of the page, you'll also see a notation of the date the information was submitted and the ID of the person who submitted the information.

When you click on a person's name in the pedigree chart view, it will bring up that person's vital information on the left. The View Tree link (in the upper left) brings up the pedigree chart for that person as well. (Note: These pedigree charts do not act like the pedigree charts you see when you enter your own family tree information in the Family

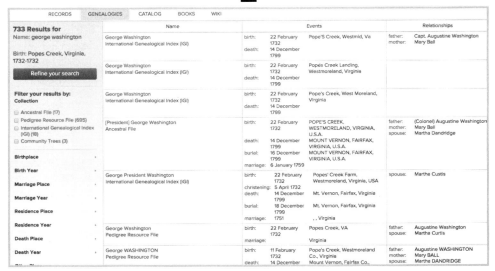

	Name	Events			Relationships	
733 Results for	George Washington	birth:	22 February 1732	Pope'S Creek, Westmld, Va	father:	Capt. Augustine Washington
Name: george washington	International Genealogical Index (IGI)	death:	14 December 1799		mother:	Mary Ball
Birth: Popes Creek, Virginia, 1732-1732	George Washington	birth:	22 February 1732	Popés Creek Landing, Westmoreland, Virginia		
[Refine your search]	International Genealogical Index (IGI)	death:	14 December 1799			
Filter your results by:	George Washington	birth:	22 February 1732	Pope's Creek, West Moreland, Virginia		
Collection	International Genealogical Index (IGI)	death:	14 December 1799			
☐ Ancestral File (17)	[President] George Washington	birth:	22 February 1732	POPE'S CREEK, WESTMORELAND, VIRGINIA, U.S.A.	father:	(Colonel) Augustine Washington
☐ Pedigree Resource File (695)	Ancestral File				mother:	Mary Ball
☐ International Genealogical Index (IGI) (18)		death:	14 December 1799	MOUNT VERNON, FAIRFAX, VIRGINIA, U.S.A.	spouse:	Martha Dandridge
☐ Community Trees (3)		burial:	16 December 1799	MOUNT VERNON, FAIRFAX, VIRGINIA, U.S.A.		
Birthplace ▸		marriage:	6 January 1759			
Birth Year ▸	George President Washington	birth:	22 February 1732	Popes' Creek Farm, Westmoreland, Virginia, USA	spouse:	Martha Custis
Marriage Place ▸	International Genealogical Index (IGI)	christening:	5 April 1732			
Marriage Year ▸		death:	14 December 1799	Mt. Vernon, Fairfax, Virginia		
Residence Place ▸		burial:	18 December 1799	Mt. Vernon, Fairfax, Virginia		
Residence Year ▸		marriage:	1751	, , Virginia		
Death Place ▸	George Washington	birth:	22 February 1732	Popes Creek, VA	father:	Augustine Washington
	Pedigree Resource File				spouse:	Martha Curtis
Death Year ▸		marriage:		Virginia		
	George WASHINGTON	birth:	11 February 1732	Pope's Creek, Westmoreland Co., Virginia	father:	Augustine WASHINGTON
	Pedigree Resource File				mother:	Mary BALL
		death:	14 December	Mount Vernon, Fairfax Co.,	spouse:	Martha DANDRIDGE

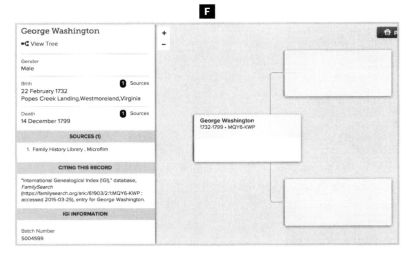

George Washington

▪ View Tree

Gender
Male

Birth ❶ Sources
22 February 1732
Popes Creek Landing,Westmoreland,Virginia

Death ❶ Sources
14 December 1799

SOURCES (1)

1. Family History Library , Microfilm

CITING THIS RECORD

"International Genealogical Index (IGI)," database,
FamilySearch
(https://familysearch.org/ark:/61903/2:1:MQY6-KWP :
accessed 2015-03-25), entry for George Washington.

IGI INFORMATION

Batch Number
5004599

George Washington
1732-1799 • MQY6-KWP

Tree section of the website: There are no hints, no way to add more details, and no auto-mated way to add the information to your Source Box or attach it to your family tree.)

Probably the most important information you'll see in a search result is source infor-mation. Click the source link or scroll to the Sources section of the entry to view the sources cited. If the sources look credible and thorough, you've just hit the genealogy jackpot (though you should still verify data in original sources).

To save that record, you'll need to print it. You can print a copy by selecting the Print button. This will print the record for the person whose information appears on the left (not the pedigree chart in the right portion of the window), so you'll need to print this page for each person whose information you want to save.

If you don't find family history information for ancestors you search in the Genealogies section, it's likely no one has submitted or compiled a genealogy including that person. In that case, consider searching for genealogies in FamilySearch.org's Family Tree (under the Family Tree tab), which contains family trees users are currently working on. Alternatively, you could search family trees located on other websites, such as MyHeritage **<www. myheritage.com>**, Ancestry.com **<www.ancestry.com>**, and Geni **<www.geni.com>**

Case Study: The Robert and Unity Wines Family

Genealogist Clare Brown, who runs the website **<www.winesfamilyhistory.wix.com/ wines>**, was looking for information on the children and parents of her fifth-great-grandparents Robert and Unity Wines when she came across FamilySearch.org's genealogies.

"Wines is not a common name, and being familiar with many of the names, I was able to home in quite quickly on who I was looking for," Brown says. "The user-submitted genealogies were useful; it's good to see others with the same info. It gives you hope that you are on the right track."

Brown already knew some details about the family, including two of the sons' names. To search for the Wines, Brown entered their names, birth years, and birthplaces to start. Her search turned up one of the Wines' sons, John. "His story would prove to be fascinating, if tragic. Eventually it led me to meet up with descendants of the third brother, Frederick Wines, which was a wonderful outcome from all this research."

From her research, Brown says she learned that cross-referencing is important—in particular, checking other sites listed as sources or notes/references in genealogies. "This proved to be useful for many in the Wines family. It was a useful hint to have sources and notes given, as this provided suggestions as to where else to look and research. From other websites listed and referred to, I have been able to find info on marriages, children, baptisms, and so much more," Brown says.

"Websites such as FamilySearch.org are ... my favorite websites for researching my family tree. The Wines history has proved to be fascinating for our family, and John Wines' story turned out to be one of crime, transportation, and a tragic end," Brown adds.

SEARCHING THE INTERNATIONAL GENEALOGICAL INDEX

The IGI is not necessarily a separate section of FamilySearch.org; it is considered one of the site's Historical Records collections and is included with the searchable user-submitted genealogies collection. The IGI was part of the original FamilySearch.org when the website launched in 1999. It contains entries of vital events such as births, baptisms, marriages, and deaths collected since the IGI was first available on microfiche in 1973.

Throughout the years, people from the genealogical community extracted and contributed details from vital records and church records, and LDS members submitted information about their ancestors to the index. The collection has two parts:

- the Community Contributed IGI, which contains approximately 430 million names from personal family information that people submitted to the LDS Church
- the Community Indexed IGI, which contains approximately 460 million names from vital records and church records dating from the 1500s to 1885. Duplicates of many records in the index are common.

Before you begin your IGI search, remember that this collection is an index only and that this file is no longer being updated. This means search results will contain no record images, and after you complete a thorough search of these records, there's no need to search this particular collection again in the future for the same ancestors.

Also before you begin a search, consider checking what records the index actually covers. How? Go to the FamilySearch Wiki at **<www.familysearch.org/learn/wiki/en/ International_Genealogical_Index_Coverage>**. This Wiki page has detailed information on what information is contained for each US state. Note that the information on this Wiki entry is dated—the information is valid as of 1998, whereas new data were contributed to the IGI until 2008. Still, the page will give you a good enough idea of geographic and date coverage to help you determine whether searching the collection is worth your time.

Two Ways to Search the IGI

The first way to search the IGI is using the Genealogies search form at **<www.family search.org/family-trees>**: Before you hit the Search button, click on the All button (with a down arrow) and select just the IGI. You'll want to select the tab to Search With a Relationship, since AF numbers don't apply to the IGI records. For information on viewing search results using this search form, see the Viewing Genealogies Search Results section earlier in this chapter.

The second way to search the IGI is to go to **<www.familysearch.org/search/collection/ igi>** (image **G**). This search form allows you to get a little more detailed with your IGI search because here, you can select whether or not to include both parts of the collection, just the Community Contributed IGI, or just the Community Indexed IGI. The form also has fields for searching

- on first and last names
- with a life event (such as a birth, marriage, residence, or death place and year range)
- with a relationship (such as spouse, parents, or other person)
- by batch number, film number, or serial/sheet number

When using this second option for searching, the results window separates the results into two tabs: one for the Contributed IGI and one for the Indexed IGI (image **H**). Each tab has columns for Name, Events, and Relationships. Under the person's name in each entry in the Name column, it lists what records collection the information originated in. This could be the IGI (for Community Contributed IGI results) or a vital-records or church collection (for Community Indexed IGI results). The Events column includes any combination of birth, marriage, or death dates and locations. The Relationship column typically lists any spouse, children, or parents associated with the IGI entry.

To view a full entry from your search results, you can click on the person's name linked in the Name column in either results tab. For results under the Indexed IGI tab, there's one additional column: Preview, where you can click the down arrow to preview the record without having to jump to an entirely new viewing window.

If you click the person's name to view an entry in the Community Contributed IGI results, you'll see a portion of a pedigree chart with vital-records information and family

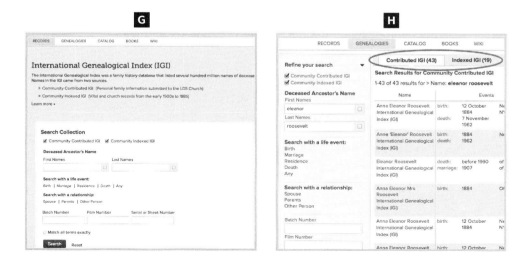

connections (image **I**). It also shows the submitter's name and/or number. To save this record, the only option available is to print a hard copy.

Under the Indexed IGI tab, results windows will show a record transcription, as you would see for other historical records you find. You can then copy the information, print it, add it to your Source Box, share it via social media or e-mail, or attach it to your family tree. Note the Indexing Project (Batch) Number and GS Film Number at the bottom of each record. If you click on the batch number link, you'll see other individuals indexed from the same batch of records as the entry you viewed. If you click the film number link, it will take you to other listings online from the same microfilm reel (image **J**).

It's important to verify any information you find in the IGI in the original records or other primary sources.

IGI Search Strategies

So how should you start your search of the IGI? Here are four tactics.

POWER-USER TIP

Searching by Number

What are the numbers at the bottom of the Indexed IGI results? The film number represents the number of the FamilySearch microfilm containing the original record. You can search for this microfilm number in the FamilySearch Catalog, then order a copy to view at your local FamilySearch Center. Batch numbers were numbers assigned to records extracted from a particular church for inclusion in the IGI. You can refine your search in the IGI by batch number.

START BROAD

As with any online search, start your search with broad criteria. Include both parts of the collection in your search, and do not use exact matches. You can always refine your criteria later after you see what type of results you get from an initial search. If you need to narrow results to only one part of the IGI collection, you'll need to use the IGI collection search form at

<www.familysearch.org/search/collection/igi> (not the Genealogies search form at <www.familysearch.org/family-trees>).

SEARCH FOR FAMILY MEMBERS

If you can't find your ancestor's name in the results, try searching for relatives such as the ancestor's parent, child, or sibling.

USE WILDCARDS

As on other search forms, you can use wildcard characters when searching the IGI. Using wildcards (an asterisk for more than one letter, a question mark for only one letter) can help you find entries with misspelled names.

TRY BATCH NUMBERS

All records from the same source, such as a church's baptism registers, should have the same batch number. Why is this useful? By searching on the batch number, you could potentially find other family members who attended the same church and were recorded in the same source. Third parties have created lists to help you find batch numbers to search. See a list of batch numbers for Canada and the United States at <freepages.genealogy.rootsweb.ancestry.com/~hughwallis/IGIBatchNumbers.htm>. Alternatively, if you find a record when searching the Community Indexed IGI, clicking on its batch number will add the batch number to the Refine Your Search box at the left. You can then enter a name or other search criteria to search only that batch. To use these search strategies, you'll need to search using the IGI collection search form (not the Genealogies form).

SEARCHING THE FAMILYSEARCH CATALOG

FamilySearch's Family History Library in Salt Lake City has billions of genealogy records in books and on microfilm. Only a small portion of those records are available online, so if you don't find the records you seek in an online collection on FamilySearch.org, try using the FamilySearch Catalog to locate other possible sources. If you find a microfilm containing records you want to look at, you can order it for viewing at a local FamilySearch Center near you. (Use the form at <www.familysearch.org/films> to order microfilm.)

You can access the FamilySearch Catalog (image **K**) by clicking on the Search tab, then selecting Catalog from the drop-down menu (or go to <www.familysearch.org/catalog-search>). You can search the catalog by Places, Surnames, Titles, Author, Subjects, and Keywords. If you already know the microfilm or microfiche number or the book call number you need, there are search fields for entering those numbers as well. Here's a quick summary of what each catalog search category helps you find.

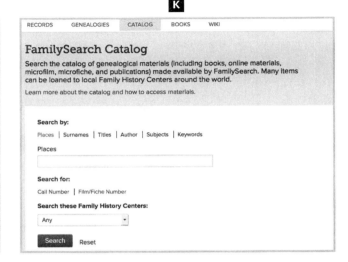

- **Places:** Use this to search for sources for the places where your ancestor lived. This helps you determine what records exist for you to research for your ancestor.
- **Surnames:** Search for family histories or genealogies for your family name.
- **Title:** Look for a source by a specific title, such as the name of a book or microfilm.
- **Author:** If you want to find publications by a specific author or corporation, use this option.
- **Subjects:** Look for works on a particular topic.
- **Keywords:** If you're not sure about a title or your other searches fail to yield relevant results, try inputting a word or phrase that might appear in the catalog entry.

Strategies for Searching the Catalog

Searching the FamilySearch Catalog is similar to searching any other library catalog, but here are a few strategies to make your searching more successful.

TRY MORE THAN ONE SEARCH

If you don't get any results the first time you search, adjust your search terms, and remove or add search fields. For example, if a Surnames search doesn't get any hits, try a Keywords search.

USE MORE THAN ONE CATEGORY

The FamilySearch Catalog lets you combine the categories you're searching for, so you could search for a place and surname at the same time, for instance. This is helpful if your catalog search results are too broad and you need to narrow the results.

When using the Surnames field, try using different name spelling variations.

SEARCHING FAMILY HISTORY BOOKS

You can search more than 150 thousand digitized genealogies, family histories, county and local histories, genealogy periodicals, gazetteers, school yearbooks, and more on FamilySearch.org. The Family History Books collection contains digitized publications from the Family History Library and other libraries and historical societies, including

- Allen County Public Library in Fort Wayne, Indiana
- Brigham Young University Harold B. Lee Library in Provo, Utah
- Brigham Young University Idaho David O. McKay Library
- Brigham Young University Hawaii Joseph F. Smith Library
- Church History Library for The Church of Jesus Christ of Latter-day Saints
- Historical Society of Pennsylvania
- Houston Public Library's Clayton Center for Genealogical Research in Texas
- Mid-Continent Public Library's Midwest Genealogy Center in Independence, Missouri
- Onondaga County Public Library in Syracuse, New York

Search Fields

You can search the digitized book collections using a Simple Search or Advanced Search form (image **L**). I recommend using the Advanced Search form because it will give you more control over the search terms you enter, therefore improving the results you get.

The Advanced Search form lets you enter search terms in two different boxes, as well as select a Material Type (periodicals/serials, gazetteer, or book) and Language (English, German, French, Hungarian, or Spanish). Next to the boxes where you enter search terms, drop-down menus let you select options to broaden or narrow your searches.

POWER-USER TIP

Viewing Digital Books

If you get the message "you don't have sufficient rights to view the requested object" when you click on a digital publication you want to explore, you'll need to access it at the Family History Library, a local FamilySearch Center, or a FamilySearch partner library. Why? Not all digitized books are available for you to view online at home because they are copyrighted and may have limited access.

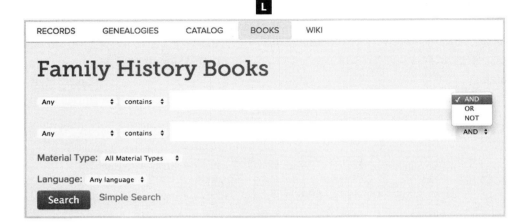

Under the Any menu, you can opt to look for any materials that have your search terms, or select a specific type of material or place where your search term should appear, such as in Reviewed Materials, as the Primary Subject, as the Periodical Title, or in the Full Text of the entry.

Under the Contains menu, you can select either Contains or Is Exact. Contains means that your search term could be anywhere in the search result or digitized publication. Is Exact means the search term must appear in the publication entry exactly as you type it into the search box. The Is Exact option can be helpful for narrowing your search results.

Under the And menu, you can select And, Or, or Not to broaden or narrow your search results. This option refers to how search terms you've entered in both search boxes should appear in results.

Strategies for Searching Family History Books

Searching more than 150 thousand digital publications sounds great, but how exactly do you find your ancestors in those resources? Use these strategies to up your odds of success.

START BROAD

It's usually best to start your search broad, then narrow if you get too many results. Having too narrow of a search to begin with could make you miss out on relevant resources.

TRY DIFFERENT SEARCH TERMS

You can enter any word or phrase as a search term. Try searching for a surname only or for a surname and a location where an ancestor lived to find genealogies. As always, experiment with spelling variations of surnames. Search for a location to find local and country histories. Additionally, try putting both the first and last name in one search field, or search on just the surname. Also try inputting the record or book type (such as year-book or marriage records) that you're looking for in one of the search fields. When you search for just a surname, consider selecting the Full Text option from the drop-down menu next to the search box.

USE WILDCARDS

The same wildcards that work for searching Historical Records collections work for Family History Books. An asterisk (*) will replace multiple characters, and a question mark (?) will replace a single character. For example, a search for the surname *John*n* finds publications with the name Johnson, Johnsen, and Johnston.

REFINE SEARCH RESULTS

At the time of this writing, there were limited ways to refine your search results, but as FamilySearch.org and its searching capabilities evolve, that could change. To the left of the search results, you'll see a column with several options for refining your search. Click the down arrow next to a category to check the appropriate boxes to narrow your search.

DOWNLOAD THE PDF

When you find a publication to review, download it as a PDF. You can then search within the PDF for your ancestor's name or other search terms so you don't have to spend tons of time going page by page through the entire publication.

KEYS TO SUCCESS

⭐ Always double-check the information you find in the genealogies on FamilySearch.org so you can ensure what you find is accurate.

⭐ Start searching all genealogies on FamilySearch.org at **<www.familysearch.org/family-trees>**. If you need to narrow your IGI results further, use the IGI search form at **<www.familysearch.org/search/collection/igi>**.

⭐ Use the FamilySearch Catalog to identify microfilms of records you can't find online. You can order the microfilm to view at your local FamilySearch Center.

⭐ If you can't find genealogies already submitted to FamilySearch.org, check the Family Trees section of the site **<www.familysearch.org/tree>** (which contains trees people are actively working on) or check other major genealogy family tree websites.

⭐ Remember to search the digitized book collections on FamilySearch.org for any type of record you're searching for, as well as for local or church histories.

5

US Census Records

love census records. These are some of the most widely available records for US genealogy researchers, and I've had great luck finding census records for my own ancestors on
my maternal and paternal sides.

FamilySearch.org not only has federal census records, but also several state and territorial censuses. In this chapter, we'll explore what US census records exist, what you
can learn from them, which records are available on FamilySearch.org, and strategies for
searching the census collections on FamilySearch.org. Let's get started.

ABOUT FEDERAL CENSUS RECORDS

The United States' first federal population census was taken in 1790, the same year that
President George Washington delivered the first State of the Union address and founding
father Benjamin Franklin died. The federal government has conducted censuses every
ten years since then. Between 1790 and 1870, US Marshals were tasked with taking the
census. Beginning in 1880, specially trained enumerators were hired to go door to door to
take the decennial census. It wasn't until 1960 that the government began mailing census
questionnaires to households. US census records are, by law, not released to the public

until seventy-two years after a census is taken. The most recent US census available to researchers is 1940.

Information collected on the censuses varied by year. The 1790 census recorded

- the head of household's name
- the number of free white males under age sixteen and age sixteen and over
- the number of free white females
- the number of other free persons
- the number of slaves

The 1850 census was the first census to request the name of each member of the household, as well as age, sex, and color. Each person's listing also included

- profession, occupation, or trade (for people older than fifteen)
- the value of real estate owned
- place of birth
- whether the person was married within in the last year
- whether the person was at school within the last year
- if the person (age twenty or over) could read or write
- if the person was "deaf, dumb, blind, insane, idiotic, pauper, or convict"

The 1880 census was the first to record the birthplace of the person's mother and father, as well as include a category to identify the relationship to the head of household, and marital status. The 1890 census (of which only fragments survive; the rest was water-damaged after a 1921 Commerce Department fire) recorded a person's Civil War service—Union or Confederate. The 1900 census was the first to include the year of immigration and citizenship status for foreign-born individuals. According to Ancestry.com, 1900 "is the only available census that provides columns for including the exact month and year of birth of every person enumerated." The 1910 census includes much of the same information as the previous one.

The 1920 census was the first to include a person's year of naturalization as well as a column to record the individual's father's and mother's native language. The 1930 census followed suit.

The 1940 census includes an interesting column for the person's place of residence on April 1, 1935, the number of weeks worked in 1939, and the amount earned in 1939 (reflecting the economic hardships of the Great Depression). It also includes a column for a person's highest school grade completed.

For more details on what questions each census asked, consult the chart at the end of this chapter, the U.S. Census Bureau's website **<www.census.gov/history/www/through_the_decades/questionnaires>**, and the *Family Tree Pocket Reference* (Family Tree Books).

Clues in Federal Census Records

Census records are important in genealogy research because they help you confirm where your ancestor lived during a particular time period. By knowing an ancestor's place of residence, you can then begin to look for other records he may have generated during that time, such as birth, death, marriage, land, probate, church, and other records. The 1850 and later censuses are particularly helpful because they list the names of all members of the household.

A census record can tell you a lot about your ancestors—more than just their age. For example, a 1930 census record for my great-grandfather Goffredo Gemignani (yes, he was Italian!) that I found on FamilySearch.org shows Goffredo's brother-in-law was living with him at the time of the census. The 1900 census record for my ancestor Frank H. Rolfes showed him living with his wife and six kids in Iowa, but it also showed me a clue I

Official Census Days

The date a census taker wrote on his form isn't as important as the official census date: Enumerators were supposed to list individuals' ages as of a date specified by the U.S. Census Bureau. Suppose your ancestor was born February 12, 1909, and the 1920 census taker visited in April. Your ancestor should still be recorded as ten years old, based on the official census day of January 1. Consult this chart when calculating ages from the census.

Census Year	Official Census Day	Census Year	Official Census Day
1790	August 2	1870	June 1
1800	August 4	1880	June 1
1810	August 6	1890	June 1*
1820	August 7	1900	June 1
1830	June 1	1910	April 15
1840	June 1	1920	January 1
1850	June 1	1930	April 1**
1860	June 1	1940	April 1

* Census taking began Monday, June 2.
** In Alaska, Census Day was October 1, 1929.

didn't know before: the years they immigrated to the United States—Frank in 1870 and his wife Mary in 1868. I can use this information to help narrow the date range of immigration records I can search for.

Depending on the census year you're researching, the records also could tell you

- whether your ancestor was naturalized and the date he became a citizen
- how much property (if any) your ancestor owned
- your ancestor's field of employment
- whether your ancestor served in the Civil War
- the language(s) your ancestor spoke (mother tongue and whether he spoke English)

US CENSUS RECORDS ON FAMILYSEARCH.ORG

FamilySearch.org has more than seventy-five collections of US census records to search and/or browse—and growing. Here's an overview of the available records.

Federal Censuses

FamilySearch.org has searchable indexes to all publicly available censuses, 1790 to 1940, including the 1890 census fragments for Alabama, the District of Columbia, Georgia, Illinois, Minnesota, New Jersey, New York, North Carolina, Ohio, South Dakota, and Texas. In addition, FamilySearch.org gives you access to record images for all censuses but the 1890 census. Here's the catch: Only record images from the 1850, 1870, 1900, and 1940 censuses are accessible for free directly on FamilySearch.org. For the remaining censuses, the FamilySearch.org listings link to images on the partner websites Ancestry.com (1790, 1800, 1810, 1820, 1830, 1840, 1880, 1910, 1920, 1930 censuses) and Fold3 **<www.fold3.com>** (1860 census). To access those images, you have to visit a FamilySearch Center or have a subscription to the partner site. To access specific US federal census collections, as well as learn more about the US federal census records available on FamilySearch.org, go to **<www.familysearch.org/census/us>**.

State and Territorial Censuses

State census records are great resources for trying to locate your family in between the decennial federal censuses. FamilySearch.org has searchable indexes to population census records for eighteen states, including

- Alabama: 1855, 1866
- California: 1852
- Colorado: 1885
- Florida: 1885, 1935, 1945
- Illinois: 1855, 1865

- Iowa: 1885, 1895, 1905, 1925 (1925 is browsable only)
- Massachusetts: 1855, 1865
- Michigan: 1894
- Minnesota: 1865, 1875, 1885, 1895, 1905, 1857 (territorial)
- Missouri (state and territorial): 1732–1933
- Nebraska: 1885
- New Jersey: 1885, 1905, 1915
- New Mexico (territorial): 1885
- New York: 1855, 1865, 1875, 1892, 1905, 1915, 1925
- North Dakota: 1915, 1925
- Rhode Island: 1885, 1905, 1915, 1925, 1935
- South Dakota: 1905, 1915, 1925, 1935, 1945
- Wisconsin: 1855, 1865, 1875, 1885, 1895, 1905

Most of these states' census collections include record images, but some images may be viewable only at a local FamilySearch Center or via partner subscription-based sites such as Ancestry.com.

To see the number of records available for each state census or to link directly to the state collection you want to search, follow these easy steps:

1. Click on the Search tab, then the Browse All Published Collections link to get to **<www.familysearch.org/search/collection/list>**.
2. Under the Place heading, click United States, then click the state's name.
3. In the Filter By Collection Name search box, type in *census*.

Special Census Records

In addition to the regular decennial population census, the federal and state governments conducted other non-population schedules and special censuses.

MORTALITY SCHEDULES

These schedules record information about people who had died during the year preceding the enumeration. They pre-date official recording of vital statistics in most states. Mortality schedules were taken in the United States in 1850, 1860, 1870, 1880, and 1885; the 1850 mortality schedule is available (and searchable) on FamilySearch.org **<www.familysearch.org/search/collection/1420441>**.

VETERANS SCHEDULES

Veterans were recorded separately during several decennial enumerations. These schedules include information on Revolutionary War or Civil War service. FamilySearch.org has a searchable collection for the United States Census of Union Veterans and Widows of the Civil War, 1890 **<www.familysearch.org/search/collection/1877095>** (these did not suffer the fate of the 1890 population schedules).

SLAVE SCHEDULES

The 1850 and 1860 censuses enumerated slaves separately. Slaves were identified by number, not by name, but each slave's age, sex, color, and owner was included. FamilySearch.org has a searchable collection for the 1850 slave schedule at **<www.familysearch.org/search/collection/1420440>**.

MERCHANT SEAMEN

An index with 1930 schedules listing merchant seamen—individuals who served in the Merchant Marine—is searchable at **<www.familysearch.org/search/collection/1821205>**. No record images are available for this collection.

STRATEGIES FOR SEARCHING US CENSUS RECORDS ON FAMILYSEARCH.ORG

You can search censuses on FamilySearch.org several different ways. One option is to use the main Historical Records collection search form. Another is to search specific census collections for one census only. When you search in census-specific collections, the search fields may vary based on the information collected in each census. For example, the 1800 US census search form has search fields for

- First Names and Last Names
- Residence Place

In contrast, the 1940 US census has search fields for

- First Names and Last Names
- Marital Status
- Residence in 1940 (with state; county; and city, township, or other civil division)
- Residence in 1935
- Birth (place and year)
- Family Relationships (father, mother, spouse, any household member)

All the census search forms have an option to Match All Terms Exactly for the entire form; most individual fields (such as a name or a place field) also provide a match-exactly check box.

Where to start? Here are some strategies to launch your search and refine your searches to home in on the records you want to find.

START GLOBAL

Begin by using the general search form, not search forms for a single census year. To do this, go to the main Historical Records collections search form at <**www.familysearch.org/search**>. In the Restrict Records By box, select Type, then Census, Residence, and Lists. A global search could return none or several hits for your ancestor in multiple censuses. For census years you don't find, proceed with searching individual census collections, rather than all census collections at once.

ENTER A LOCATION

There could be a John Schmidt (or multiple ones) living in every state. Especially if you have an ancestor with a common name, enter the Residence location for the city, county, and/or state where you believe your ancestor lived.

SEARCH FOR SOMEONE ELSE

If your search for one member of the household doesn't get results, try looking for a different person. This worked for me when searching the 1930 census on FamilySearch.org. A search for my great-grandfather Goffredo Gemignani in Illinois returned zero results, but when I searched for my grandfather (Goffredo's son), Tuly Gemignani, I found the entire household on Tuly's record. Also, when searching for ancestors in the 1840 and earlier censuses, remember to search using the head of household's name only, because other household members were not listed by name in those censuses.

BROWSE FOR EXTENDED FAMILY

It wasn't uncommon for our ancestors to live next door to other relatives. In fact, as an adult, my grandfather lived two houses down from his sister, and other family members lived on a nearby block. Because censuses were taken door to door, households from the same street and neighborhood appear on the same or consecutive pages of the census. When you get a search hit for one of your ancestors that has a free record image on FamilySearch.org, click Open in a new window and use the forward and back arrows in the record image toolbar to move through the records page by page.

USE ALTERNATE SPELLINGS AND WILDCARDS

Do you know why I couldn't find Goffredo Gemignani in the 1930 census? After searching for his son's name and getting a search hit, I discovered Goffredo's first name was spelled incorrectly: Golfred. Wildcard characters can help you find ancestors even if their name was spelled differently than you expect. You also can try searching for different spellings of the name. If I had tried an alternate spelling or used wildcards, I probably would have found Goffredo without having to search for a relative.

Log In Before Searching

Before you start a search, log in to FamilySearch.org so you can save any records you find to your Source Box or attach them to your family tree.

AVOID EXACT MATCHING

While in some instances using Match This Term Exactly could be helpful, most of the time it may restrict your searches too much. In my searches for Goffredo and Tuly Gemignani, not only was Goffredo's first name spelled incorrectly in the record, but his and Tuly's last name was misspelled, too. Their last name was spelled Gemignania, instead of Gemignani. If I had used the Match This Term Exactly option, my search for Tuly would not have been successful.

SEARCH 1890 CENSUS SUBSTITUTES

Fragments exist for only ten states, plus the District of Columbia. If your ancestors aren't listed in these fragments, search alternative sources on FamilySearch.org, such as the 1890 Veterans Schedule or state censuses from the same time period. Other websites, such as Ancestry.com and Fold3, may have city directories that could serve as census alternatives if you don't have luck finding ancestors in the substitutes on FamilySearch.org.

Step-by-Step Example: Searching All US Census Collections

Now let's put the strategies discussed above into practice. In this step-by-step example, we'll look for census records for my ancestor Daniel Schwer. He was born in 1864, was the son of Blasius Schwer, and lived in Cook County, Illinois. Daniel died in 1925, so he should have been recorded in six federal censuses: 1870, 1880, 1890, 1900, 1910, and 1920. Let's see what we can find on FamilySearch.org.

1 NAVIGATE TO THE MAIN SEARCH FORM. Click on the Search tab, then select Records from the drop-down menu (or go to **<www.familysearch.org/search>**).

2 ENTER SEARCH INFORMATION. In the First Names and Last Names boxes, type the ancestor's name—in this case, *Daniel Schwer*. Under the Search With a Life Event heading, click on Residence. Enter the location and a date range. Here, we'll type *Illinois* and the date range of 1860 to 1930 to capture all entries, plus or minus a few years of Daniel's birth and death.

3 RESTRICT THE SEARCH TO CENSUSES. Under the Restrict Records By heading, click the Type link. Check the box next to Census, Residence, and Lists. Hit the Search button.

4 REVIEW AND PREVIEW YOUR RESULTS. The search results bring up fifteen results. The first three results—one each for the 1880, 1900, and 1910 censuses—look like good matches. The information in the Name, Events, and Relationships columns all seem to match my Daniel. Click the down arrow in the Preview column next to each of the first

two results. Each will show a detailed transcription of the record. It also shows that to access the record images for 1880 and 1910, I'll need to view those on Ancestry.com (a subscription is required) or at a local FamilySearch Center.

5 VIEW THE RECORD IMAGE ON FAMILYSEARCH.ORG OR A PARTNER SITE. To view Daniel's record on Ancestry.com, click the Visit Partner Site link. If you are logged into your Ancestry.com account, it will bring up the census record image in a new browser tab. You can then access Ancestry.com's toolbars for adjusting the image and zooming in or out to better view the image. It also gives you options to save the record image to your computer, to an Ancestry.com family tree (if you have one), or to your Ancestry.com Shoebox. If the image is available for free on FamilySearch.org, click the View the Document link.

6 SAVE IT ON FAMILYSEARCH.ORG. Go back to the FamilySearch.org search results window and choose to save the record transcription to your Source Box. You also could

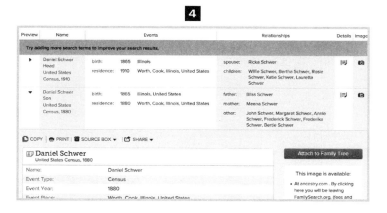

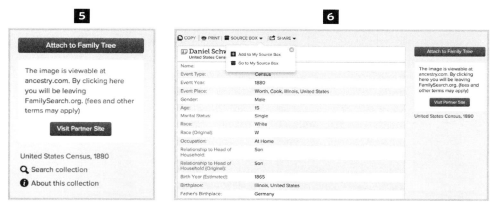

attach it to your family tree using the Attach to Family Tree button, print a hard copy, copy the text from the transcription and put it in a Word (or other word processing) document, or share your find with others via social media or e-mail. If saving to your Source Box, an Add to Source Box window will pop up. Fill in the Notes, select the folder, edit the Source Title, and click the Save button.

7 KEEP SEARCHING. So far, we've only found three of the six censuses Daniel Schwer should be in, so let's quickly scroll to the remaining results to see if any are a match. They're not, so now it's time to refine our search to see if we can find Daniel in the other censuses. Let's broaden our search first to catch any possible misspellings. In the Refine Your Search column, put the first three letters of Daniel's first name, plus an asterisk: *dan**. This should find any listings for nicknames, such as Dan or Danny, or a misspelling. Hit the Search button.

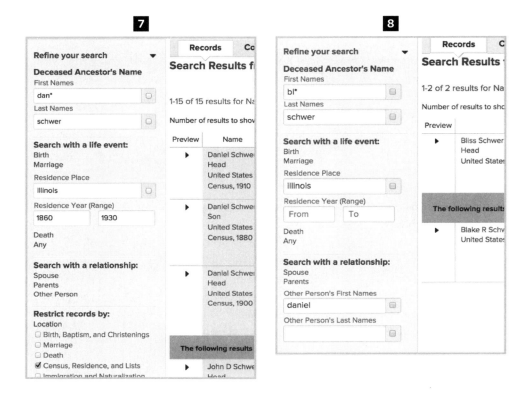

8 CONTINUE REFINING YOUR SEARCHES. No luck using the wildcard for Daniel's first name to broaden results: Our hits show only the same three censuses we already had found. Keep trying different combinations of search terms and wildcards. If you're still having no luck, try switching strategies. For example, instead of searching for Daniel, search for someone else who lived in the same household. I tried searching for his father, Blasius, using *bl** for the first name, Schwer for the last name, and Illinois as the Residence Place. I still couldn't find Daniel in other censuses. It might be time to search for him in a specific census collection.

Step-by-Step Example: Searching a Single Census

Now let's try searching an individual census collection. For this example, we'll look for census records for my ancestor Susanna Schmidt in the 1900 US census. Susanna lived in Mosalem Township, Dubuque County, Iowa. Her husband, Charles, died in 1899, so Susanna may be a head of household. Her son Ferdinand (my great-grandfather) could be living with her, since he was only about sixteen years old in 1900. Let's get started.

1 **LOCATE THE 1900 CENSUS SEARCH FORM.** Under the Search tab, select Records from the drop-down menu. Scroll down to and click on the Browse All Published Collections link to get to **<www.familysearch.org/search/collection/list>**. From the column of links on the left, select United States of America under the Place heading, then type *census 1900* in the Filter by Collection search box, then click United States Census, 1900.

2 **ENTER AN ANCESTOR NAME AND PLACE.** Type *Susanna* in the First Names box, and *Schmidt* in the Last Names box. Do not check the exact search boxes. Under the Search By Life Events heading, click on Residence Place. A search field will appear. Enter *Iowa*. Hit the Search button.

3 **REVIEW THE SEARCH RESULTS.** Look through the search results listed. There are columns for Name, Birth (month, year, and place), Parents, Spouse, Children, Other, and Residence. The first two hits don't appear to be my Susanna, but the third looks promising. Even though it lists the name as Susan (not Susanna), the Children column lists a Ferdinand, and the Residence column shows the town where I know Susanna lived. Time to explore further, so click on the name Susan Schmidt.

4 **ANALYZE THE RESULTS AND VIEW THE RECORD IMAGE.** At this point, you should see a page with a transcription of the census record for Susan Schmidt. Upon closer inspection, you'll see Susan listed as head of household and Ferdinand as age sixteen. The other

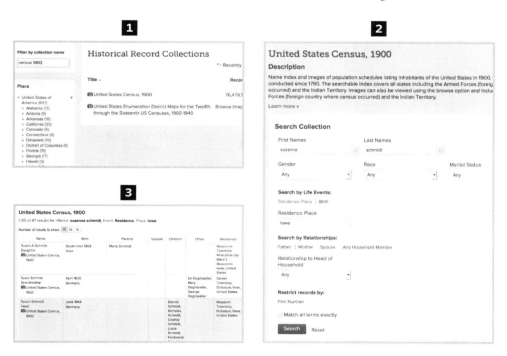

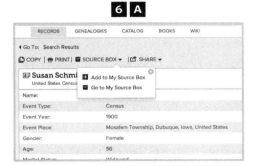   

POWER-USER TIP

Free Census Forms
Download free census extraction forms from <familytreemagazine.com/info/census-forms> to record your findings from federal censuses.

information—her birth date and place, and Widowed marital status—matches up, too. Click the View the Document link (under the Camera icon) to view the record image.

5 **ADJUST THE IMAGE.** Use the Zoom tools (plus and minus signs) to zoom in or out to better view the image. Click on the census image to drag it up or down, left or right to view the lines you need to see. Also use the Adjust Image option (under the Tools icon) to play with the brightness and contrast or the Invert button to invert the image colors, if needed, to read the image. Susanna Schmidt is on line 93 of this page, and her son Ferdinand is on line 98. Under the Tools icon, click the Print link to print a hard copy of the record, or click the Download link to download a JPEG version of the image. If you want to look for other possible family members living nearby, click the Open in a new window link and use the left and right arrows (next to the image box in the toolbar) to navigate to adjacent census pages.

6 **SAVE IT TO YOUR SOURCE BOX OR FAMILY TREE.** To add the record to your Source Box or attach it to your FamilySearch Family Tree, click the back arrow in your web browser. On the page with the record transcription, click on the Source Box down arrow, then click Add to My Source Box from the drop-down menu (image **6** **A**). Select the Source Box folder where you want to save it and enter any notes you'd like (image **6** **B**). In my case, I changed the Source Title to be Susanna instead of Susan. I entered in the notes that the record listed her as Susan. To attach the record to your family tree, click the blue Attach to Family Tree button just above the camera.

KEYS TO SUCCESS

⭐ Search for your ancestors in every federal census taken during their lifetimes. US censuses were taken every ten years starting in 1790.

⭐ Inform your searches by understanding which questions were asked in which census years. For example, you won't bother looking for your third-great-grandfather as a child in the 1830 census when you know that pre-1850 censuses listed names of heads of household only.

⭐ Look for your family in state and special censuses in addition to federal enumerations.

⭐ Start your census research on FamilySearch.org with the main search form to find your ancestor in multiple censuses at once. Follow up by searching the individual databases for any specific census years that don't come up in your global search.

⭐ Be prepared to try different spellings and search tactics to find your family. Information in census records doesn't always match exactly what you expect.

Consult this handy chart to see which key ancestor details were recorded in which census years. The stars in each column represent important genealogical clues you can expect to find about your ancestor in that census.

		1790	1800	1810	1820	1830	1840
Names	Head of household's name	★	★	★	★	★	★
	All household members' names (except slaves)						
Birth Information	Age ranges of free white males	★	★	★	★	★	★
	Age ranges of free white females	★	★	★	★	★	★
	Ages of all household members						
	Birthplace						
	Month and year of birth						
Parents	Foreign-born parents						
	Parents' birthplaces						
	Mother tongue						
	Parents' mother tongues						
Marriage	Married in the census year						
	Marital status						
	Years married						
	Age at first marriage						
Immigration and Citizenship	Number of aliens/non-naturalized residents				★	★	★
	Year of immigration						
	Years in the United States						
	Naturalization status						
Other	Number of free colored				★	★	★
	Relationship to head of household						
	Veteran status						
	Number of children mothered (living and total)						

1850	1860	1870	1880	1890	1900	1910	1920	1930	1940
★	★	★	★	★	★	★	★	★	★
★	★	★	★	★	★	★	★	★	★
★	★	★	★	★	★	★	★	★	★
★	★	★	★	★	★	★	★	★	★
					★				
		★							
			★	★	★	★	★	★	★
						★	★	★	★
							★	★	
★	★	★	★	★					
			★	★	★	★	★	★	★
					★	★			
								★	
					★	★	★	★	
				★	★				
				★	★	★	★	★	★
			★	★	★	★	★	★	★
				★		★		★	
				★	★	★			

US CENSUS RECORDS CHECKLIST

Ancestor's name: _____

Ancestor's maiden name (if female): _____

_____

Residence/location(s): _____

Date of birth: _____ Birthplace: _____

Mother's name: _____

Mother's date of birth: _____

Mother's birthplace: _____

Father's name: _____

Father's date of birth: _____

Father's birthplace: _____

Other member(s) of household: _____

_____

_____

_____

Look for your ancestor in all US censuses taken during his or her lifetime. Put a check mark next to the year after you've found his or her census listing and saved a copy for your records. Cross off any censuses that occurred before your ancestor was born or after he or she died.

Federal Census

☐ 1790	☐ 1830	☐ 1870	☐ 1910
☐ 1800	☐ 1840	☐ 1880	☐ 1920
☐ 1810	☐ 1850	☐ 1890	☐ 1930
☐ 1820	☐ 1860	☐ 1900	☐ 1940

Saved in Source Box folder: _____

State/Territorial Censuses

Do a little research to learn about censuses taken in your ancestor's state. You can use the FamilySearch Wiki **<www.familysearch.org/learn/wiki>** to locate this information. Write in the years of these state and/or territorial censuses below. Put a check mark next to the year after you've found his or her census listing and saved a copy for your records. (If the state census isn't on FamilySearch.org, make a note to check later, or list another website where it's available.)

State Name: _____

State Census Dates to Check:

☐ _____

☐ _____

☐ _____

☐ _____

☐ _____

☐ _____

☐ _____

☐ _____

Saved in Source Box folder: _____

Special Censuses on FamilySearch.org

If you think your ancestor might be in a special census, search those collections on FamilySearch.org. Put a check in the box next to the census once you've searched it.

☐ 1850 Mortality Schedule

☐ 1850 Slave Schedule

☐ 1890 Veterans Schedule

☐ 1930 Merchant Seamen Census

☐ _____

☐ _____

Saved in Source Box folder: _____

US Vital Records

In addition to census records, I've experienced much luck finding vital records for my ancestors on FamilySearch.org. My finds include many records for my Iowa ancestors, including the 1905 marriage record for my ancestors Elizabeth Rolfes and Joseph Heims, the 1896 death record for Henry Buschelman, and the 1925 death record for Frank H. Rolfes. Finding these records has not only confirmed the dates of vital events in my ancestor's lives, but they've helped me add branches to my family tree because many of these records list information such as the parents' names (including mother's maiden name) and birthplaces.

Searching for vital records on FamilySearch.org can be exciting and provide essential clues to help fill in the blanks on your pedigree charts and family group sheets. In this chapter, we'll explore what US vital records exist, what you can learn from them, which records are available on FamilySearch.org, and strategies for searching vital-records collections on FamilySearch.org.

VITAL RECORDS IN THE UNITED STATES

When we talk about vital records, civil registrations—records kept by local or county governments—are often the first records that come to mind. These include birth certificates, death certificates, marriage licenses, marriage certificates, and divorce records.

Most US states mandated vital-record keeping in the late 1800s and early 1900s. Massachusetts, Hawaii, New Jersey, and Rhode Island were the first to require statewide record keeping for births in 1841, 1842, 1848, and 1853, respectively. The same four were also some of the first states to adopt statewide marriage records: Massachusetts in 1841, Hawaii in 1842, New Jersey in 1848, and Rhode Island in 1853. Delaware started recording marriages at the state level in 1847. Early adopters of statewide death records include Massachusetts (1841), New Jersey (1848), and Rhode Island (1853). Find the beginning date for statewide vital-records registration in your ancestor's state by referring to *Family Tree Magazine*'s Vital-Records Chart, downloadable for free from **<www.familytreemagazine.com/upload/images/pdf/vitalrecords.pdf>**.

Keep in mind that earlier records of vital events may exist: Counties or towns often kept vital records (especially marriage records) earlier than the state mandates. On the flip side, some locations were slow to comply, so records may be spotty for the first several years after statewide record keeping began.

You can glean a lot of important genealogical information and clues from vital records, including birth dates, death dates, burial places and dates, church affiliations, family relationships, locations of residence, maiden names, information about previous marriages or previous children born, and parents' names. Some records even have street addresses for the people listed in them, which could be extremely helpful if you're having trouble finding those relatives in a particular census, if you want to locate their old home on a map, or if you want to research land records.

Alternative Vital-Statistics Sources

Of course, government civil registrations aren't the only places to find birth, marriage, and death information for your ancestors. Several other records may contain this information as well. For example, church records may contain baptism/christening records, marriage bonds, or confirmation records. County or town records may contain vital records prior to state-mandated record keeping. Newspapers often printed obituaries or death notices,

POWER-USER TIP

Global Vital Records

FamilySearch has digitized vital records not just from the United States, but also from countries around the world. After you've found your ancestor's US vital records, remember to check for their vital records in other countries, too.

as well as wedding announcements. Cemeteries have their own records of tombstone inscriptions. Estates that went through probate courts produced record files. Ancestors may have been listed in the Social Security Death Index.

In addition, you may have documents in your home (or your relatives' homes) that provide additional vital-statistics clues or sources. For example, you might have copies of vital certificates, prayer cards, funeral/memorial cards, wedding albums, wills, or newspaper clippings. Be sure to check your home sources before beginning your online vital-records search.

US VITAL RECORDS ON FAMILYSEARCH.ORG

FamilySearch.org has hundreds of vital-records collections covering forty-seven states and the District of Columbia (only Alaska, North Dakota, and South Dakota had no vital records on FamilySearch.org at the time of this writing). The searchable and unindexed vital-records collections encompass

- birth certificates and indexes
- cemetery records/cemetery inscriptions
- church records, parish registers, and diocese records (baptisms/christenings, confirmations, marriage banns)
- county records
- death certificates and indexes
- divorce/annulment records
- estate files
- funeral sermons
- gravestone indexes (such as the Find A Grave Index and BillionGraves Index)
- marriage licenses/certificates and indexes
- marriage bonds
- newspaper announcements of births, marriages, and deaths
- obituaries
- synagogue registers
- town records
- US Social Security Death Index
- wills

To see which vital records are available for your state, go to **<www.familysearch.org/search>** (from the home page, click the Search tab, then select Records from the drop-down menu). Next, click the Browse All Published Collections link. Use the Place filters to navigate to your state, then use the Collections filter for Birth, Marriage, & Death to see the available civil-registration and church records that contain vital statistics. Be sure to

Vital-Records Glossary

If you're unfamiliar with vital-records research, here's a summary of common record types you may encounter and the information you may find in those sources:

- **baptism/christening certificates:** These records were kept by the church and usually include the full name of the person baptized, date of birth, place of birth or baptism, parents' names and residences, and names of and relationship to the baptismal sponsors.

- **birth certificates:** State, county, or local governments kept these records; they generally contain the person's full name, date of birth, place of birth, parents' names, and parents' place of residence. They also might list the parents' ages and the father's occupation.

- **death certificates:** State, county, or local governments kept these records; they typically include the full name of the deceased, as well as the deceased's place of birth, age, death date and place, and cause of death. Death certificates also may contain information on the deceased's martial status, occupation, and burial place.

- **death notices:** These are exactly what they sound like. Published in newspapers, notices provided basic announcements of a person's death and funeral arrangements.

- **marriage banns:** Prior to marrying, a pastor would read or post banns on the church's door; it notified the community that the couple intended to marry and gave people in the community a chance to come forward if they knew a reason why the couple legally could not marry (for example, if one of them was already married, if they were too closely related, or if they were not of age).

- **marriage bonds:** Whereas marriage banns are church records, marriage bonds are civil records. Grooms took out bonds to ensure there was no legal obstacle to the marriage.

- **marriage certificates:** These civil documents were recorded after the marriage ceremony was performed. The person who performed the ceremony filed the certificate with the clerk of court, and it contains that celebrant's name; often the information certifying the marriage took place was recorded in a separate section of the marriage license.

- **marriage licenses**: Also kept by the state, county, or local government, marriage licenses typically include the groom's and bride's names, ages, and places of residence, along with the marriage date and location. Licenses also may include the names of the couple's parents and/or witnesses to the marriage, as well as the couple's occupations, race, or birth dates.

- **obituaries:** These are newspaper articles written about a person who died. Historically, obituaries were written by newspaper staff; families could request one be written for their relative, but in some cases they were written only about well-known individuals in a town.

check under the Probate & Court and Other filtering options, too, as you might find collections for wills, estate files, county records, and more that the Birth, Marriage, & Death filter doesn't show.

State-specific collections aren't the only vital-records collections on FamilySearch. org. Your ancestors' vital statistics could also appear in the following indexes or sections of the website.

Social Security Death Index

Searchable from **<www.familysearch.org/search/collection/1202535>**, this index contains names and other details about people whose deaths were reported to the Social Security Administration beginning in 1962. The database does not include every person who died since Social Security numbers were first issued in 1936, but is a good resource to check for anyone born in the 1900s (even some people born in the late 1800s are in the database). The index may include the deceased person's name, birth date, death date, death residence (or zip code), and the state where the Social Security number was issued. You can search this database using the deceased's first and last names, birth year range, and death place and year range.

Find A Grave Index

This index contains tombstone transcriptions and images covering the years 1500 to 2013, courtesy of Find A Grave **<www.findagrave.com>**, a free website owned by Ancestry.com. The database covers more than 124 million records. On FamilySearch.org, you can search this index via a form with fields for the deceased's first and last names, a life event or residence location, or with a relationship. Results on FamilySearch.org list the person's name, event type, event date and place, birth date, death date, and cemetery, along with a note about whether a photo was included in the listing on the Find A Grave website. To see the actual Find A Grave record or the image, you'll need to click the Visit Partner Site button in the record page.

The information on Find A Grave may be more comprehensive than what's listed in the index on FamilySearch.org. For example, the entry on the Find A Grave website for my Iowa ancestor Frank H. Rolfes, who died in 1925, contains not only birth and death information, but also tombstone photos, a transcription of Frank's obituary, and links to other family members' records on Find A Grave.

POWER-USER TIP

Searching Obituaries
FamilySearch plans to add tens of millions of obituaries, mainly from the United States, to FamilySearch.org. The records will be added through a partnership with NewsBank **<www.newsbank.com>**.

BillionGraves Index

With more than ten million records, this collection indexes burial records from the free BillionGraves website <**www.billiongraves.com**>. You can search by the deceased's first and last names, birth year range, and death place and date. Each record page provides the ancestor's name, event type and place, cemetery name, birth date, death date, and GPS coordinates of the gravestone. To view a tombstone image or the full BillionGraves listing, click the Visit Partner Site button.

User-Submitted Genealogies

Don't overlook the genealogies on FamilySearch.org at <**www.familysearch.org/family-trees**>. These contain around 240 million records of births, marriages, and deaths submitted by website users and LDS church members. These records are separate from the Historical Records collection on FamilySearch.org. Because the information is user-submitted, be sure to check the sources to verify the information about any ancestor matches you find. For more information on searching genealogies, see chapter 4.

International Genealogical Index

The IGI has more than 892 million records. It's a searchable index of vital event entries (such as births, baptisms, marriages, and deaths) contributed by others. Learn more about this collection and searching this index in chapter 4.

FamilySearch Books

Numerous books compiling town, county, and church vital records have been published over the years—and they are increasingly being digitized. You can search some of these digitized books through the FamilySearch Books collection. For example, a simple search for the word *marriage* finds books such as *Marriage Records of Vermillion County, Indiana, Volume 3, 1844–1861* and *Marriage Records of Washington Country, Arkansas: 1880–1890, Book 3*. When you look for vital records in the digitized book collection, try searching by the location and the type of record. For more FamilySearch Books search tips, see chapter 4.

STRATEGIES FOR SEARCHING VITAL RECORDS

When searching for any records on FamilySearch.org, always start with the main search form. For vital records, use these additional strategies to find your ancestors.

Limit by Record Type

As always, it's best to start your records search as broadly as possible, and then narrow your search criteria from there. To find only vital records when you use the main Historical Records search form <www.familysearch.org/search>, enter your ancestor's name, and under the Restrict Records By heading, select the Type link. You'll need to check all three boxes to search all types of vital records:

- Birth, Baptism, and Christenings
- Marriage
- Death

Case Study: The Search for John H. Pennington's Last Marriage

Rick Crume, a contributing editor for Family Tree Magazine *with a website at* <www.onelibrary.com>, *used FamilySearch.org's vital records collections to uncover the marriage record for his relative John H. Pennington. Here he explains how he did it.*

A news item titled "On His Wedding Trip" in the April 22, 1897, *Milwaukee Sentinel* had sparked my curiosity. It reported, "J.H. Pennington, president of the North and South American Transportation company, was at the Plankinton yesterday. His residence is New York and he is rated a multi-millionaire. He is said to be on his wedding trip." This would be the last of my second-great-grand-uncle John H. Pennington's four known marriages, and I was curious to find out when and where he was married and who the bride was.

A search of FamilySearch.org's Historical Records collection for John H. Pennington's marriage in the year range 1897 to 1897 turned up no relevant matches on the first page of results. I filtered the results by location to the United States, and further narrowed it to the state of Wisconsin. The three resulting matches in the Wisconsin, Marriages, 1836–1930 collection all pertained to my relative's marriage. The records provided the place of birth and parents' names for both the bride and groom, but each record was slightly different. They say that John Howard Pennington and Florence Howard Denby were married April 18, 1897, in Milwaukee, Wisconsin. The groom was a native of Ho[u]lton, Maine and a son of William Edward Pennington and Isabell Slipp, while the bride was a native of "Brooklyn, U.S." and a daughter of Thomas Denby and Maria Howard. This is the only record I've seen that gives William Pennington's middle name, Edward.

Include a Year Range and Place

To get more relevant search results, enter information into one or more of the Search With a Life Event search fields. Unless you're searching for a specific record (such as a marriage license), start by entering just a birth year range and place, because most vital records give the person's age or birth information. For the year range, consider using a span of at least two or three years, since age or birth year reported on later records (like a death record) is only as accurate as the informant.

Use Wildcards

Wildcard characters can help you find ancestors even if their names were spelled incorrectly. FamilySearch.org supports the asterisk (*) and question mark (?) as wildcards. You can put these characters anywhere in your search term (beginning, middle, or end).

No images of these marriage records were available on FamilySearch.org, but the records did cite the microfilm numbers (the GS Film number) of the source records. Two of the records came from microfilm 1013997, and the other one came from microfilm 1292307. To find out what's on these microfilms, I selected Catalog from the Search tab on FamilySearch.org then clicked on Film/Fiche Number. A search on microfilm number 1013997 showed it contains Milwaukee County, Wisconsin, marriages records from 1838 to 1911 and an index from 1838 to 1918. The other film, number 1292307, has Milwaukee County registration of marriages from 1837 to 1907 and an index of marriages from 1852 to 1907.

If a record on FamilySearch.org isn't linked to a digital image, it's a good idea to view the original record to verify that the information on FamilySearch was transcribed correctly and to see if it provides any additional details. For a small fee, you can borrow most microfilms and view them at a Family History Library near you. Just click on the microfilm number in the FamilySearch Catalog to place your order and pay by credit card.

So far, I have viewed microfilm 1292307, and the marriage record on it reveals a few more details: The groom's occupation was listed as Transportation, and he was a resident of Chicago. The ceremony was performed by Charles S. Lester at a "Presb. Episc." Church, and the witnesses were Marie Denby and Elisa C. Lester.

I feel the date and place of marriage in these records is very reliable, but some of the other details in the transcriptions could be wrong. According to other sources, John H. Pennington's middle name was Hudson, not Howard. Also, one of the records says the bride's father was Thomas Denby, but the other two mistakenly call him Thomas Howard. All in all, these records were highly informative.

Search for Maiden and Married Names

Remember to search on both your female ancestor's married name and maiden name. Death and burial records will usually be in her married name, while birth and marriage records will use her maiden name.

Use Relationships

Especially if your ancestor has a common name, you may want to enter a spouse or parent's name in the Search With a Relationship field. For a marriage record, put the spouse's name in the Spouse's First Names and Spouse's Last Names search boxes. For a birth record, put the mother and/or father's names in the Parents search boxes.

Skip Exact Matching

On your initial searches for vital records, do not check the Match All Terms Exactly check boxes on the search form. This will help keep your search broad to catch all possible records that your ancestor may be listed in (even some with spelling errors).

Search for a Parent or Next of Kin

Sometimes a specific ancestor's name doesn't come up in an online search, but the record may still be there and you could find it by searching for the other people listed on the record. For example, if you can't find a birth record for your ancestor, try searching for records for the mother by entering the mother's name in the main first and last names search fields. When you search for records, results will turn up records where the woman is listed as the mother.

Remember Alternative Sources

The main Historical Records collection search form will return results not just for civil registrations, but also for other records that list birth, marriage, and death information. To ensure you don't miss any possible records, be sure to follow up with searches in specific collections that could substitute for vital records. Find possible records collections

---

POWER-USER TIP

Vital Records Beyond the Website

No luck finding vital records on FamilySearch.org? Don't forget to look in the FamilySearch Catalog to see available books or microfilm for your ancestor's location and time period. If you find a microfilm reel that fits your ancestor's location and vital-event dates, you can order a copy to view at your local FamilySearch Center.

to search for your ancestor's time period and location by going to **<www.familysearch.org/search/collection/list>**. Filter the collections listed by Place and Date.

Step-by-Step Example:
Searching the Historical Records Collection for Vital Records

In this example, let's search for my ancestor Daniel Schwer, who was born June 10, 1864, and died March 22, 1925, in Illinois. Information passed through the generations from my relatives doesn't include a marriage date on the pedigree chart, but in other records he's found with his wife, Fredaricka (who went by the nickname Ricka).

1 **DO A GLOBAL SEARCH.** Under the Search tab, select Records from the drop-down menu to get to **<www.familysearch.org/search>**. Type in the ancestor's name in the First Names and Last Names search boxes. Under Search With a Life Event, choose Birth and enter the Birthplace and Birth Year range. For this example, I've entered *Daniel Schwer* in the names boxes, *Illinois* for the birthplace, and *1860* to *1865* for the birth year range. Under Restrict Records By, be sure to click on Type, and select three options: Birth, Baptism, and Christenings; Marriage; and Death. Hit the Search button.

2 **PREVIEW RESULTS.** On the results page, we get sixty-five results. The first five look pretty promising for this search, including a couple from death records collections and one from a marriage records collection. None of the results for Daniel Schwer have record images (no camera icons appear in the far right column). To save time, instead

3

4

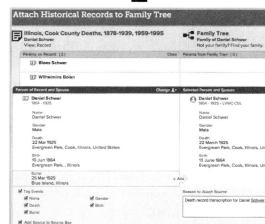

of clicking on Daniel's name, click the Preview down arrow next to the Name for each record that appears to be a possible match. Preview each record one by one.

3 ANALYZE MATCHES. As you preview the records, analyze the quality of the match. Is it really your ancestor? In this example, there appear to be two death records for Daniel. Both records look to match the information I have (such as parent's name, death date and place), but the one from the Illinois, Cook County Deaths collection seems to have more detail, including his address, marital status, occupation, and the informant's name. I compare this information with the information I've collected on Daniel and make note of new information.

4 SAVE EACH RECORD FOUND. Once you've determined a record is truly a match to your ancestor, save the record. To do that, you can copy the information from the records page, print a hard copy of the record, add it to your Source Box, share it via social media or e-mail, or attach it to your family tree. When you click the Attach to Family Tree button,

FamilySearch automatically matches the record to the appropriate person in your family tree and also lets you add it to your Source Box at the same time. Simply click the Add Source to Source Box check box to do both. You also can enter a Reason to Attach Source to this particular person in your tree.

Step-by-Step Example: Searching a Single Vital-Records Collection

After you've done a global search, it's usually a good idea to follow up by looking at specific records collections, especially if there's a certain record you want to find but weren't able to in a global search. Although I found a death and marriage record for my ancestor Daniel Schwer in the previous step-by-step example, I still didn't find his 1864 birth record. Could he be in a birth record on FamilySearch.org? Let's see if we can locate an appropriate collection to search.

1 BROWSE THE PUBLISHED COLLECTIONS LIST. To find a relevant collection to search, go to **<www.familysearch.org/search/collection/list>**. Filter the list of collections to ones in the right location first using the Place filters. For this example, I've chosen United States and Illinois as filters.

2 CHOOSE A COLLECTION TO VIEW. Review the list of Historical Records collections that meet your filtered criteria. Click the Birth, Marriage, and Death filter under Collections to further refine the list of collections. The list for this example shows three birth-records collections for Illinois—two for Cook County (where Daniel Schwer lived) and one statewide collection. Which one would be best to search? Look at the date in the collection title. The two Cook County collections start in the 1870s, which is after Daniel

was born, so he won't be in there. I select the Illinois Births and Christenings, 1824–1940 collection by clicking on the collection title.

3 **ENTER SEARCH TERMS.** Enter at least the ancestor's first and last names in the collection's search form. Also fill in a birth year range as well. Remember, start your search broad. You can always refine it later. Here, I've entered *Daniel Schwer* in the First Names

and Last Names fields, and *1860* to *1865* in the Birth Year range fields. Hit the Search button. This returns no search results.

4 **ADJUST YOUR SEARCH CRITERIA.** Our first search didn't find Daniel (or any results), so it's time to employ some new strategies. Let's start first with using wildcards for the names. Enter *dan** in the First Names field and *sch** in the Last Names field the same. Hit the Update button.

5 **REVIEW AND ANALYZE THE RESULTS.** My latest search criteria deliver forty results. The first one is for a Daniel Christian Schaide born in 1863. This isn't my ancestor. Scroll through the entire list to see if any of the information in the Name, Events, and Relationships columns could be a match. Unfortunately, none of these are my Daniel either.

At this point, you could continue trying different search criteria combinations until you are satisfied you've tried all possible combinations that could find your ancestor. Sometimes, our ancestors just aren't in an online collection we search. It's bound to happen, but at least you gave it a valiant effort and can now turn your energy to looking for that particular record via other traditional sources, such as by requesting a vital record directly from a state vital-records office. And keep in mind that it's possible the record you're seeking for your ancestor simply does not exist.

KEYS TO SUCCESS

★ Know the dates when your ancestors' state (and county or town) started keeping vital records so you don't waste time searching for records that don't exist.

★ Expand your research beyond official vital records—you'll find ancestors' birth, marriage, and death details in many other sources. On FamilySearch.org, be sure to search the Probate and Court, Social Security Death Index, and Books collections (among others) for vital statistics.

★ Consider the right search parameters for the records you want to find. Don't include death dates in a search for your great-grandparents' marriage record, for example. Look for Great-grandma's birth record under her maiden name and her death record under her married name.

★ Review the source information in your ancestor's vital record on FamilySearch.org to track down originals when there's no record image. Use the FamilySearch Catalog to identify and order microfilms of original records.

US VITAL-RECORDS CHECKLIST

Ancestor's name: _____

Ancestor's maiden name (if female): _____

Residence/location(s): _____

Religion (if known): _____

Fill in the following information as you discover it and confirm it in your research.

Birth

Date birth records started in birthplace: _____

Date of birth: _____ Birthplace: _____

Mother's name: _____

Father's name: _____

Source(s): _____

Marriage

Date marriage records started in marriage place: _____

Date of marriage: _____ Place of marriage: _____

Spouse's name: _____

Source(s): _____

Death/Burial

Date death records started in death place: _____

Date of death: _____ Place of death: _____

Cause of death: _____

Source(s): _____

Date of burial: _____ Place of burial: _____

Cemetery name: _____

Cemetery plot information: _____

Records to Search on FamilySearch.org

☐ civil registrations

☐ birth certificates

☐ marriage licenses/certificates

☐ death certificates

☐ divorce/annulment records

Alternate Vital-Statistics Sources

☐ birth, marriage, or death announcements in newspapers

☐ church records, parish registers, and diocese records (baptisms/christenings, confirmations, marriage banns)

☐ synagogue registers

☐ county records

☐ town records

☐ cemetery records/cemetery inscriptions (burial records)

☐ gravestone indexes

☐ obituaries

☐ Find A Grave Index

☐ BillionGraves Index

☐ Social Security Death Index

☐ estate files

☐ wills

☐ funeral sermons

US Immigration and Naturalization Records

"Remember, remember always, that all of us, and you and I especially, are descended from immigrants and revolutionists." Franklin D. Roosevelt gave these remarks in 1938 when he addressed a gathering of the Daughters of the American Revolution.

For many genealogists, discovering and documenting their immigrant heritage is a key goal of their research—it may be what inspired them to begin their search in the first place. It's a thrill to see your ancestor's name on a passenger list documenting his journey from the old country. As experienced researchers know, finding your ancestor's immigration record isn't always as easy as searching the Ellis Island database at **<www. libertyellisfoundation.org>**. In fact, many of our ancestors came to America before and after Ellis Island operated, and not all immigrants came through New York.

In my case, I did somewhat easily find my maternal grandfather and great-grandfather and their family's passenger list records when they came through Ellis Island in the 1920s. In contrast, I haven't yet succeeded in finding the immigration records for ancestors in my paternal family line. That research is still a work in progress. As I continue to find other records for my ancestors via FamilySearch.org and other genealogy websites, I'm uncovering additional clues to help me pinpoint the time period and possible ports of entry where my paternal ancestors could have entered the United States.

In this chapter, we'll take a look at immigration and naturalization records—what records exist, what records are available on FamilySearch.org, and how to find your immigrant ancestors' records. We'll start with a short history lesson and work our way to the nitty-gritty details about the FamilySearch.org collections.

A BRIEF HISTORY OF IMMIGRATION TO AMERICA

Since the first permanent settlement was established at Jamestown, Virginia, in 1607, people from Europe and other countries have immigrated to America. Early colonists often sought religious freedom. Most early immigrants were German, English, Welsh, or Dutch. These early immigrants typically settled in New England and Virginia.

The 1800s saw the largest waves of immigration as millions sought a better life and new economic opportunities in the newly formed United States of America. In the 1820s alone, more than ten million immigrants from northern Europe, the United Kingdom, and Scandinavia were drawn to America, followed by a wave of Irish and Germans who came to America in the 1840s, largely to escape the Irish Potato Famine as well as political and social turmoil. The California Gold Rush in the mid-1800s lured many immigrants from China. From 1880 to 1920, more than twenty-five million immigrants came from southern and eastern Europe.

Many nineteenth-century immigrants intended to find work in America and send their earnings to families back in the old country. As a result, you may find passenger lists for a male relative traveling by himself, rather than with his family. Sometimes a husband traveled to America first, then sent for the family to come once he was established. So a husband, wife, and children may not all appear on the same passenger list.

Ports of Entry

While most of us immediately think of Ellis Island in New York when we first think of ports of entry into the United States, immigrants entered through dozens of US and Canadian ports. The most popular US ports of entry were New York, Boston, Baltimore, Philadelphia, and New Orleans. Other popular ports of entry include several cities in Atlantic and Gulfport states (such as New Bedford, Massachusetts; Key West, Florida; and Gulfport and Pascagoula, Mississippi), as well as a few Pacific ports such as Honolulu and San Francisco. In fact, the West Coast had its own immigration processing station, Angel Island, which was nicknamed the "Ellis Island of the West." Angel Island in the San Francisco Bay area operated from 1910 to 1940 and processed hundreds of thousands of immigrants from eighty-four different countries, but primarily China, Japan, and Russia. Castle Garden, the precursor to Ellis Island in New York, processed immigrants from 1855 to 1890. Ellis Island processed immigrants from 1892 to 1954.

Ports of Departure

If you can't find records for your ancestors at their port of entry into the United States, consider taking your search overseas. In addition to the US passenger-arrival lists filled out at the ports of embarkation, those exit ports sometimes kept their own records of departing passengers. Among those with existing records are Bremen and Hamburg in Germany, London and Liverpool in England, Amsterdam and Rotterdam in The Netherlands, Antwerp in Belgium, and Le Havre and Marseille in France. FamilySearch.org has some searchable port of departure records for Antwerp and Bremen, as well as for New Zealand. Passenger lists, passports, and other records are browsable for emigrants from Spain and Portugal, and passengers who rode on the Holland-America line (1900–1974).

Some ancestors may have arrived in Canada first and then made their way to the United States. If that was the case with your ancestor, you may need to look for him or her in US–Canadian border crossing records or in passenger lists at Canadian ports of entry.

Types of Records Created

Finding ancestors' immigration records prior to 1820 is hit-or-miss because ships were not required to provide a list of passengers upon arrival to America until that year. Here are a few types of records you might find for early immigrants.

PASSENGER LISTS/MANIFESTS

Passenger lists, as well as crew lists, were created at the port of departure and were presented at the port of arrival. Passenger lists may include information such as the immigrant's name, place of birth, age, physical description, occupation, place of last residence, names and address of relatives he was joining in the United States, and even the amount of money he was carrying.

PASSPORTS

Passports were first issued to American citizens traveling abroad in 1789. The information collected on passport applications was standardized in the 1860s, when a printed form was used. The applicants typically were men. If a man's wife and children accompanied him, their names, ages, and relationships to the applicant would be included on the passport application. If a mother traveled with her children only (and not her husband), the children's names would be on her passport. Early passports were often valid for only two years or less, so the same person could have applied for a passport on many different occasions throughout his lifetime.

US Immigration and Naturalization Timeline

1790 The first naturalization laws require two years of residency for "free white persons" of "good moral character."

1798 Immigrants must register arrival in a local court; this continues until 1828.

1808 A new law bans the importation of slaves.

1819 Congress requires shipmasters to begin providing manifests of all individuals aboard arriving ships.

1840s The Irish Potato Famine (1845–1852), crop failures in Germany, and social and political unrest in Europe spur mass immigration.

1848 The United States extends citizenship to eighty thousand Mexicans living in Texas, California, and other southwest areas after the Mexican-American War; California Gold Rush spurs Chinese immigration.

1855 The Castle Garden immigration station opens at the port of New York.

1870 Citizenship is expanded to African-Americans; Asians are still excluded.

1875 Supreme Court declares regulation of immigration a federal responsibility.

1881–1885 German immigration peaks, with more than one million arriving

1881–1920 Two million Eastern European Jews arrive in the U.S.

1882 The Chinese Exclusion Act restricts Chinese immigration.

1892 Ellis Island opens in New York.

1897 A fire at Ellis Island destroys some immigration records dating from 1855.

1906 The Naturalization Act of 1906 standardizes the process throughout the country.

1907 The Expatriation Act causes American women who marry foreign nationals to lose their citizenship; Ellis Island arrivals peak at more than one million.

1910 The Angel Island immigration station opens in San Francisco Bay area.

1911–1920 Italian immigration peaks, with more than two million arriving.

1917 he United States enters World War I, restricts immigration from Asia, grants citizenship to Puerto Ricans, and enacts a literacy requirement for citizenship.

1922 The Cable Act partially repeals the Expatriation Act, but American women who marry Asians still lose their citizenship.

1924 The Immigration Act of 1924 limits European immigration via quotas; the United States creates the U.S. Border Patrol to police borders with Canada and Mexico.

1933 The Bureau of Immigration and the Bureau of Naturalization combine into one agency: the Immigration and Naturalization Service.

1945–1946 The War Brides Act of 1945 and Fiancées Act of 1946 permit spouses and families of returning US soldiers to come to America.

1954 The Ellis Island immigration station closes.

1965 The Immigration and Naturalization Act eliminates quotas based on nationality.

Passport applications often included the applicant's name, birth date, birthplace, and a physical description. They may also include the applicant's foreign destination and occupation. Additionally, emigrants leaving a country may have had a passport issued by their home country.

BORDER CROSSINGS

Border crossings into and out of America from Canada first began to be tracked in 1895, with lists of passengers arriving at Canadian seaports who declared they were proceeding to the United States. These border crossings from Canada were compiled into the so-called St. Albans Lists, which cover border crossings from 1895 to 1954. United States-Mexico border crossings have been tracked since about 1906. Along the Mexican border, crossings were recorded on border-crossing cards, which typically contained the person's full name, age, sex, marital status, occupation, point of arrival in the United States, and final destination.

THE NATURALIZATION PROCESS

The requirements for naturalization have changed over the years in America. At a minimum, requirements included residency in the country for a specified time period and an oath of loyalty or allegiance. From about 1790 to 1906, people could go to any courthouse in the United States to file papers and complete the naturalization process. Each form in each location was different. The Naturalization Act of 1906 changed that. It standardized requirements for citizenship and created the agency that's now called the U.S. Citizenship and Immigration Service. The Naturalization Act of 1906 required immigrants to learn English in order to become citizens and permitted only certain state and federal courts to process naturalization papers.

The naturalization process for most ancestors involved filing two papers: a declaration of intention (image **A**, also called first papers) and a petition for naturalization (image **B**, also called second or final papers). The information contained in naturalization records could vary depending on when your ancestor filed his papers. Declarations of intention filed before 1906 often include less information than the standardized forms used in and after 1906, which recorded

- immigrant's name
- country of birth or allegiance
- application date
- applicant's signature
- applicant's age, birth date, and birthplace
- applicant's occupation

- personal description
- citizenship status
- current address
- last foreign address
- port of embarkation
- US port of entry and date of arrival

Naturalization petitions after 1906 may be labeled as petitions for citizenship and generally include

- petitioner's name
- residence
- occupation
- birth date and place
- citizenship
- personal description
- the date the applicant emigrated
- the arrival and departure ports
- marital status (with wife's name and date of birth, if married)
- names, dates, and places of birth and residence of the applicant's children
- the date when US residence began

- applicant's length of residence in the state
- name change
- applicant's signature
- photo (included after 1929 only)

For more history on the naturalization process, visit **<www.familysearch.org/learn/wiki/en/United_States_Naturalization_and_Citizenship>**.

IMMIGRATION AND NATURALIZATION RECORDS ON FAMILYSEARCH.ORG

FamilySearch.org has not only collections of US immigration and naturalization records, but also some passenger arrivals, naturalizations, immigration cards, and emigration lists from countries worldwide. In this section, we'll focus on records from US locations. In addition, keep in mind that FamilySearch.org adds new records daily, so be sure to check the Historical Records collections list at **<www.familysearch.org/search/collection/list>** for recent additions that may cover your ancestors.

Passenger-Arrival List Collections

Indexed (and searchable) record collections on FamilySearch.org include passenger-arrival and ships' crew lists for these US ports of entry:

- Atlantic and Gulf Ports (1820–1874)
- Baltimore (1820–1948; 1954–1957)
- Boston (1820–1943)
- Detroit (1906–1954)
- Eagle Pass, Texas (1905–1954)
- Eastport, Idaho (1924–1956)
- El Paso, Texas (1905–1927)
- Honolulu (1900–1953)
- Key West, Florida (1898–1945)
- Los Angeles (1907–1948)
- New England (1911–1954)
- New Orleans (1820–1945)
- New York (1820–1957)
- Philadelphia (1800–1948)
- San Francisco (1893–1957)
- Seattle (1890–1957)
- Tampa, Florida (1898–1945)
- Wilmington and Morehead City, North Carolina (1908–1958)

You may need to search multiple collections for each port to cover all the available records and dates. Individual databases were created from different sources—some data come from original records, others from compiled sources such as indexes. So the level of detail and availability of record images varies from collection to collection.

In addition, FamilySearch.org has twentieth-century passenger and/or crew arrival lists that aren't yet searchable for several locations. You'll need to browse the record images for these collections, similar to scrolling through a microfilm reel. Some of the browsable collections on FamilySearch.org include

- Alexandria, Virginia (1946–1957)
- Ashtabula and Conneaut, Ohio (1952–1974)
- Boston (1899–1940)
- Brownsville, Texas (1943–1964)
- Georgetown, South Carolina (1904–1942)
- Knights Keys, Florida (1908–1912)
- Laredo, Texas (1903–1955)
- Manitowoc, Wisconsin (1925–1956)
- Milwaukee (1922–1963)
- New York (1906–1942)
- Port of Del Rio, Texas (1906–1953)
- Robbinston, Maine (1947–1954)
- San Francisco (1954–1957)
- Texas and Arizona, various ports (1903–1910)
- Wisconsin, six ports (1925–1956)

European Immigration to America

If you're looking for Irish, German, Russian, or Italian ancestors, FamilySearch.org has digital collections specifically for ancestors from those ethnic backgrounds. These indexes were compiled by extracting data from original records. They're not complete (so don't be alarmed if you don't find your ancestor), but can serve as a handy shortcut to finding an actual passenger-arrival record.

- United States Famine Irish Passenger Index, 1846–1851 <www.familysearch.org/search/collection/2110821>
- United States Germans to America Index, 1850–1897 <www.familysearch.org/search/collection/2110801>
- United States Italians to America Index, 1855–1900 <www.familysearch.org/search/collection/2110811>
- United States Russians to America Index, 1834–1897 <www.familysearch.org/search/collection/2110813>

Chinese and Japanese Records

FamilySearch.org has a collection of more than sixty thousand Philadelphia case files for Chinese immigrants spanning 1900 to 1923 <www.familysearch.org/search/collection/1888682>. These case files include the ancestor's name, occupation, age, birthplace, ship name, arrival date, and more. The site offers a few more collections covering Japanese immigrants.

For San Francisco arrivals between 1928 and 1942, FamilySearch.org has an unindexed collection of immigration registers <www.familysearch.org/search/collection/2427230>. The records contain names of people who were detained for special inquiry, as well as the date of arrival.

During World War II, millions of Japanese Americans were relocated to internment camps. FamilySearch.org has a searchable collection of more than ten million Japanese Americans who were relocated between 1942 and 1946 at <www.familysearch.org/search/collection/2043779>. The search form here includes a unique search field category: Move Place.

Border-Crossing Records

You can search a collection of 4.3 million US border crossings from Canada to the United States on FamilySearch.org <www.familysearch.org/search/collection/1803785>. These records cover the years 1895 to 1956. More than 4.1 million records from the St. Albans Lists covering 1895 to 1924 also are on FamilySearch.org, but they're not searchable. You can browse them from <www.familysearch.org/search/collection/2185163>.

In addition, a searchable database of 3.6 million border crossings from Mexico to the United States (1903–1957) is available at <www.familysearch.org/search/collection/1803932>.

Passports

Ancestors who applied for US passports could be in FamilySearch.org's United States Passport Applications, 1795–1925 collection <www.familysearch.org/search/collection/2185145>, which contains more than three million digital images. The records contain a wealth of information, including the applicant's name, application date and place, birth date and place, residence, occupation, travel plans (including port of departure, ship name, and date of departure), age, physical description, and photograph. A passport also may include a spouse or father's birth date and place, residence, and citizenship status.

FamilySearch.org also has a few collections of passport applications ancestors applied for in their home country. For example, you can browse unindexed collections of passport registers from Portugal (Aveiro 1882–1965 and Leiria 1861–1901) and passports from the Province of Cádiz, Spain (1810–1866).

Naturalization Collections

FamilySearch.org has more than forty collections containing US naturalization records. The records in those collections encompass indexes, petitions for naturalization, and naturalization cards. There may be multiple collections for each state that cover different areas of the state or overlap in coverage, so you may need to search more than one collection to find your ancestors' records. FamilySearch.org's searchable naturalization records cover the following states:

- California (Northern 1852–1989; San Diego 1868–1958; Southern 1915–1976)
- Illinois (1840–1950; 1926–1979)
- Indiana (1848–1992)
- Maryland (1797–1951, 1906–1931)
- Minnesota (1930–1988)
- New England (Connecticut, Maine, Massachusetts, New Hampshire, Rhode Island, and Vermont 1791–1906)
- New York (1791–1980; Eastern 1865–1957; Southern 1824–1941 and 1917–1950, Western 1907–1966)
- Ohio (1800–1977)
- Pennsylvania (1795–1952)
- Texas (1906–1989)
- West Virginia (1814–1991)
- Wisconsin (Milwaukee 1848–1990)

Several collections are not yet indexed, but you can browse the records. Browsable naturalization record collections cover these states:

- Colorado (1876–1990)
- Delaware (1796–1958)
- Illinois (1800–1962; 1906–1994)
- Louisiana (1831–1906)
- Maine (1800–1990)
- Missouri (1883–1927)
- Montana (1868–1999)
- New England (Maine, Massachusetts, New Hampshire, Rhode Island, and Vermont 1787–1906)
- New Hampshire (1771–2001)
- New Jersey (1749–1986)

- New Mexico (1882–1983)
- New York (1792–1906; Southern 1824–1946)
- Ohio (Northern 1855–1967; Southern 1852–1991)
- Pennsylvania (1795–1931)
- South Dakota (1865–1972)
- Utah (1906–1930)
- Virginia (1906–1929)
- Washington (1850–1982)
- Wisconsin (1807–1992, 1848–1991, Dane County 1887–1945)

Mormon Migration Database

A unique collection on FamilySearch.org contains an index to pioneer immigrants from 1840 to 1932. The index links to images of journals, autobiographies, letters, and other narrative works. The database covers British, Scandinavian, Dutch, and Swedish immigrants. Records contain information such as the immigrant's name, gender, marital status, birth date and place, baptism date, and residence, as well as names of other people traveling with the immigrant. Entries also state whether the person was a member of the LDS church, a child of a member, or held a priesthood office.

STRATEGIES FOR SEARCHING IMMIGRATION AND NATURALIZATION RECORDS

The first step in finding your ancestors' immigration and naturalization records is trying to determine the approximate date they came to America and the port of entry they may have used. Use these strategies to find immigration and naturalization records for your ancestors in the digitized records on FamilySearch.org.

Consult Censuses First

Censuses are a great help for pinpointing your ancestor's immigration and naturalization dates, which will help you fine-tune your search criteria when looking for immigration or naturalization records. Beginning with the 1900 census, year of immigration to the United States and naturalization status were recorded. The 1920 census also reported the year the person was naturalized. By combining the birthplace with year of immigration, you can make an educated guess about which port they may have left from in the old country and which port they may have entered in America. By knowing the naturalization status or year, you can focus your naturalization record searches accordingly and know whether record years covered in certain digitized collections may include your ancestors.

Check Collection Date Ranges

No one wants to waste time or stay up hours past their bedtime researching ancestors online only to come up empty-handed. Before you begin a search for your ancestor's immigration and naturalization records on FamilySearch.org, look at the list of Historical Records collections **<www.familysearch.org/search/collection/list>** and filter by Collection type (Migration & Naturalization). Browse the list of collections to identify which ones your ancestor may be included in, then look at the date range for those collections. For example, if you see collections from 1882 to 1957, but your ancestor arrived in the 1850s, he won't appear in those collections.

Start Broad, Then Refine

When entering your initial search criteria, enter just the person's first and last names. This will cast the widest net possible to locate your ancestor's immigration or naturalization records. If you get too many results to sort through, narrow your search using the options in the Refine Your Search box to the left of the results. Try adding a birth date range, or use the Any field under the Search With a Life Event heading and input the immigration year. Don't include a death date, since immigration and naturalization records don't include death information. Also, use caution when restricting results by relationships, because many males traveled alone and the rest of the family followed at a later date.

Search for Male Ancestors

Historically, married women and children got their citizenship status from their spouse or father. Citizenship stopped being available to women through marriage in 1922. When looking for naturalization records, search for the husband's or father's name. For immigration records, search for male and female ancestors separately, as they may have arrived at different times, even if they were married.

Try Alternate Locations for Naturalization Records

Before 1906, ancestors could start the naturalization process in one court and finish it in another. If they moved between filing first and second papers, the papers could be filed in different locations. In addition, if you can't find your ancestor's naturalization records in a collection for a specific state or region, try looking for records in another state or area nearby; your ancestor may have filed papers in the closest courthouse, not necessarily the courthouse in his county.

Try Alternate Names and Wildcards

As with any record you look for, consider that misspellings of given names and surnames could have occurred, as well as the fact that ancestors may have used nicknames in records. In addition, it's possible a woman could have immigrated to America before she

More Free Online Immigration, Emigration, and Naturalization Databases

If you strike out in searching for your ancestors in immigration collections at FamilySearch.org, don't give up. Try searching one of these free online databases for immigrant ancestors.

- **Boston Passenger Manifest Lists (1848–1891) <www.sec.state.ma.us/Archives Search/passengermanifest.aspx>**: Search more than one million Boston arrivals.
- **Bremen Passenger Lists <www.passengerlists.de>**: Search surviving passenger and emigration lists from Bremen, Germany, a popular port of departure.
- **Castle Garden <www.castlegarden.org>**: Find records of eleven million immigrants who arrived in New York prior to the opening of Ellis Island, from 1820 to 1892.
- **The Danish Emigration Archives <www.emiarch.dk/info.php?l=en>**: Access approximately 394 thousand records from 1869 to 1908.
- **Ellis Island <www.libertyellisfoundation.org>**: Search more than fifty-one million passenger records from 1892 to 1957.
- **Finnish Institute of Migration Emigrant Register <maine.utu.fi/emregfree/nimihaku_e. php>**: This site has a free limited search of the Finnish emigrant register, which includes 318 thousand passenger lists and 268 thousand passports, among other emigration records.
- **Galveston Immigration Database <www.galvestonhistory.org/attractions/maritime-heritage/galveston-immigration-database>**: Search this database of more than 130 thousand passengers who arrived in Galveston, Texas, from 1846 to 1948.

married, so be sure to look for female ancestors under their maiden name, unless you have proof she was married before she came to America. Remember also to use wildcards (an asterisk for more than one letter; a question mark for one letter) to search for name variations.

And while it's a myth that officials at Ellis Island changed immigrants' names, your ancestor could have "Americanized" his or her name after arriving. So be sure to look for the ethnic spelling of your ancestor's name (the way it would have been spelled in the old country) as well as how it may have been spelled in America. For example, one of my ancestors' first names is Henrietta, but records I found on FamilySearch.org spell her name as Hindrikje. Depending on her nationality, other spellings could have been Harriet, Harietta, Henriette, Henrike, Henrikka, Heinrike, or Henryka. Use BehindtheName.com <www.behindthename.com> to find ethnic spellings of your ancestors' names.

- **German Emigrants Database <www.deutsche-auswanderer-datenbank.de/index. php?id=51>**: Access records for five million emigrants from 1820 to 1897, 1904, and 1907.
- **Immigrant Ship Transcribers Guild <www.immigrantships.net>**: Search for ancestors in more than sixteen thousand passenger manifests.
- **Irish Emigration Database <www.dippam.ac.uk/ied>**: The majority of the records on this site are from 1820 to 1920 and materials include letters from emigrants.
- **Library and Archives of Canada: Immigration Databases <www.bac-lac.gc.ca/eng/ discover/immigration/Pages/introduction.aspx>**: If your ancestors arrived first in Canada, check out the databases here for records dating back to the mid-1800s.
- **_Mayflower_ (1620) Passenger List <www.mayflowerhistory.com/mayflower-passenger- list>**: Browse a list of _Mayflower_ passengers, then follow links for additional information.
- **New Orleans Ship Passenger List Online Index: January to July 1851 <www.sos.la.gov/ HistoricalResources/ResearchHistoricalRecords/Pages/PassengerManifests.aspx>**: This database contains only a portion of available New Orleans passenger lists.
- **One-Step Webpages <www.stevemorse.org>**: Use the special search forms here to find ancestors in a variety of online immigration databases.
- **The Scottish Emigration Database <www.abdn.ac.uk/emigration>**: This database has more than twenty-one thousand passengers who departed at Glasgow and Greenock in 1923, as well as from other Scottish ports between 1890 and 1960.
- **TheShipsList <www.theshipslist.com>**: Passenger lists, ship descriptions and pictures, fleet lists, and marriages at sea—this site has plentiful material to search and browse.

Look at a Map

Boundaries of countries in Europe, especially Eastern Europe, changed frequently throughout the years. Consult a map from the time period your ancestor would have lived overseas to confirm what the country was called at that time. Then look in any collections for the appropriate country (or countries).

STEP-BY-STEP EXAMPLE: SEARCHING IMMIGRATION AND NATURALIZATION RECORDS

The key to successful searches, as you've heard me say before, is to start your search broadly. Always start using the main Historical Records search form and use the search fields to narrow your criteria as needed. If you still can't find your ancestor, try searching (or browsing) records in a specific collection.

Let's look at an example of how to search for immigration and naturalization records on FamilySearch.org. In this example, I'll look for an immigration record for my great-grandfather Goffredo Gemignani, who was born in 1892 in Bargecchia, Italy. From family stories, I know he came to America from Italy in the 1920s and lived in Chicago once he was here.

1 ENTER SEARCH CRITERIA. Using the Historical Records search form at **<www.familysearch.org/search>**, enter the ancestor's first and last name: *Goffredo Gemignani*. Under the Restrict Records By heading, click the Type link and check the box next to Immigration and Naturalization. Hit the Search button.

2 REVIEW THE RESULTS. The search results page has columns for Preview, Name, Events, Relationship, Details, and Image. Review the information in each column to see if it matches what you know about your ancestor. In this case, FamilySearch.org returned five matches (four immigration and one naturalization) that the system thinks match my ancestor. Four of the matches appear to have the right birth date and/or birthplace, as well as place of residence in America for my ancestor. I decide to investigate the other record first to see if I can rule it out.

3 PREVIEW A RECORD. Under the Preview column, click the arrow next to the name on the record you want to view more closely, in this case the record that has a 1907 immigration date. This brings up a preview of the transcription for the record. In addition to the immigration date, the preview shows the immigrant's age. In this example, the age of the immigrant in 1907 was twenty-three years old. My ancestor was born in 1892, so he would have been fifteen years old in 1907. I determine this is not a match and go on to preview other possible record matches. When you do find a match, click on the link for the person's name to see the page with the full record.

1

RECORDS GENEALOGIES CATALOG BOOKS WIKI

Search Historical Records

Search for a deceased ancestor in historical records to uncover vital informat

Deceased Ancestor's Name

First Names — goffredo
Last Names — gemignani

Search with a life event:
Birth | Marriage | Residence | Death | Any

Birthplace
Birth Year (Range) — From / To

Search with a relationship:
Spouse | Parents | Other Person

Restrict records by:
Location | Type | Batch Number | Film Number

Country
State or Province

Type
☐ Birth, Baptism, and Christenings   ☑ Immigration and Naturalization
☐ Marriage   ☐ Military
☐ Death   ☐ Probate
☐ Census, Residence, and Lists   ☐ Other

☐ Match all terms exactly

[Search] Reset

2

3

4

The image is viewable at ellisisland.org. By clicking here you will be leaving FamilySearch.org. (fees and other terms may apply)

[Visit Partner Site]

5

RECORDS GENEALOGIES CATALOG BOOKS WIKI

◀ Go To: Search Results

COPY | PRINT | SOURCE BOX ▾ | SHARE ▾

Goffredo Ge...
New York, Passenge...

⊕ Add to My Source Box
🗄 Go to My Source Box

Given Name:	
Surname:	Geminiani
Last Place of Residence:	Bargecchia, Lucca
Event Date:	01 Sep 1910
Age:	18y
Nationality:	Italian, South
Departure Port:	Genoa
Arrival Port:	New York
Gender:	Male
Marital Status:	S
Ship Name:	Verona

[Attach to Family Tree]

The image is viewable at ellisisland.org. By clicking here you will be leaving FamilySearch.org. (fees and other terms may apply)

[Visit Partner Site]

New York, Passenger Arrival Lists (Ellis Island), 1892-1924
🔍 Search collection
ⓘ About this collection

4 **VIEW THE RECORD IMAGE.** If a record image is included, your next step is to view the image. For this example, the record image is available via a FamilySearch partner's website, so click the Visit Partner Site button. This should open a new browser tab. You may have to log in (or set up an account) at the partner site, in this case the Ellis Island website. If possible, download the record image to your computer. Remember to click Open in a new window and click forward and back through images surrounding the image for your ancestor—you might find a second page to the record or a record for an ancestor traveling with him.

POWER-USER TIP

Visiting Partner Sites for Images

If the record image for your ancestor is on a FamilySearch.org partner website, it is often easiest for you to go to that website first and log in to your account before you click on the View Partner Site button on FamilySearch.org. This will let you go directly to the record image after you click the button.

5 **RETURN TO FAMILYSEARCH.ORG TO SAVE.** Click on the tab with your FamilySearch.org search results in it. For the record you found, click the Attach to Family Tree button to add it to your family tree. If you don't want to attach it to your Family Tree right away, click the down arrow next to the Source Box link to add it to your Source Box. You also could print the record transcription, if desired.

Next, return to the search results page and repeat steps 3 through 5 for each record you find that may match your ancestor.

KEYS TO SUCCESS

★ Start with a broad search of FamilySearch.org's entire Immigration and Naturalization category, especially if you are unsure of your immigrant ancestor's port of arrival.

★ Focus on naturalization records first if you don't know your ancestor's arrival date or port. Naturalization records often give the applicant's specific place of origin. Glean immigration clues from US census records, too.

★ Search on various spellings of your ancestor's names, and keep in mind that immigration records will use her original name used in the old country—not an Americanized version she may have adopted later.

★ Check for departure records as well as arrival records. FamilySearch.org has several collections of emigration records; others are available on microfilm through the FamilySearch Catalog.

CHECKLIST AND WORKSHEET

Ancestor Profile

Ancestor's name: _____

Ancestor's maiden name (if female): _____

Birth date: _____ Birthplace: _____

Residence/location(s) in United States: _____

Last known country of residence (prior to immigration): _____

Age at immigration: _____

Estimated date of immigration: _____

Possible ports of entry: _____

Possible ports of departure (from old country): _____

Estimated date of naturalization: _____

Other family members (including children) who may have immigrated at same time:

_____

_____

_____

Records Search Checklist

☐ Consult the following US censuses for clues to your ancestor's immigration date:
   ☐ 1900 federal census
   ☐ 1910 federal census
   ☐ 1920 federal census

☐ Start with a broad search of all Historical Records collections on FamilySearch.org **<www.familysearch.org/search>** (select Immigration and Naturalization as Type), then search individual collections.

☐ Identify specific collections to search on FamilySearch.org. Go to **<www.familysearch.org/search/collection/list>** and filter by collection type (Migration & Naturalization).

☐ In the table below, list the collection titles you want to search for your ancestor, then record your searches.

Collection Title and Record Coverage Dates	Date You Searched This Collection	Search Terms/ Criteria Used	Notes (e.g., found record, next steps)

EXTRACTION WORKSHEET

When you find a record for your ancestor, record the information from the record(s) here.

Immigration Record Extraction

Ancestor's name: _____ Age at immigration: _____

Country of origin: _____

Last known residence/city (prior to immigration): _____

Date of US arrival: _____ Ship name: _____

Port of entry: _____ Port of departure: _____

Names and relationships of other family on same ship:

_____

_____

Other information learned from record:

_____

_____

_____

Naturalization Record Extraction

Ancestor's name: _____

Address: _____

Name/location of court: _____

Country of birth/allegiance: _____ Birth date: _____

Date of US arrival: _____ Port of arrival: _____

Date of naturalization: _____

Names and addresses of witnesses of naturalization:

_____

_____

Other information listed on the record:

_____

_____

US Military Records

Military service is part of many Americans' family trees, including mine. My grandfather Harold Schmidt, an Iowa farmer and skilled carpenter, fought in World War II. During the war, he was assigned to a cavalry unit and became a gunner. He never talked much about his war experience, but his sister convinced him to write down part of his story. His first-person account gives a bleak picture of war. After months of training, he was sent to the Admiralty Islands and later Leyte Island in the Philippines. There, his unit battled not only suicidal enemy groups, but also mountain rains and typhoons, and hunger—once going four days without food.

If you don't have a great first-person account written by your ancestor or a relative like I had, or even if you do, the US military records on FamilySearch.org can provide a wealth of details about your ancestor, his military service, and even his dependent family members such as a wife/widow and children.

In this chapter, I'll provide some background about US military records, outline the military records available on FamilySearch.org, and offer strategies to search those records most efficiently.

ABOUT US MILITARY RECORDS

Military records can tell you a lot about your ancestor—more than just his service information. As you analyze the records you find, you may glean additional information or discover new avenues for research. For example, death information in a service or pension record can help you pinpoint a specific date and location to track down a death certificate. A widow's pension application often gives a marriage date and place in the supporting documents—she had to prove she was married to the soldier to be eligible for his pension. Let's review three common types of US military records and the clues they contain.

Service Records

These records chronicle the service of each soldier or sailor. Service records could include muster rolls, pay vouchers, and other records. Typically the information in these records covers the serviceman's rank, unit, dates of service, and some basic biographical and medical information.

Pensions

Pensions were given to veterans, widows, and their heirs. Pension records typically include the name of the person submitting the claim and his/her status (invalid, widow, or minor); the soldier's service record (including rank, company, regiment, and enlistment and discharge dates), application number, certificate number, and date and place of the soldier's death.

Available records may include pension applications and pension payment records. According to the National Archives and Records Administration, pension files are the most genealogically rich of all military records—they contain supporting documents such as narratives of events during service, vital-records certificates (for births, marriages, and deaths), family letters, witness depositions, affidavits, and discharge papers.

Draft Registration Cards

Draft registration cards are available for relatives who served in the two World Wars. In May 1917, the Selective Service Act authorized the president to temporarily increase the size of the military and launched a registration process overseen by district boards. That process created records for your ancestors who were drafted for service in World War I. Not all men who registered for the draft served in the military. Men registered on various dates according to their age group:

- June 5, 1917, for men ages twenty-one to thirty-one
- June 5, 1918, for men who had turned twenty-one since the first registration occurred
- September 12, 1919, for men ages eighteen to forty-five

The information collected on World War I draft registration cards for each registration date varied. The registration cards may include the person's name, home address, date and place of birth, race, country of citizenship, occupation, employer name, a physical description, and information on the nearest relative, dependent relatives, marital status, father's birthplace, or previous service exemption.

The Selective Training and Service Act was issued in 1940 after the United States entered World War II. There were several different draft registration dates:

- October 16, 1940, for men ages twenty-one to thirty-six
- July 1, 1941, for men who had turned twenty-one since the first registration occurred
- February 16, 1942, for men ages twenty to twenty-one and thirty-five to forty-four
- April 27, 1942, for men ages forty-five to sixty-four
- June 30, 1942, for men ages eighteen to twenty
- December 10–31, 1942, for men who had turned eighteen since the last registration
- November 16–December 21, 1943, for American men ages eighteen to forty-four who were living abroad

The information on World War II draft registrations may include the person's name, address, age, birth date and place; the name of a "person who will always know your address" (usually a relative); his employer's name and address; and a physical description.

US MILITARY RECORDS ON FAMILYSEARCH.ORG

FamilySearch.org has a growing collection of US military records. The bulk of the records relate to Civil War service, but some collections cover records from the Revolutionary War, War of 1812, Mexican-American War, World War I, World War II, the Korean War, and the Vietnam War. Some records are in nationwide collections, while others are in collections for specific states.

Civil War Records

Collections of Civil War records cover soldiers from both the Union and Confederate armies. They encompass service records, pensions, cemetery records, veterans' organization records, prisoner-of-war records, and papers about the war.

SERVICE RECORDS

Confederate service records from 1861 to 1865 are available for these states:

- Alabama
- Arizona
- Arkansas

- Florida
- Georgia
- Kentucky
- Louisiana
- Maine (in the state archive collections from 1718 to 1957)
- Maryland
- Mississippi
- Missouri
- North Carolina
- South Carolina
- Tennessee
- Texas
- Virginia

Union service records from 1861 to 1865 are available for these locations:

- Alabama
- Arkansas
- Dakota Territory
- Delaware
- Florida
- Georgia
- Kentucky
- Louisiana
- Maryland
- Mississippi
- Missouri
- Nebraska
- Nevada
- New Mexico
- New York
- North Carolina
- Oregon
- Tennessee
- Texas
- Utah
- Virginia
- West Virginia

TIMELINE OF MAJOR US MILITARY CONFLICTS

1775-1783 Revolutionary War

1812-1815 War of 1812

1846-1848 Mexican-American War

1861-1865 Civil War

1898 Spanish-American War

1899-1902 Philippine Insurrection

1917-1918 World War I

1941-1945 World War II

1950-1953 Korean War

1959-1973 Vietnam War

You'll find a few specialized databases as well, including a searchable collection of service records for "Union colored troops" and a browsable collection of Vermont militia enrollment records from 1861 to 1867—basically any man between eighteen and forty-five who served or was eligible for service.

In addition, FamilySearch.org has its own searchable index of the United States Civil War Soldiers Index, 1861–1865 **<www.familysearch.org/search/collection/1910717>**, which contains 6.3 million records outlining the soldier's name, regiment, company, rank, and whether he fought for the Union or Confederate sides. The information in this collection is the same information from the Civil War Soldiers and Sailors Database available at **<www.nps.gov/civilwar/soldiers-and-sailors-database.htm>**.

PENSIONS

Whereas the federal government administered pensions for Union soldiers, Confederate pensions were issued by the state. As a result, the dates for Confederate pensions vary by state. FamilySearch.org has several indexed and unindexed Civil War pension collections for both the Union and Confederacy.

Among the browsable Confederate pension collections:

- Arkansas (1901–1929 and 1891–1939)
- Florida (1885–1955)
- Kentucky (1912–1950)
- Louisiana (1898–1950)
- Mississippi (1900–1974)
- Missouri (1911–1938)
- North Carolina (1885–1953)
- Tennessee (1891–1965)

FamilySearch.org's searchable Union Civil War pension collections cover approximately nine million records; most of the associated record images are accessed via FamilySearch.org partner site Fold3.com (requires subscription).

- United States Civil War Widows and Other Dependents Pension Files, 1861–1934 **<www.familysearch.org/search/collection/1922519>** contains case files for widows and other dependents primarily of Civil War soldiers and sailors; some pension files for Spanish-American War service are included.
- United States Civil War and Later Pension Index, 1861–1917 **<www.familysearch. org/search/collection/1471019>** comprises information such as the soldier's name, application number, and the regiment in which he served, as well as the soldier's date and place of death. Though the majority of these records pertain to Civil War veterans, you'll find some for the Spanish-American War, Indian wars, the Philippine Insurrection, and World War I (1917 only) as well.

- United States General Index to Pension Files, 1861–1934 <www.familysearch.org/search/collection/1919699> also pertains mainly to Union Civil War service, but includes records from various other conflicts such as the Spanish-American War, Philippine Insurrection, and Boxer Rebellion.

PRISONERS OF WAR

FamilySearch.org has two unindexed collections of prison and prisoners-of-war records: more than four thousand Andersonville, Georgia, prison records (including hospital admissions, death and burial records, and other prisoner records) from 1862 to 1865 <www.familysearch.org/search/collection/2019835>, and more than fifty-one thousand records of Confederate prisoners of war from 1861 to 1865 <www.familysearch.org/search/collection/1916234> containing lists and registers of prisoners, prisoner deaths and burials, Confederate deserters, and more.

VETERANS RECORDS

In 1890, the federal government took a census of Union veterans and widows, and nearly nine hundred thousand of these records are in a searchable collection on <www.familysearch.org/search/collection/1877095>. Because much of the 1890 US federal census was destroyed, this surviving collection is an excellent population census substitute. The records list the name of the surviving solider, sailor, or widow; martial status; age; number of children; birthplaces for members of the household; occupation; number of years lived in the United States; and the service member's dates of enlistment and discharge, length of service, rank, and company/regiment of service. In addition, a collection of Minnesota Grand Army of the Republic records <www.familysearch.org/search/collection/2239221> documents Civil War veterans.

PARDONS

Former Confederates excluded from a May 29, 1865, proclamation of amnesty and reconstruction could seek a pardon from President Andrew Johnson. FamilySearch.org has a searchable collection covering nearly eighty thousand of the applications for these pardons from 1865 to 1867 <www.familysearch.org/search/collection/1936545>. The applications created lots of paperwork: affidavits, oaths of allegiance, recommendations for clemency, and more. Records may contain the petitioner's name, date, and place of residence.

Revolutionary War Records

FamilySearch.org has two searchable collections of records from the American Revolution: The first has more than two million compiled service records from 1775 to 1783

<www.familysearch.org/search/collection/1849623>, and the second has nearly seven million pension and bounty-land war applications from 1800 to 1900 <www.familysearch.org/search/collection/1417475>. The compiled service records contain information such as the soldier's name, rank, regiment, state from which he served, term of enlistment, and payment records. The pension and bounty-land warrant records each contain about thirty pages with the application and supporting documents. The documents may include the veteran's name, birth date and place, residence, death date and place, marriage date and place, names and ages of children, and the name of the person applying for the pension.

The remaining Revolutionary War collections are unindexed, so you'll have to browse those image by image. One of those collections contains Revolutionary War pension payment ledgers from 1818 to 1872 <www.familysearch.org/search/collection/2069831> and also includes a few records from the War of 1812. Another covers war rolls from 1775 to 1783 <www.familysearch.org/search/collection/2068326>, and the last one is a more narrowly focused collection of Virginia pension applications from 1830 to 1875 <www.familysearch.org/search/collection/2070137>. If you browse the war rolls collection, you'll need to know your ancestor's state and military unit. The FamilySearch Wiki has a coverage table that can help you figure it out <www.familysearch.org/learn/wiki/en/Revolutionary_War_Rolls_Coverage_Table>.

War of 1812 Records

FamilySearch.org has two main collections of War of 1812 records. In addition, a few War of 1812 records are included in the Revolutionary War payment ledgers (1818–1872) collection mentioned above, and a few pension records for soldiers from Louisiana are available at <www.familysearch.org/search/collection/1527724>.

The only searchable War of 1812 collection is an index to pension application files from 1812 to 1910 <www.familysearch.org/search/collection/1834325>. The index includes the soldier's name, military service information, the widow's name, and pension and bounty land numbers. It may be helpful to use the soldier's birth date or name of the widow in searches. The original pension files are not on microfilm or online, so to access the full application you'll need to request those records from the US National Archives and Records Administration <www.archives.gov>.

The browsable collection of interest to most is an index to War of 1812 service records <www.familysearch.org/search/collection/1916219>, with more than 620 thousand record images arranged alphabetically. In addition to the soldier's name, the index gives the soldier's rank/position, military unit, and state of enlistment.

Mexican-American War Records

For the Mexican-American War, you'll find two main collections: one searchable pension index covering 1887 to 1926 **<www.familysearch.org/search/collection/1979390>** and a browsable collection with an index and service records from 1846 to 1848 **<www.familysearch.org/search/collection/1987567>**. Within the pension index, expect to find the soldier's name, rank, dates of service, application number, and the name of the soldier's spouse. The service-records collection contains records from five states: Iowa, Mississippi, Pennsylvania, Tennessee, and Texas. Those records list the soldier's name, rank, unit, state from which he served, and more. Another searchable collection covers pension applications for the Mormon Battalion (who enlisted in Iowa), dated 1846 to 1923 **<www.familysearch.org/search/collection/1852758>**.

World War I and II Records

World War I draft registrations are a key source for tracing male relatives in the early 1900s because all men had to register for the draft. So it's worth looking for your ancestor in draft records even if he did not ultimately serve in World War I. FamilySearch.org's United States World War I Draft Registration Cards, 1917–1918 collection at **<www.familysearch.org/search/collection/1968530>** contains more than twenty-four million records. All of the images are available to browse directly on FamilySearch.org, but only 96 percent of them are searchable: The index is incomplete for Illinois, Indiana, Michigan, Nebraska, Nevada, Ohio, Puerto Rico, Utah, Washington, and Wisconsin. For indexed records, you can enter your ancestor's name, gender, birthplace and year range, or draft registration place and year range in the search form.

For World War II, FamilySearch.org's collection of United States World War II Draft Registration Cards, 1942 **<www.familysearch.org/search/collection/1861144>** contains more than ten million records for men ages forty-five to sixty-four who registered in the fourth draft registration, called the Old Man's Registration. Only twenty-three states' records are indexed. A browse-only collection by the same name contains about a million more records than the searchable collection. You can view record images directly on FamilySearch.org. Note that World War II draft registrations exist for only forty states; cards were destroyed for Alabama, Florida, Georgia, Kentucky, Mississippi, North Carolina, South Carolina, and Tennessee.

If you have Georgia ancestors who served in World War II, check the collection of more than 173 thousand Georgia-only World War II draft registration cards for 1897 to 1942 **<www.familysearch.org/search/collection/1880573>**. (The collection's start date may seem too early for World War II, but these records cover people born as early as 1897.) The records may contain the person's name, place of residence, date and place of birth, employer's name and address, race, and physical description—and the collection includes record images.

If you had an ancestor who served in the Army or Women's Army Auxiliary Corps, try the United States World War II Army Enlistment Records, 1938–1946 index **<www.familysearch.**

org/search/collection/2028680>. Although the database doesn't have corresponding record images, the index typically gives the person's full name, date and place of birth, race, county of residence, date of enlistment, occupation, and marital status.

The final World War II collection <www.familysearch.org/search/collection/2127320> covers nearly thirty thousand American military personnel and civilians who were prisoners of Japan from 1941 to 1945. Records from this searchable collection contain the prisoner's name, rank, service number, branch of service, and source of information. Record images are not included.

Additional Military Records

FamilySearch.org also has collections for the Korean War and Vietnam War. Four searchable collections cover more than 150 thousand Korean War deaths from 1950 to 1957 and American prisoners of war during the Korean War from 1950 to 1954. Two searchable collections cover more than one hundred thousand records for casualties from the Vietnam War and military personnel who died during the war from 1956 to 2003.

In addition, you'll find a hodgepodge of other searchable collections for particular military branches, agencies and conflicts, including:

- United States Headstone Applications for US Military Veterans, 1925–1949 <www.familysearch.org/search/collection/1916249> covers hundreds of thousands of veterans from the Civil War and later.
- United States Index to General Correspondence of the Pension Office, 1889–1904 <www.familysearch.org/search/collection/1834308> covers volunteers and soldiers; inquiries may pertain to soldiers as far back as the Revolutionary War.
- United States Index to Indian Wars Pension Files, 1892–1926 <www.familysearch.org/search/collection/1979427> is a card index that may contain a soldier's name, rank and unit, dates of service, and more.
- United States National Homes for Disabled Volunteer Soldiers, 1866–1938 <www.familysearch.org/search/collection/1916230> documents veterans admitted at twelve regional homes. Records may contain rank, discharge date, date admitted to the home, birthplace, age, religion, residence, marital status, name and address of nearest relative, pension information, date and cause of death, and place of burial.
- United States Muster Rolls of the Marine Corps, 1798–1937 <www.familysearch.org/search/collection/1916228> has more than one million records with the soldier's name, rank and unit, date of enlistment (as well as re-enlistment), and name of ship.
- United States Naval Enlistment Rendezvous, 1855–1891 <www.familysearch.org/search/collection/1825347> contains recruiting station records that include the recruit's name, enlistment date and term, rank, ship assignment, previous Naval experience, age, birthplace, and a physical description.

- United States Navy Widows' Certificates, 1861–1910 **<www.familysearch.org/ search/collection/1852605>** covers more than twenty thousand approved pension application files.
- United States Old War Pension Index, 1815–1926 **<www.familysearch.org/search/ collection/1979425>** lists the names of the veteran and his dependents, the veteran's rank and military unit, his dates of service, the date of the pension filing, and more.
- **United States Registers of Enlistments in the U.S. Army, 1798–1914 <www. familysearch.org/search/collection/1880762>** compiles data from various military records, including the soldier's name, rank, regiment, commander, age, occupation, birthplace, date and place of enlistment, and a physical description.
- United States Remarried Widows Index to Pension Applications, 1887–1942 **<www. familysearch.org/search/collection/1979426>** includes records from the Civil War and later, and may contain the name of the claimant, soldier's name, military unit, application number, and date filed.
- United States Veterans Administration Pension Payment Cards, 1907–1933 **<www. familysearch.org/search/collection/1832324>** has cards created for Army and Navy invalids and widows.

Be sure to check the collections list at **<www.familysearch.org/search/collection/list>** for more US military collections (under Place, select United States of America, and under Collections, choose Military). FamilySearch.org is constantly adding new records and collections, so check back occasionally to look for new databases relevant to your research.

SEARCH STRATEGIES FOR MILITARY RECORDS

The key to US military records searches is the key to any other search at FamilySearch. org: Start broadly, then narrow your options by adding filters or additional search criteria. If you know your ancestor served in a specific conflict and he doesn't turn up in a broad search, review the list of Historical Records collections **<www.familysearch.org/search/ collection/list>** for specific collections to search. In some cases, the records for a certain conflict may not yet be searchable, so you may come across collections to browse. Below are a few additional strategies to employ as you look for your ancestors' military records on FamilySearch.org.

Include Residence

Including a residence will help you determine whether the John Smith listed is your ancestor John Smith. In addition, many military records were recorded or arranged by state, and most military records typically include the soldier's residence location. Combining the name with the residence will help yield more relevant results.

Add a Family Relationship

Particularly when searching for pension records, try adding a family relationship. Why? Pensions in particular included family members such as the soldier's widow or children. Other military records may include family members' names, too, since soldiers often had to provide information on their next of kin or a contact person back home.

Date Ranges

When entering a life event to your search criteria, FamilySearch.org provides a date range field. Even if you know the exact year of your ancestor's birth, enter dates a couple of years before and after that date so you catch records that are off by a year or two due to incorrect transcriptions or errors when the event date was first recorded.

Check Location Coverage

If you're searching in a specific collection, be sure to check the locations the records cover. For example, some collections have records for only one state or a couple dozen states—but not all states. So if your New York ancestor served in the Mexican-American War, he's probably not in the unindexed collection of service records at **<www.familysearch.org/search/collection/1987567>** because that collection covers only service records from Iowa, Mississippi, Pennsylvania, Tennessee, and Texas.

Account for Name Variations

According to Ancestry.com, some Italian immigrants wrote their last names first on World War I draft registration cards, which resulted in cards being filed alphabetically by first name, rather than last name. World War I cards for Hispanics may be filed under the mother's maiden name (if it was part of the person's surname). Try entering the names in reverse order (first name in the Last Names search box, and last name in the First Names search box), or search for the solider using his mother's maiden name as the last name. Also try searching for your ancestor using various nicknames. If your ancestor has a common name, try entering the first initial of his middle name in the First Names box after his first name (for example, Harold E).

In addition, remember to use wildcards to account for any spelling errors in the records or transcriptions. An asterisk replaces multiple characters, while a question mark replaces only one character.

STEP-BY-STEP EXAMPLE: SEARCHING MILITARY RECORDS

For this step-by-step example, let's follow the strategies above and start with a broad search. I'm going to search for my ancestor Ferdinand Schmidt. He was from Iowa and was born May

29, 1884. He married Catherine Geber (who also went by Kate and Katie) in 1915, so if he did serve in a conflict, it was likely World War I. Follow the steps by replicating the search or by entering your ancestors' information in the appropriate places.

1 **USE THE MAIN SEARCH FORM.** Go to <www.familysearch.org/search> to access the main Historical Records search form.

2 **ENTER SEARCH CRITERIA.** Enter information in the First Names and Last Names boxes. In this case, enter *Ferdinand Schmidt*. Also under Search With a Life Event, click on the Residence link and enter the location where he lived: *Iowa*.

3 **RESTRICT RECORDS.** Under the Restrict Records By heading, click the Type link, then check the box next to Military. This will restrict your search to only the military records on FamilySearch.org. Hit the Search button.

4 **NARROW RESULTS.** This search returned 313 results. Apparently, quite a few Iowa men had the last name Schmidt and the first or middle name Ferdinand. To find the most relevant results, use the Refine Your Search box on the left to add search criteria. In this case, let's add Ferdinand's birth date. To do this, under the Search With a Life Event heading, click on the Birth link. Enter a birthplace and date range: *Iowa* and *1880* to *1885*. Hit the Update button.

5 **REVIEW AND PREVIEW THE RESULTS.** Scroll down the list of possible matches until you find a relevant match. The second Ferdinand listed has the same birth date as my ancestor, and the county in Iowa listed (Dubuque) matches the area where he lived. Click the down arrow in the Preview column to see a preview of the record.

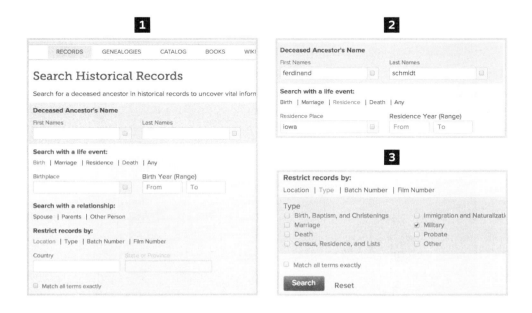

6 **VIEW THE DOCUMENT (IF AVAILABLE).** The information appears to match up with my Ferdinand, so it's time to view the record image. In this instance, the record image is directly on FamilySearch.org, so the record has a View the Document link. Click that link to see the record image. (Alternatively, you can click on Ferdinand's name from the original results listing to go to a new page with the same information. This way, when you get to step 7, you'll go right back to his listing.)

7 **ANALYZE THE RECORD.** Is the record really a match for your ancestor? Look at the information provided. The record for Ferdinand is a World War I draft registration card. It lists his name, permanent home address (St. Donatus, Iowa), birth date (May 29, 1884), age (34), occupation (farmer), and nearest relative (Katie Schmidt). All of these details match the information I know or have seen in other places about my ancestor, so this is a match.

8 **SAVE THE RECORD.** On the record image page under the Tools icon, click the Download link to download a copy of the image to save on your computer, or click the Print link to print a copy. If you want to attach it to your family tree or save it to your Source

Box, you'll need to go back a step by clicking your browser's back arrow or clicking the X in the upper-right corner of the image. From the record Preview pop-up box or the full transcription window, you can select the Attach to Family Tree button or Add to My Source Box link.

9 KEEP SEARCHING FOR MORE RECORDS. Once you complete your search, don't forget to keep going. Your ancestor could be in other records. Click the Collections tab to look for more applicable databases to search.

KEYS TO SUCCESS

★ Before searching for military records, determine which conflicts your ancestor may have fought in based on his birth and death dates and the dates of major US conflicts.

★ Familiarize yourself with the types of military records available for each conflict. Consult the FamilySearch Wiki to find this information.

★ Use the typical search strategies to find your ancestor in searchable collections: Start broadly, then narrow results to home in on your ancestors. If needed, search a specific collection to pinpoint your ancestor's record.

★ Remember to browse record collections that can't yet be searched.

US MILITARY RECORDS CHECKLIST

Ancestor's name: _____

Residence/location(s): _____

Birth Date: _____

Birthplace: _____

Spouse's name: _____

Children's names: _____

_____

_____

_____

US Wars/Conflicts to Research

Check all the wars that occurred during your ancestor's lifetime.

☐ Revolutionary War (1775–1783)

☐ War of 1812 (1812–1815)

☐ Mexican-American War (1846–1848)

☐ Civil War (1861–1865)

☐ Spanish-American War (1898)

☐ Philippine Insurrection (1899–1902)

☐ World War I (1917–1918)

☐ World War II (1941–1945)

☐ Korean War (1950–1953)

☐ Vietnam War (1959–1973)

☐ Other _____

FamilySearch.org Collections to Search

Go to **<www.familysearch.org/collection/list>**. Under Place, select United States of America, and under Collections, choose Military under Collections. Browse the resulting list of US military collections to find ones relevant to your ancestor. List which collections you want to search and track your search progress below.

Collection Title and Record Coverage Dates	Date You Searched This Collection	Search Terms/ Criteria Used	Notes (e.g., found record, next steps)

US Probate
and Court Records

After you've exhausted your searches for immigration, census, military, and vital records, don't forget to check the US probate and court records on FamilySearch. org for additional details and research clues. US probate and court records are a hodgepodge of official documents, covering everything from estate files and wills to land purchases and citizenship papers to tax lists and vital records. Each state had different laws, so the types of records and date ranges vary by state.

In this chapter, we'll look at the records you might encounter when researching probate and court files, the types of probate and court records available on FamilySearch.org, and strategies for searching and browsing these records.

TYPES OF US PROBATE AND COURT RECORDS

As mentioned above, US probate and court records encompass almost any type of record, including estate files and wills, land records, naturalization records, tax lists, and vital records. Here's a crash course in the documents and ancestral details you can expect to find within this record group.

Probate Records

Estates went through probate if a person died and left behind an estate worth more than a certain value and/or if no will had been created. Probate records were typically filed and kept at county courthouses, and they can include all sorts of juicy genealogical items: estate inventories of property, wills, guardianship records for minors or others deemed legally incompetent, letters assigning an administrator of an estate, a surety bond, petitions to the court, oaths from estate executors, claims against the estate, and a final settlement statement.

These documents may reveal information about relatives' names, family relationships, residences of your ancestors, property owned, and more. They also may contain information about organizations the deceased belonged to. For example, a will might designate a certain portion of the estate to go to a local church or other charity.

Land Records

Land records were issued by states or the federal government, depending where your ancestor lived. In state-land states (the original thirteen colonies, as well as Hawaii, Kentucky, Maine, Tennessee, Texas, Vermont, and West Virginia), the records are often located at a state archives, and if they are on FamilySearch.org, would likely appear in a state-specific collection.

In public-land states, the federal government sold or granted land to individuals. For instance, your ancestor might have received free land following the Homestead Act of 1862 or as a reward for military service (known as bounty land). Records of those transactions are most likely to appear in a nationwide record collection covering the entire United States. Here's a brief overview of the different types of American land records.

LAND GRANTS

A land grant was issued by a state to an individual purchasing land. Grants typically include information on the person receiving the grant and a description of the property. Some collections on FamilySearch.org refer to *headright grants*. A headright grant is a document that legally allotted land to settlers, particularly in the Colonial era. Headrights were given to people willing to travel to the New World to help populate the colonies.

LAND PATENTS

These federally issued legal documents transfer land ownership from the government to an individual. Patents include the patentee's name, a legal land description, and the date the patent was issued, among other information. Land patents were issued to people who took advantage of the Homestead Act of 1862 by settling on land for five years and making improvements to the land, as well as to other individuals who purchased land from the federal government.

DEEDS

Deeds track the ownership of land from person to person. After a land grant or patent was issued, subsequent owners received a deed to confirm their legal right to the land.

BOUNTY-LAND WARRANTS

A bounty-land warrant is a type of land patent. Bounty land was given to men who served in certain US wars, including the Revolutionary War, the War of 1812, and the Mexican-American War. Records include the number of acres granted and the congressional act that authorized the grant. Bounty-land warrants also often include the soldier's service rank and regiment.

TRACT BOOKS

These books contain summaries documenting official land transactions. Entries typically include a legal description of the land, the applicant's name, the application date, the amount of land purchased/granted, a copy of the final certificate, and the patent number.

Naturalizations

As discussed in chapter 7, from about 1790 to 1906, immigrants could go to any courthouse in the United States to file citizenship papers and complete the naturalization process. The forms in each location were different, so the genealogical information in those naturalization records varies. After 1906, the US government standardized the naturalization process, and papers could be filed only in certain state and federal courts. As a result, many county courthouses have naturalization records prior to 1906.

Some of these county-level naturalizations have been digitized and are available on FamilySearch.org among the US probate and court records collections. You may find these records in collections titled generally as "county records" or "court records" or more specifically as "naturalizations."

Tax and Voter Lists

Various taxes have existed in America since Colonial days. On the federal level, one of the earliest direct taxes was collected during the Civil War in order to raise funds to pay for the war. States, counties, and cities/towns also collected various taxes. Tax records for cities/towns and counties are typically kept by county courthouses, so any digitized tax records on FamilySearch.org are typically in collections organized by state and/or county. Like naturalizations, you may find these records in collections titled generally as "county records" or "court records" or more specifically as "tax records," "tax lists," or "revenue assessments."

The information in tax records and lists varies, but these records typically note the value of the property (personal property and/or land) a person owned. A tax list can serve as a census substitute when a census is missing, when you can't find your ancestors in an extant census, or when you want to place your ancestors in a certain location between state and federal censuses.

Voter lists and other voting records (kept by county courthouses) also can serve as census substitutes or place your ancestors in a specific location during a certain time.

Vital Records

Vital records on FamilySearch.org aren't limited to birth, marriage, and death collections. You'll also find vital statistics in county or court record collections for certain states and counties because the records typically were first recorded on the county level.

US PROBATE AND COURT RECORDS ON FAMILYSEARCH.ORG

FamilySearch.org has more than 130 collections of probate and court records from the United States. Among these records are estate files, Freedmen's Bureau records, county naturalizations, will books, land records, tax lists, and even some county vital records. Coverage is spotty and location-specific. The records are typically in collections organized by state.

The majority of these collections are unindexed and won't be included in search results. To access the unindexed records (all but about twenty collections), you'll need to browse through the record images, similar to scrolling through microfilm.

Records by State

Here's a summary of the types of probate and court records available by state:

- **Alabama:** estate files (1830–1976), probate records (1809–1985), Jefferson County circuit court papers (1870–1916), Madison County chancery and circuit court records (1829–1968), Sumter County circuit court records (1840–1950)
- **Arizona:** probate records for Maricopa County (1870–1930)
- **Arkansas:** probate records from several counties (1817–1979) and Freedmen's Bureau Field Office records (1865–1872)
- **California:** "Great Registers" of county clerk voting records (1866–1910) and probate estate files (1833–1991)
- **Colorado:** Denver County probate records (1900–1925)

- **Delaware**: orphan court records (1680–1978) and Freedmen's Bureau Field Office records (1865–1872), which are combined with records from Maryland
- **Florida:** probate records from several counties (1784–1990)
- **Georgia:** Hall County marriages (1950–2005); headright and bounty land records (1783–1909); probate records from various counties, including estate files, inventories, wills, minutes, and guardianships (1742–1990); Freedmen's Bureau Field Office records (1865-1872)
- **Idaho:** county naturalizations from thirty-six counties (1861–1974); county records for Elmore County (1889–1972), Gem County (1877–1962), Gooding County (1879–1962), Lemhi County (1868–1964), and Twin Falls County (1906–1988)
- **Illinois:** probate records, with some counties including guardianship, naturalization, and/or military records (1819–1988), DeKalb County land records (1838–1927), and Lee County probate and naturalization records (1830–1954)
- **Iowa:** probate records for Fayette County (1851–1928), Polk County (1914–1924), and Poweshiek County (1850–1954), as well as land records for Poweshiek County (1855–1934)
- **Kentucky:** probate records, including wills, bonds, and estate inventories from Caldwell, Henry, Hickman, Russell, and Trimble counties (1727–1990)
- **Louisiana:** Orleans Parish estate files (1804–1846), will books (1805–1920), and court records (1822–1880), as well as Freedmen's Bureau Field Office records (1865–1872) and Eastern District naturalization petitions (1838–1861)
- **Maine:** probate records and estate files for Androscoggin County (1854–1918), Aroostook County (1837–2007), Kennebec County (1779–1915), Knox County (1861–1915), Oxford County (1805–1915), Somerset County (1809–1915), York County (1690–1917); and a general probate collection containing records from multiple counties (1760–1979), as well as deed books for Aroostook County (1865–1900) and Piscataquis County (1838–1902)
- **Maryland:** probate estate and guardianship files (1796–1940), register of wills (1629–1999), and Freedmen's Bureau Field Office records (1865–1872)
- **Massachusetts:** probate and estate files for Plymouth County (1686–1915 and 1633–1967) and Worcester County (1731–1925), Boston tax records (1822–1918), a naturalization index (1906–1966), and land records covering all counties in the state (1620–1986)
- **Michigan:** probate records (1797–1973)
- **Minnesota:** wills (1849–1985) and land records for Clay County (1872–1947) and Roseau County (1892–1930)

Detailed Record Coverage Charts

To find out the specific counties and years of coverage for a record collection, click on the collection title, then click the Learn More link to view the FamilySearch Wiki entry about the collection. The Wiki entries may include coverage tables with specifics, such as in this Wiki entry for Illinois probate records <**www.familysearch.org/learn/wiki/en/ Illinois_Probate_Records_(FamilySearch_Historical_Records)**>.

- **Mississippi:** Tippah County deed and probate case files (1836–1923) and Freedmen's Bureau Field Office records (1865–1872)
- **Missouri:** probate records and a few civil and criminal case court records for multiple counties (1750–1998) and for Andrew and Cole counties (1826–1945), as well as Freedmen's Bureau Field Office records (1865–1872)
- **Montana:** primarily probate, land, naturalization, divorce, and vital records from Granite County (1865–2009), Meagher County (1866–2012), and Toole County (1913–1960), as well as naturalizations from twenty other counties (1856–1979)
- **Nebraska:** homestead records from the Broken Bow Land Office (1890–1908)
- **New Hampshire:** various probate and estate files for ten counties with dates ranging from 1660 to 1973; not all counties have records for all dates
- **New Jersey:** probate and estate files for Middlesex County (1830–1921) and from multiple counties (1678–1980)
- **New York:** probate records and estate files for Orange County (1787–1950), Bronx County (1914–1931), Queens County (1785–1950), and Kings County (1866–1923), plus some from other counties from 1629 to 1971; land records (1630–1975); naturalization index (1907–1966)
- **North Carolina:** estate files (1663–1979), probate records (1735–1970), and Freedmen's Bureau Field Office records (1863–1872)
- **Ohio:** tax records (1800–1850); probate records and estate files for Cuyahoga County (1813–1932) and Montgomery County (1850–1900), as well as various counties from 1789 to 1996; court records for Jefferson County (1797–1947) and Stark County (1809–1917); various county records such as naturalization, probate, vital, land, and military records for Hamilton County (1791–1994)
- **Oklahoma:** probate records (1887–2008) and land records from when land was allotted to members of the Five Civilized Tribes (1899–1907)
- **Pennsylvania:** probate records (1683–1994) and records from Philadelphia of seamen's proof of citizenship (1791–1861)
- **Rhode Island:** district court naturalization indexes (1906–1991)

- **South Carolina:** probate records (bound volumes 1671–1977; loose files 1732–1964) and Freedmen's Bureau Field Office records (1865–1872)
- **South Dakota:** Minnehaha County probate records (1873–1935)
- **Tennessee:** probate books and files (1795–1955) and Putnum County records including wills, divorces, and estates (1842–1955), as well as Freedmen's Bureau Field Office records (1865–1872)
- **Texas:** probate records (1800–1900), Concho County deed and probate records (1849–2008), Nolan County civil court files (1881–1938), and county tax rolls for 231 Texas counties (1846–1910)
- **Utah:** land and probate records for Juab County (1847–1948); naturalization, land, and vital records for Utah County (1850–1962); probate, naturalization, court, and divorce records from the state archives for nearly twenty counties (1848–2001); territorial court case files (1870–1896)
- **Vermont:** probate and estate files for Addison County (1845–1915), Bennington County (1779–1935), Orange County (1790–1935), Washington County (1862–1915), and Windham County (1781–1921), as well as for Chittenden and Essex counties (1800–1921); land records (1600–1900)
- **Virginia:** Isle of Wight County records including marriages, guardianships, military lists, and other court records (1634–1951); Freedmen's Bureau Field Office records (1865–1872)
- **Washington:** probate records for King County (1854–1927) and for multiple counties (1832–1950 and 1853–1929); land records (1850–1954); naturalization records (1853–1957)
- **West Virginia:** will books from all fifty-five counties (1756–1971)
- **Wisconsin:** probate estate files (1848–1948)

Nationwide Collections

Next, let's look at probate and court records collections that cover multiples states within a single collection.

FREEDMAN'S BANK RECORDS

This searchable collection contains an index and images of registers for sixty-seven thousand individuals who had accounts at the Freedman's Saving and Trust Company from 1865 to 1874 <www.familysearch.org/search/collection/1417695>. To open an account, the applicant had to provide personal information about his family and heirs, so the registers may give details such as the depositor's name, birthplace, residence, age, complexion, occupation, and employer, plus the names of spouses, children, parents, and siblings. The early books may also include the name of the depositor's former master or mistress, plantation, and Civil War service.

TAX LISTS

FamilySearch.org has a browsable collection of more than four hundred thousand record images from annual tax lists spanning 1862 to 1874 **<www.familysearch.org/search/collection/2075263>**. Referred to as "internal revenue assessment lists," these records were created to raise money for the Civil War. These records list the person's name, residence, property/goods owned, amount of taxes owed, and occupation.

LAND RECORDS

Two browsable probate and court record collections contain land records. One has nearly one million images from Bureau of Land Management tract books covering the years 1820 to 1908 **<www.familysearch.org/search/collection/2074276>**. The tract books recorded land status and transactions of public lands. Look for the name of the landowner, the location, and a physical description of the land, along with the date the land was sold, purchase price, number of acres, and other information. The FamilySearch Wiki has a table outlining state and township coverage **<www.familysearch.org/learn/wiki/en/United_States,_Bureau_of_Land_Management_Tract_Books_Coverage_Table_(FamilySearch_Historical_Records)>**.

The other collection has "cancelled, relinquished, or rejected" land entry case files from 1861 to 1932 **<www.familysearch.org/search/collection/2170637>**. The more than ninety-one thousand record images include applications for homesteads, mining claims, and land preemptions that were not approved.

NATURALIZATIONS

America's wartime military wasn't limited to naturalized citizens—immigrants fought for their adopted country, too. A searchable index documents more than eighteen thousand World War I soldiers who were later granted citizenship through an expedited process **<www.familysearch.org/search/collection/1858291>**. To attain citizenship, the soldiers had to meet certain requirements, but the declaration of intent may have been waived or residence requirements reduced (see chapter 7). As a result, soldiers may have been granted citizenship on the same day they filed their petition for naturalization. The online index record will list the soldier's name, date of naturalization, court of naturalization, certificate number, and the military base the soldier was assigned to on the date of naturalization. You can search this collection by the ancestor's name or by the naturalization life event place and date range.

SEARCH STRATEGIES

If you are looking specifically for US probate and court records, consider employing these search techniques.

Focus on a Specific Location

US probate and court files were typically recorded on the county or state level, and thus are usually organized by state and/or county. Because of this, if you're using the main Historical Records search form at **<www.familysearch.org/search>** to locate these records, you'll need to be sure to include a Residence location in your search, in addition to entering your ancestor's first and last names.

Also, consider looking at historical maps (which you can access online by googling the term *historical map* along with the city, county, or state name) before you start your searches. County and state boundaries have changed over time, so it's important that you know the correct county/state name during the time period your ancestor lived there. For example, if your ancestor lived near a state border, it could mean the difference between looking for records in one state or the other. And that could make a huge difference in whether or not you can find your ancestor in the records.

Search Specific Collections

Out of more than 130 US probate and court record collections, only about two dozen of them are searchable. Because of that, you may want to forego doing a broad, sitewide search when looking specifically for probate or court records. Instead, go to the list of published Historical Records collections **<www.familysearch.org/collection/list>**, and, using the filtering options, select United States of America from the Place heading, and choose Probate & Court from the Collections section. Scroll through this list (or narrow further by selecting a specific state name as the Place) to see which records are available for the location and time period your ancestor lived. If a collection matches the time and location of your ancestor, go ahead and search it. If not, you can save time and move on to do research in other, more relevant collections or record types.

Account for Spelling Errors

As with any other searchable collection on FamilySearch.org, be sure to account for spelling and transcription errors in your ancestor's name. Use wildcards in your searches and try alternate spellings and nicknames.

Browse and Browse Some More

Because only a fraction of the US probate and court records on FamilySearch.org are searchable, you'll likely need to spend time browsing records if you're going to find ancestors in them. Some of these browsable collections contain millions of records—yikes! But don't fret: Most have ways to help you narrow your options.

For example, the unindexed collection Missouri, Probate Records, 1750–1998 **<www.familysearch.org/search/collection/2399107>** has more than six million record images. When you click on the first link to browse the images, it takes you to a list of counties to narrow your search. After you select a county name, it lists types of records available and coverage date ranges. If you're lucky, one of the types of records might be an index, so check the index first if it's available, then click on the other record type listings to find the records you're searching for.

Depending on the collection, you may even come across alphabetized record types, which makes it easier to jump around the images and pinpoint your ancestor's record. Simply guess an image number to start with and enter it in the Image box in the collection you're browsing. For example, if the portion you're browsing has two thousand images and covers surnames from A–M, and your ancestor's name was Miller, don't start at Image 1. Start at an image number near the end, such as 1,500, then click the forward and back arrows (or guess another number to enter) to advance to other record images as necessary.

STEP-BY-STEP EXAMPLE: SEARCHING US PROBATE AND COURT RECORDS

The majority of my ancestors lived in Iowa and Illinois, so for this example I'm going to see if I can find any probate records for my ancestors in these two states. My ancestors primarily lived in Dubuque County, Iowa, dating back to the mid-1800s, and Cook County, Illinois, beginning in about the 1820s or 1830s.

You can follow along by replicating the click-by-click instructions below or by applying the strategies outlined in these steps to find your own ancestors living in other states.

1 BROWSE THE HISTORICAL RECORDS COLLECTIONS LIST. First, we need to figure out what records exist for the location and time period our ancestors lived. In this case, I want to see what records exist for Iowa and Illinois. On **<www.familysearch.org/search/collection/list>**, filter the collections list. Under the Place heading, select United States of America. Under the Collections heading, select Probate & Court. To narrow by state, either type the state name in the Filter by Collection search box or click on the state name under the Place heading. The collections in the list for Iowa are not for any counties that my ancestor lived in. Out of the three collections for Illinois, one of them is not county-specific, and it covers the time period in which my ancestors lived in Illinois. So I choose to search that collection: Illinois Probate Records, 1819–1988. Click on the collection title to begin the search.

2 LEARN MORE ABOUT THE RECORDS COVERED. The record collection I chose is not indexed, and it covers a wide range of years. In fact, it contains more than a million images. Before browsing through the images, it's important to learn more about the records covered. Click the Learn More link on the collection's landing page. In this example, the Learn More link (image **A**) takes you to a description of the record collection, which includes a table of records coverage (image **B**). Unfortunately, this table (which was current as of October 2011) does not list any records for Cook County, where my ancestors lived. Since it's possible records could have been added since 2011, I take my search one step further.

3 BEGIN BROWSING RECORDS. To begin browsing record images in an unindexed collection, click on the link to Browse Through 1,316,299 Images. This typically will take you to a page with links to narrow your browsing efforts. Unfortunately, the list of links here still shows no Cook County, so my records search in this collection stops here. If my ancestors' county did appear, however, I would click on the county name. For this example, let's explore records for DeKalb County, so click on that link.

4 CHOOSE A RECORD TYPE OR YEAR RANGE. Depending on the collection, your next screen may include a list of links for year ranges, record types, and/or date ranges for specific record types. It also may include a list of records by town/city. In this example, the DeKalb County collection has a list of records by record type, volume, and year range for administrator's records, appraisement records, circuit court records, court records, estate inventories, executor's records, guardian's inventory records, petitions, bonds, probate case files, and more. Let's take a look at the estate inventories. Scroll down and click on the link to Estate Inventories 1868–1877 vol. B.

5 SELECT A STARTING PLACE. Click through a couple of record images using the forward and back arrows next to the Image box at the top of the record image page. Observe how the records are arranged. This collection appears to be organized alphabetically, based on the lettered tabs on the right-hand pages. On each page, only a few individuals' names are listed next to a number. This is an index to the record images. Since these records have an alphabetical index, make a guess of the index image number that your ancestor may appear on, based on your ancestor's surname. For example, in this collection, there are 616 images. If we were searching in the index for an ancestor with the last name Schmidt, we'd guess the index record image would be toward the end of the index, perhaps around record number 30. Enter *30* in the Image box and hit Enter (or click the Go button).

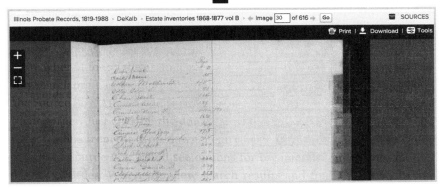

1

Filter by collection name

Collection name

Place

- United States of America (3)
  - Illinois (3)   ✕
    No further place filters found

Date

- 1800 - 1849 (3)
- 1850 - 1899 (3)
- 1900 - 1949 (3)
- 1950 to present (2)

Collections

- Probate & Court (3)   ✕
  No further collections filters found

Availability

☐ Only collections with images

Historical Record Colle

Title ▴

📷 Illinois Probate Records, 1819-1988

📷 Illinois, DeKalb County Land Records, 183?

📷 Illinois, Lee County Records, 1830-1954

2 A

Illinois Probate Records, 1819-1988

Description

Collection of probate records, which includes will, indexes, and other documents created to track the distribution of estates of deceased individuals who lived in Illinois. Probates were generally recorded in the county of residence. This collection cove probate records created by Illinois courts, 1819-1970, but the content and time period of the records will vary by county. Som county probate courts also include guardianship, naturalization, and/or military records. Additional records may be added to collection. Check the wiki or browse the collection to determine current coverage.

Learn more ›

View Images in this Collection

Browse through 1,316,299 images

Citing this Collection

"Illinois Probate Records, 1819-1988." Images. FamilySearch. http://FamilySearch.org : accessed 2015. County courthouses, I

2 B

Coverage Table

The Coverage Table shows the places and time periods covered in the records for this collection. Most of the records in the collection are from the time periods listed in the table; however, the collection may have a few records from before or after the time period. This table is current as of October 2011.

Illinois Probate Books Year Ranges

Name of County	Recorded Year Range	Will Registers	Probate Records	Bonds and Letters
Alexander	1829–1902	1850–1902	1829–1867	1860–1886
Brown	1817–1936	1869–1890	1849–1923	1849–1936
Calhoun	1829–1916	1870–1916	1829–1874	1859–1904
Champaign	1851–1921	1851–1921	N/A	N/A
Coles	1866–1946	1866–1925	1900–1923	N/A
De Witt	1862–1923	1862–1923	N/A	1850–1901
DeKalb	1837–1921	1862–1921	1837–1924	N/A
Effingham	1838–1920	1838–1920	1838–1893	1871–1894

3

| RECORDS | GENEALOGIES | CATALOG | BOOKS | WIKI |

Illinois Probate Records, 1819-1988

County

Alexander

Brown

Calhoun

Champaign

Coles

De Witt

DeKalb

Effingham

4

| RECORDS | GENEALOGIES | CATALOG | BOOKS | WIKI |

Illinois Probate Records, 1819-1988 › DeKalb

Record Type, Volume, and Year Range

Estate inventories 1868-1877 vol B

Estate inventories 1877-1892 vol C

Estate inventories 1885-1896 vol D

Estate inventories 1898-1904 vol E

Estate inventories 1904-1910 vol F

Estate inventories 1910-1920 vol G

Estate ledger 1897-1911 vol 4

Estate record 1911-1922 vol 1

5

Illinois Probate Records, 1819-1988 › DeKalb › Estate inventories 1868-1877 vol B   ◄   Image 30 of 616 ► Go   🖴 SOURCES

🖶 Print | ⬇ Download | ⊞ Tools

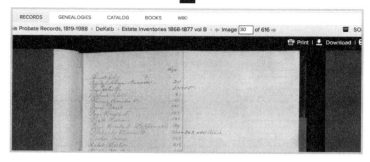

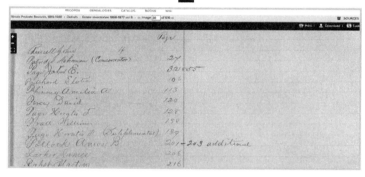

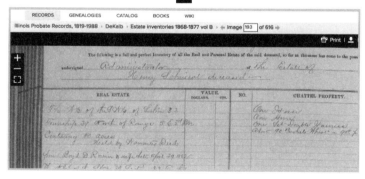

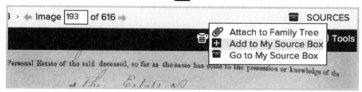

6 MOVE FORWARD AND BACKWARD. The record image on page 30 appears to have last names that start with P. We're getting close. Try entering another image number in the Image box, then as you get closer to the S surnames, hit the forward arrow to move until you get to a page that lists the S surnames. Use the zoom tools (the plus or minus sign in the top left corner) to zoom in or out to view the records, if needed.

7 GO TO THE INDEX PAGE NUMBER. Image 36 has the S surnames, and the page lists a Henry Schmidt. The index says his record is on page 74 of the records. Note: This number is not necessarily the same as the record number, so if you type in 74 in the Image box, you may not find the record. Instead, you need to make another guess. There are 616 record images, and Henry Schmidt's is the 74th one listed. Let's try entering *100* in the Image box and see how close we get.

8 MOVE FORWARD AND BACKWARD AGAIN. Zoom out to see the full page. The top right corner shows a record number: 27. We've still got about fifty pages to go to get to Henry Schmidt's record. Enter another image number guess in the Image box. Then use the forward and back arrows to pinpoint record number 74. Finally, we see Henry Schmidt's record when we get to Images 193 and 194. The record lists the real estate he owned, "chattel" property owned, and property value on the first page. Use the forward and back arrows to move to the other pages of the record. In this record collection, additional pages include information on "notes and accounts" such as the amount of debts the deceased owed.

9 SAVE THE RECORD. If you find a record for your ancestor, be sure to save it. Click the Download link to save a copy of the image to your computer. Click the Sources link to add the record image to your Source Box and/or attach it to your family tree. Remember to save each record image, not just one image, so you have the entire record for your ancestor and not just part of it.

KEYS TO SUCCESS

★ Look for probate and court records on the state and/or county level, because that's typically where the records were originally recorded.

★ Remember that county and state boundaries changed over time, so be sure to look for records in both the current-day and parent counties. Check period maps to confirm the right county or state/territory for the records you're searching for.

★ Be open to browsing record collections image by image to find your ancestors because the majority of probate and court records on FamilySearch.org are not yet searchable.

US PROBATE AND COURT RECORDS CHECKLIST

Ancestor's name: _____

Residence/location (include town/city, county, and state names): _____

_____

_____

Dates lived in that location: _____

Spouse's name: _____

Children's names: _____

_____

Types of US Probate and Court Records to Look For

Put a check mark next to each record type after you've searched available records on FamilySearch.org for the ancestor listed above. Cross off any record types that aren't available on FamilySearch.org for your ancestor's residence location and time period.

Record Type	Date Searched
☐ Bonds	_____
☐ Civil court case records	_____
☐ Criminal court case records	_____
☐ Estate files/records	_____
☐ Estate inventories	_____
☐ Freedman's Bank records	_____
☐ Freedmen's Bureau Field Office records	_____
☐ Guardianship records	_____
☐ Land records (deeds, grants, patents, tract books)	_____
☐ Naturalizations	_____
☐ Orphan records	_____
☐ Probate files	_____
☐ Tax lists/records	_____
☐ Vital records (births, marriages, deaths, divorces)	_____
☐ Voter lists/records	_____
☐ Wills/will books	_____
☐ Other _____	_____

10

European Records

America is a melting pot. The majority of the population has ancestry overseas, particularly in Europe. The most prevalent European ancestries in the United States today are German, Irish, English, Italian, Polish, French, and Scottish.

Happily, FamilySearch.org isn't limited to just US records. The website has more than six hundred digitized records collections from the United Kingdom, Ireland, and continental Europe. Among them are some of the most valuable records for tracing ancestors across the pond: church records and civil registrations, documenting births, deaths, and marriages. Census records for some countries are available. All of these records can help you pinpoint your ancestors' location during different periods of time.

Don't forget you also can use FamilySearch.org to streamline your search for offline European records, too. FamilySearch has millions of microfilmed records from European countries that you can rent for viewing at a local FamilySearch Center. You'll use the FamilySearch Catalog on the website to identify and order those records.

Let's take a closer look at the records available online, strategies for searching and browsing them, and tips to tap into microfilmed records via the FamilySearch Catalog.

UK AND IRISH RECORDS
ON FAMILYSEARCH.ORG

FamilySearch.org has more than 120 collections of historical records for the United Kingdom and Ireland. These records cover mostly England, Ireland, Scotland, and Wales, with some for Guernsey, the Isle of Man, and Jersey (the Channel Islands).

England

You'll find collections of vital records (births/christenings, marriages, and deaths) dating back to 1538, several civil registration indexes, census records for each decennial enumeration from 1821 to 1851, and church records, as well as some land tax assessments, school records, probate records, workhouse records, marriage bonds, and wills. In all, the site has nearly three-quarters of a billion indexed and searchable English records; a few collections are still unindexed, meaning you'll need to browse through record images in order to find your ancestors' records.

Ireland

You can research your Irish ancestors in more than forty million searchable records on FamilySearch.org. The Irish record collections include censuses (1821, 1831, 1841, and 1851), civil registrations, wills, estate court files, and prison registers.

FamilySearch.org also offers an important Irish resource called the Tithe Applotment Books. Compiled mostly between 1823 and 1837, these records are great for researching ancestors prior to the 1840s Potato Famine. According to FamilySearch.org, the Tithe Applotment Books cover about 40 percent of family heads in Ireland. The digital collec-

What's in a Name

Records on FamilySearch.org are labeled as being from the United Kingdom, Great Britain, or England. To find your ancestors, you may need to look for records under each name. But what's really the difference between these three terms?

- **United Kingdom:** historically refers to the union of the four separate countries of England, Scotland, Wales, and Ireland (now only Northern Ireland, as the remainder of Ireland is independent)

- **Great Britain:** the island west of continental Europe with the countries England, Wales, and Scotland

- **England:** the largest country in the United Kingdom

tion on FamilySearch.org **<www.familysearch.org/search/collection/1804886>** spans the years 1814 to 1855. When using this collection, be sure to search only for heads of families—other household members were not recorded by name.

Scotland

Search more than thirty million records for Scottish ancestors, including births and baptisms dating back to 1564, marriages back to 1561, and the every-ten-years census enumerations from 1841 to 1891.

Wales

Parish registers make up the bulk of the millions of Welsh records on FamilySearch.org. Other records cover births/baptisms, marriages, deaths, burials, electoral registers, probate abstracts, and some court records. All of the vital and parish records are searchable; the remaining records are not indexed and must be browsed. In addition, Welsh ancestors may be included in the England and Wales census collections covering 1821 to 1851.

More UK Records

A searchable collection of births and baptisms for the Channel Islands has forty-one thousand records from 1820 to 1907. Searchable collections for the Isle of Man cover parish registers, births/baptisms, deaths/burials, and marriages dating back to the early 1600s.

Several military collections cover the entire United Kingdom. Those include World War I service records (1914–1920), World War I Women's Army Auxiliary Corps records (1917–1920), militia service records (1806–1915), Merchant Navy seamen records (1835–1941), and some Chelsea pensioners' service records (1760–1913).

CONTINENTAL EUROPEAN RECORDS ON FAMILYSEARCH.ORG

FamilySearch.org has records for most countries in continental Europe. Collections often go back to the 1400s or 1500s, and a few date as early as the mid-thirteenth and fourteenth centuries. Records range from church books/registers and civil registrations to censuses and even land, school, estate, military, emigration, passport, and court records. The most abundant records are vital records from churches and civil registers.

The availability of searchable, indexed records for continental European countries is more hit-or-miss than for the United Kingdom and Ireland, so be prepared to click through unindexed collections. And keep in mind that more records are being indexed and added all the time. Here are some of the record highlights.

Austria

Most records for Austria are unindexed, but you can find military, vital, church, court, city, and census records, as well as citizen rolls.

Belgium

FamilySearch.org has more than two million searchable records and 2.8 million unindexed images for Belgium, notably civil registrations and Antwerp immigration/emigration records (potentially useful even for non-Belgian ancestors who left from this port).

Czech Republic

Available records include censuses, church records, civil registrations, land records, school records, and even some nobility seigniorial records. The online Czech Republic collections are a new and exciting avenue for researching ancestors in a country whose records have not been widely microfilmed.

Finland

Access nearly six million searchable and more than 200,000 unindexed church records (including baptisms, marriages, and burials).

France

Records cover Catholic and Protestant parishes, civil registrations, and censuses. Most collections focus on Toulouse.

Germany

If you have German ancestors, definitely take a look at the roughly sixty collections covering areas of Hesse, Prussia, Rhineland, Westfalen, Württemberg, Saxony, Mecklenburg, Baden, Brandenburg, Bremen, and Bavaria. Collections encompass church records (including births/baptisms), Jewish records, civil registrations, military records, probate records, city directories, miscellaneous city records, emigration records, citizen rolls, and even funeral sermons.

Hungary

Record collections include church records, civil registrations, funeral notices, and a Jewish vital records index. Note that Hungarian records cover areas of the former Kingdom of Hungary that are now in other countries, such as Slovakia, Croatia, or Romania. They're not limited to ethnically Hungarian ancestors.

Italy

The good news for genealogists with Italian roots: Italy has more record collections on FamilySearch.org than any other European country (even England). The bad news: Only a few of those collections are indexed, so be prepared to browse. It's well worth the effort, though, as the records include many civil registrations and church registers, as well as some censuses.

Luxembourg

This tiny country has church, civil registration, census, and notarial records on FamilySearch.org. A few of the collections are searchable, but most are unindexed—including a database of more than a million census records dating back to 1843. In addition, don't miss the Luxembourg collection (civil registrations from 1580 to 1920) that's grouped with records for Belgium due to historical boundary changes.

The Netherlands

FamilySearch.org has mostly civil registrations and church records for the Netherlands, but its Dutch collections also include military service records, population registers, citizenship records, emigration lists, and notarial records. Most collections are unindexed.

Norway

The Norwegian collections cover baptisms, marriages, burials, and the 1875 census.

Poland

FamilySearch.org's Polish collections comprise church records from Lublin, Radom, Tarnow, Częstochowa, and Gliwice (the latter two are unindexed).

Portugal

Church records, civil registrations, and passport registers represent the bulk of Portuguese collections. Testaments (notarized wills) from 1801 to 1936 are also available. Most of these records are unindexed.

Russia

Collections for Russia include church records, tax census lists, birth/baptism records, and death/burial records (mostly unindexed).

Slovakia

A collection of church and synagogue book records contains almost fourteen million searchable records. There's also an unindexed collection for the 1869 census. Due to historical border shifts, look for Slovak ancestors in records from Hungary and Poland, too.

Spain

Millions of records cover Spanish ancestors. The collections on FamilySearch.org include vital records, church records, municipal records, emigrant records, passports, and even a collection of widows and orphans of military officers. Some collections are searchable, and some require browsing.

Sweden

Church records, as well as baptisms and burials, are plentiful for this country. The church records collections for Sweden date from the 1500s to early 1900s. Many records for Sweden are unindexed, but you'll find a few searchable collections.

Switzerland

Swiss collections comprise censuses back to 1811, baptisms dating back to 1491, marriages dating back to 1532, and burials starting in 1613. In addition, there are emigration records, as well as a collection of land and property records (called terrier records) that date all the way back to 1234.

Ukraine

The collections for this country cover nearly two million searchable (indexed) records, and more than one million unindexed (browsable) records. Records include birth records, church records, and the 1897 census.

Records for Other European Countries

Although the countries listed above have the most abundant records on FamilySearch.org, the website has limited numbers of collections for the following countries, covering records ranging from church books to censuses to estate records to vital records:

- Albania
- Armenia
- Croatia
- Denmark
- Estonia
- Gibraltar
- Iceland

- Liechtenstein
- Moldova
- Slovenia

SEARCH STRATEGIES AND TIPS

To search for records from a specific country, go to the Historical Records search form **<www.familysearch.org/search>** and type in the country name in the Residence or Any fields. Or go to the collections list at **<www.familysearch.org/search/collection/list>** and filter by Place to see what's available for your ancestor's home country, then click on the collection title to search or browse the available records. As you search collections from European countries, use these additional strategies to locate your ancestors' records.

Pinpoint the Time Frame

It's important to know the time period when your ancestors lived in Europe. After all, you don't want to waste time searching in collections that don't have any chance of listing your ancestors. Try consulting immigration and naturalization records from the United States first to pinpoint an immigration date for your ancestor. If you have trouble locating those records, try the 1900, 1910, or 1920 US census. Records from the first two of these censuses include information on year of immigration to the United States and naturalization status. The 1920 census reported the year the person was naturalized.

Look for Ethnic Name Spellings

Some immigrants Americanized their names after coming to the United States, so Johann may have became John, or Frerk may have become Fred. When you search for ancestors in records created in the old country, you'll need to look for the ethnic spelling of the name—the spelling they would have used prior to coming to America. Consult the website BehindtheName.com **<www.behindthename.com>** to research ethnic spellings of your ancestors' names.

Get Familiar With Foreign Languages

Don't expect to find European records written in English. Germans kept records in German, Italians in Italian, Russians in Russian, and so forth. Additionally, Roman Catholic records—no matter the country—often were written in Latin. Knowing some key genealogical terms in the homeland's primary language can be helpful as you sort through record results and view record images. For help learning important terms in your ancestor's native language, consult FamilySearch's Word Lists **<www.familysearch. org/learn/wiki/en/Category:Word_List>** or the digital *Genealogist's Instant Transla-*

tion Guide: At-a-Glance Glossaries for 22 Languages at **<www.shopfamilytree.com/ genealogists-instant-translation-guide-at-a-glance-glossaries>**.

Know Naming Patterns

Each country had different traditions for naming children—for both first and last names. Some names were derived from patronymics, others from occupations, and others from locations. If the culture typically used patronymics, you could find that surnames change from generation to generation. Before you begin your online searches, research which naming patterns were used during the time period your family lived in Europe. This could help you find additional surnames to search for, as well as understand family relationships. Find information on naming patterns on USGenWeb **<usgenweb.org/research/ names.shtml>** and the FamilySearch Wiki **<www.familysearch.org/learn/wiki>**.

Use Wildcards

As with any search, using wildcard characters (the question mark for one character, and asterisk for more than one character) can help broaden your search to find misspellings or alternate spellings of your ancestors' names.

Look for Relatives

If you can't find a record for one ancestor, try looking for records of another person in the family. Keep in mind that many early census records recorded the head of household only, so use the male ancestor's name when searching those records.

Embrace Browsing

Many international records have not yet been indexed on FamilySearch.org. That means you need to browse through them, like you would view microfilm. But unlike scrolling through microfilm reels, FamilySearch.org helps you focus on the right records. If you click on the title of a browsable collection, it typically gives you options to narrow records by year and/or location. Once you get to the year and/or location relevant to your ancestors, you'll need to jump from record to record to find a specific ancestor.

Before you begin looking through browsable records collections, click the Learn More link (if available) on the landing page for the collection. This will help you understand the types of records included, as well as learn how the records are organized so you can better determine your strategy for clicking through. After you get a sense of the collection's organization method, you can make better guesses about how many images to jump forward when browsing.

For example, in an Italian death records collection I was searching, I realized each year's records had an index at the beginning, and the record images for that year followed

Browsing Records Pays Off

Browsing through hundreds (or thousands) of unindexed records images may seem daunting, but it's not impossible. During one weekend, I spent several hours browsing through four different subsets of one Italian records collection. The result? I found marriage records for two couples in my family tree, death records for two ancestors, and a listing of my great-grandfather and great-grandmother in a marriage index.

the index. So I could browse the index for the year first to see if any potential ancestors were listed, then make note of a the record number. I could skip over several pages to find the record number, which was a huge timesaver for a record set of nine hundred images.

STEP-BY-STEP EXAMPLE: BROWSING EUROPEAN RECORD COLLECTIONS

I have many ancestors who lived in Italy, but so far I've found it difficult to trace them across the pond. In recent years, FamilySearch.org has added many new collections covering Italy. Plus, there's an ongoing an indexing project for Italian records **<www.familysearch.org/italian-ancestors>**, wherein 2,285 volunteers are helping to index 115 million Italian birth, marriage, and death certificates (more than 3.5 million have been indexed to date).

In this example, we'll look for my Italian ancestor Luigi Gemignani. I know he was born around 1860, but I don't know his death or marriage date. He was married to Lucia Cortopassi, and his parents were Biaggio Gemignani and Carola Lunardi. I know the family was from the village of Bargecchia, in the town (municipality) of Massarosa, in the province of Lucca. Let's see what records we can find.

1 SELECT A COLLECTION. Go to **<www.familysearch.org/search/collection/list>** to browse the list of all collections available on FamilySearch.org. Among the filter options, click on Continental Europe, then Italy. Scroll through the list to see if any locations and dates match up with the details you know about the ancestor. In this case, there are four collections I may want to check out: a searchable collection of deaths and burials (1809–1900), a searchable database of births and baptisms (1806–1900), a searchable collection of marriages (1809–1900), and one unindexed civil registration collection covering areas in Lucca (1866–1929).

2 CHECK EACH COLLECTION'S RECORD COVERAGE. Before searching a collection, find out what records it contains. Simply click the collection title and click the Learn More link. This should take you to a page that explains which records and locales the collection covers. Do this for each collection of interest. Unfortunately, the record descriptions for the indexed records don't list the area of Italy where my ancestors lived. That leaves the unindexed images, which appear to cover births, marriages, deaths, supplemental records, and marriage banns for the area and time when Luigi lived.

3 **BEGIN BROWSING.** From the collection list, click on the collection title you want to search or browse. In this instance, I chose the collection Italy, Lucca, Lucca, Civil Registration (Tribunale), 1866–1929. It's unindexed, so I'll have to browse the records by clicking the Browse Through 1,335,192 Images link.

4 **FOLLOW THE PROMPTS TO BROWSE.** Several options will appear to help you home in on the records you want to browse. In this example, click the link for the province name, Lucca. Then scroll down and click the Massarosa link. This brings up a list of record types and coverage dates for births, marriages, and deaths, as well some indexes. I decided to check the *Indici decennale matrimoni* 1876–1885 records first, since Luigi likely would have married during that time period. This brings up 2,982 pages of records.

5 **CLICK THROUGH RECORDS.** Click the forward arrow (next to the Image box) at the top of the screen to begin discerning how the records are organized. They don't appear to be in alphabetical order, but they are organized by year, which means I'll need to click through each page one by one. As I come across annual indexes, I can jump forward a few pages. To better view each record, use the zoom tools (plus or minus sign) at the top left to zoom in or out, and click on the record image to drag and drop it into view. On page 19, I see a Gemignani surname, but the first name doesn't match. I write down the image number in case it could be a possible relative, then return to clicking.

6 **KEEP CLICKING THROUGH RECORDS.** Browsing unindexed records takes patience. As I click through the records, I land on page 102 of 2,982. I recognize the last names on this record: Remedi and Simonini. I check my pedigree chart, which confirms my great-great grandmother's parents were Massimino Remedi and Amelia Simonini. Massimino was from Bargecchia, and Amelia from Corsanico. While I can't quite make out Massimino's first name from the handwriting on the record, the remainder of the details about surnames and residences match up. The year, 1879, is in the time frame where they likely would have been old enough to marry, and my great-grandmother was born in 1891, so they likely would have married prior to that. The record tells me the date of Amelia and Massimino's marriage and their ages at the time of marriage, as well as the names of their parents, which I didn't have before.

7 **ADD RECORD TO SOURCE BOX.** When you find a record that's a match for your ancestor, click the Sources link and select Add to My Source Box and/or Attach to Family Tree. I added the record for Amelia and Massimino to my Source Box.

1

Filter by collection name

Collection name

Place

▾ Continental Europe (145)
  ▾ Italy (145)   ✕
    No further place filters found

Date

▸ Pre 1700 (19)
▸ 1700 - 1749 (22)
▸ 1750 - 1799 (28)
▸ 1800 - 1849 (73)
▸ 1850 - 1899 (137)
▸ 1900 - 1949 (130)
▸ 1950 to present (4)

Historical Record Collections

*= Re

Title ▴	Rec
Italy Deaths and Burials, 1809-1900	438
🗺 Italy, Agrigento, Agrigento, Civil Registration (Tribunale), 1866-1942	Browse Im
🗺 Italy, Agrigento, Sciacca, Civil Registration (Tribunale), 1861-1929	Browse Im
🗺 Italy, Ancona, Ancona, Civil Registration (Tribunale), 1862-1929	Browse Im
🗺 Italy, Ascoli Piceno, Civil Registration (State Archive), 1740-1880, 1915-1919	Browse Im
🗺 Italy, Asti, Civil Registration (Tribunale), 1866-1910	Browse Im
🗺 Italy, Avellino, Sant'Angelo dei Lombardi, Civil Registration (Tribunale), 1866-1910	Browse Im

2

Italy, Births and Baptisms, 1806-1900

Description

Index to selected Italy births and baptisms. Only a few localities are included and the time period varies by locality. Due to privacy laws, recent records may not be displayed. The year range represents most of the records. A few records may be earlier or later.

Learn more »

3

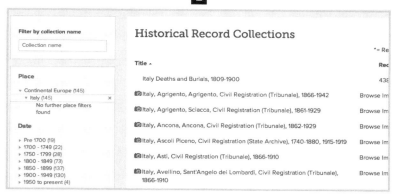

Italy, Lucca, Lucca, Civil Registration (Tribunale), 1866-1929

Description

Civil registration (stato civile) of births, marriages, and deaths within the custody of the Lucca Courthouse (Tribunale d Includes ten-year indexes (indici decennali); supplemental records (allegati); and marriage banns (pubblicazioni). Avail records is largely dependent on time period and locality.

Learn more »

View Images in this Collection

Browse through 1,335,192 images

Citing this Collection

"Italia, Lucca, Lucca, Stato Civile (Tribunale), 1866-1929." Images. *FamilySearch*. http://FamilySearch.org : accessed 201 di Lucca [Lucca Court, Lucca].

4

Italy, Lucca, Lucca, Civi...on (Tribunale), 1866-1929 › Lucca

Comune or Frazione

Castiglione di Garfagnana

Coreglia Antelminelli

Forte dei Marmi

Gallicano

Giuncugnano

Lucca

Massarosa

Minucciano

Molazzana

5

Image 19 of 2982

Atti di Matrimonio

6

Image 102 of 2982

Atti di Matrimonio

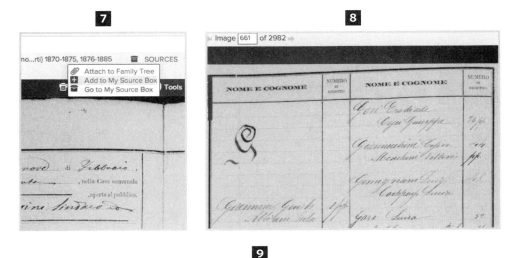

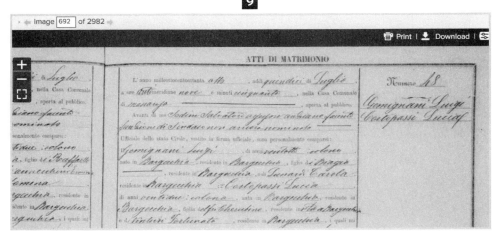

8 CONTINUE BROWSING. We still haven't found Luigi, so let's keep browsing. There are annual indexes included among the records, so instead of clicking images one by one, you can guess how many images to move forward, then type the new page number in the Image box and hit Enter (or hit the Go button). When you get to a year's index, individuals are listed alphabetically by surname of the groom. The index indicates the number of the record in the column next to the name. The bride's name is listed under the groom's. On the index for 1888 marriages, I see a Luigi Gemignani listed. The bride's name looks like it's Lucia, and the last name starts with a C. It's listed as record number 48. This could be a match. So guess how many pages ahead it might be and type in the number, then use the forward and back arrows to get to the right record.

Case Study: Finding Andreas Ochotnizcky's Family

When Family Tree Magazine *contributing editor and author of the forthcoming book* Find Your Family in U.S. Church Records *Sunny Morton began investigating the lineage of Andreas Ochotnizcky, she knew he was a naturalized US citizen who had been born around 1859 in what is now Slovakia. His US naturalization papers said his birth date was November 29, 1859. Additionally, his children's US baptismal records listed his birthplace as Forbaz or Gnazda in county Spis. Here, Sunny, whose website is* <**www.sunnymorton.com**>*, shares how she used FamilySearch. org to trace Andreas' family.*

I went to the FamilySearch Catalog and searched it by place for the villages. Forbaz doesn't come up, but Gnazda does. The first time I searched, I found microfilmed records and made a mental note to order them at some point. When I returned to order them, I found the records had been digitized and were browsable online. They have since been at least partially indexed, but I've found it more reliable to browse the images myself. I know the names I'm looking for and can more reliably spot spelling variations that way.

I found a birth and baptism in Gnazda for an Andreas Ochotniczky listed within a few days of the birth given on his naturalization papers. Both parents were named. Within a few years before and after Andreas' birth, I also found births and baptisms recorded for five other children born to that couple. I've located baptismal records for both his parents, taking the family tree back another generation. On his mother's side, I identified three siblings. Additional entries from that same church register show that Andreas' mother was likely previously married and had six children by the time she married Andreas' father and started her second family.

These fabulous finds reinforced the value of church records, especially in our search for immigrant ancestors. The imaged church records were not easy to read at first, but with a little effort I could learn to read each priest's handwriting. [Andreas'] family's surnames appeared on most pages of the parish register. It's likely that if I diagrammed out the church records completely, I could identify a lot of collateral relatives.

9 **REVIEW AND THEN SAVE RECORD.** The corresponding record for the Luigi on the index is image number 692 of 2,982. After reviewing the details, it appears to be a match. The parents' names and residences for both the bride and groom fit, and the ages appear to as well. Since I'm certain this is my ancestor, I download a copy of the image to my computer and attach it to my family tree. To save the image, click the Download link at the top of the page. To attach it to a family tree, click the Sources link and click the Attach to Family Tree link.

STEP-BY-STEP EXAMPLE:
FINDING MICROFILMED EUROPEAN RECORDS

In addition to the online records, FamilySearch has millions of microfilmed records from Europe and around the world (more than one hundred countries total). So if you strike out with the collections on FamilySearch.org—or once you've exhausted those resources—you'll want to identify relevant microfilms and order them to view at a local FamilySearch Center.

For this example, let's try to locate a microfilm with vital-records information from Bargechhia, Italy. Family stories have said that Luigi Gemignani's wife, Lucia, died of pneumonia in at age thirty-nine (approximately in 1905), but I've never been able to confirm this story. As we start searching, remember Bargecchia is a village, in the town (municipality) of Massarosa, in the province of Lucca, in the country of Italy.

1 **PULL UP THE FAMILYSEARCH CATALOG AND ENTER SEARCH CRITERIA.** Go to **<www. familysearch.org/catalog-search>**. Start by doing a Places search for the ancestor's country and a province or town. In this case, let's start broadly with the province name: *Lucca*. As you type in the location name, FamilySearch will suggest a standardized location name to search. Here, click on the suggested name: *Italy, Lucca*. Hit the Search button. Note: It's important to know the different jurisdiction names where your ancestor lived to ensure you choose the correct standardized location name to search, especially if you are looking for records from a specific village or province.

2 **REVIEW YOUR RESULTS.** A list of headings will appear, showing the different types of resources available. Click the arrow next to the heading to reveal details. Church registers and civil registrations are of primary interest for tracing European ancestors. This search returns results under four headings: one each for civil registrations, directories, history, and maps. The details show that the available civil registration records are from the state archive of Lucca and cover the years 1807 to 1814.

3 **SELECT AN ITEM OF INTEREST.** This set of civil registration records doesn't cover the date I'm looking for (1905). So let's take a look at another category: directories. Click a title to view details about that resource. For foreign records, you'll find an English description in the Notes section. This is a phone book I could use to identify potential living relatives in my ancestors' hometown. Scroll down further to the Film Notes section, which lists the records and years on each film so you can determine which specific roll or rolls you need, especially if more than one roll is available.

4 **ORDER THE FILM.** Click on the microfilm roll number to order the film, then select a rental option—short-term or extended. You may have to set your preferred FamilySearch Center. Click Add to Cart, then Proceed to Checkout. Enter your contact and payment information (there is a fee for renting microfilm), and complete your order. You'll get an e-mail notification when the film arrives.

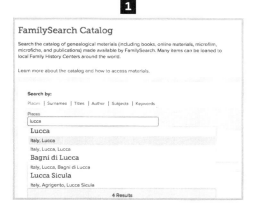

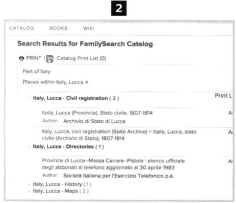

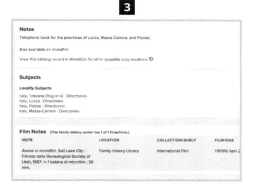

KEYS TO SUCCESS

★ Be prepared to browse European records on FamilySearch.org, as many collections are unindexed. Familiarize yourself with how the record images are arranged to save time clicking through these records.

★ Consider time and geography when choosing collections to research. Don't waste your time on a database whose records begin after your ancestor immigrated. If borders changed in your ancestral homeland, be sure to look for collections in all applicable countries (Czech ancestors in Austrian collections, for example).

★ Stay flexible with ancestral name spellings. Look for ethnic spellings and names your kin would have used in the old country, and use wildcards and alternate spellings when searching to capture variations and/or transcription mistakes.

★ Remember to search the FamilySearch Catalog for microfilmed European records you can rent to view at a local FamilySearch Center.

EUROPEAN RECORDS CHECKLIST

Ancestor's name: _____

Ancestor's maiden name (if female): _____

Date of birth: _____ Birthplace: _____

Residence/location: _____

Spouse's name: _____

Children's names: _____

European Records Search Checklist

☐ Look at the Historical Records collections list **<www.familysearch.org/search/collection/list>**. Filter by Place (select the country name).

☐ Identify collections to search or browse that cover your ancestor's location and time period. (You may need to click on the collection title, then the Learn More link to determine if the location covers your ancestor's province or town.)

☐ Search indexed collections.

☐ Browse unindexed collections.

FamilySearch.org Indexed Records Search Tracker

Collection Title and Date Coverage	Date Searched	Search Criteria Used	Results/Notes

FamilySearch.org Unindexed Records Search Tracker

If the browsable record image collection you're looking at has index pages (but hasn't been fully indexed), use these divisions to your advantage, then use this form to track your browsing efforts. Fill in these boxes with each index you find to help keep track of possible record images that list your ancestors.

Surnames to research: _____

Collection title: _____

Record type: _____

Location: _____

Year: _____

Surnames Found on Index	Record Number	Digital Record Image Page Number

Global Records

Familysearch.org's international records riches aren't limited to Europe: The website offers records from countries all around the world, including Africa, Asia, the Middle East, Australia, New Zealand, Canada, the Caribbean, Central America, Mexico, South America, and other locales.

Among these international records, you'll find civil registrations and church records for births/baptisms, marriages, and deaths, as well as census records. A few locations also have other record types, such as estate files, cemetery records, citizenship records, passenger lists, court records, probate records, and land records.

In this chapter, we'll explore the world of global records on FamilySearch.org.

CANADA

About half of the ninety-plus collections of Canadian records on FamilySearch.org are searchable. The remaining collections are unindexed, so you must browse through the records image by image. The digitized records for Canada contain quite a few vital records and censuses, along with immigration records, land records, naturalizations, church records, estate files, cemetery records, and more. Here are highlights of the Canadian collections.

Vital Records

Searchable collections of nationwide vital records include births and baptisms (1661–1959), deaths and burials (1664–1955), and marriages (1661–1949). Province-specific vital records include

- British Columbia births (1854–1903), deaths (1872–1986), and marriages (1859–1932)
- New Brunswick births and baptisms (1819–1899), deaths (1815–1938), and marriages (1789–1950)
- Newfoundland vital records, with searchable collections covering 1840 to 1949 and 1753 to 1893
- Nova Scotia births and baptisms (1702–1896), delayed birth certificates (1837–1904), deaths (1890–1955), marriages (1864–1932), and an index to a variety of vital records (1763–1957)
- Ontario births (1869–1912), births and baptisms (1779–1899), marriages (1800–1927), and deaths (1869–1947)
- Prince Edward Island baptisms (1721–1885), deaths (1721–1905), and marriages (1832–1888)
- Quebec births and baptisms (1662–1898)

Censuses

FamilySearch.org has several collections with searchable Canadian census records, including nationwide censuses from 1851, 1871, 1881, 1891, 1901, 1906, 1911, and 1916; the Lower Canada censuses from 1825, 1831, and 1842; and the Upper Canada census from 1842. Other searchable location-specific censuses include ones for New Brunswick (1861), Newfoundland (1921, 1935, and 1945), Nova Scotia (1861), Ontario (1861), Prince Edward Island (1861), and Quebec (1861). Browse-only collections include censuses for Manitoba (1831–1870). In addition, you can search a mortality schedule from 1871.

Immigration and Naturalization Records

Many passenger ships arrived in Canadian ports. Some of the immigrants on those ships later crossed the border into the United States. FamilySearch.org has a searchable collection of more than 3.8 million passenger lists from 1881 to 1922, as well as a browsable collection of Merchant

POWER-USER TIP

Lower and Upper Canadian Censuses

The three Lower Canada censuses on FamilySearch.org cover the modern-day province of Quebec, while the Upper Canada census covers records from the modern-day province of Ontario.

Marine agreements and accounts of crews from 1890 to 1921. FamilySearch.org also has a searchable collection of border-crossing records from Canada to the United States covering 1895 to 1956 **<www.familysearch.org/search/collection/1803785>**. The site has an unindexed collection of British Columbia naturalization records from 1859 to 1926.

Land Records

Available land records vary by province. There are browsable collections of Crown land grants (1851–1930), Crown land pre-emption registers (1860–1971), and Dominion land branch records (1885–1949) for British Columbia; county deed registry books (1780–1930) for New Brunswick; and deed indexes for Halifax County (1749–1958) in Nova Scotia.

Church Records

You'll find collections of church records for Manitoba (1800–1959), Newfoundland (1793–1945), Nova Scotia (1720–2001), Ontario (1760–1923), Prince Edward Island (1777–1985), and Saskatchewan (1846–1957). Only the Saskatchewan records are searchable. Some of the collections contain only Roman Catholic records, while others contain records from various Protestant churches, the Church of England, and other denominations. A separate collection contains Antigonish Catholic diocese records from the Nova Scotia province (1823–1905). The church records may contain information on births, confirmations, marriages, deaths, and burials.

Miscellaneous Records

If you're lucky, you may also find an ancestor listed in various estate files, wills, headstones, notarial records, and court records for Canada digitized on FamilySearch.org. A Canadian headstones collection contains more than one million searchable records, and a collection of Royal Canadian Mounted Police obituary card indexes and notices (1876–2007) holds more than nine thousand record images. Here's a summary of the other records you can find for various provinces:

- **British Columbia:** estate files (1859–1949), wills (1861–1981), and vital-events notices published in the *Victoria Times* (1901–1939)
- **Manitoba:** probate records (1871–1930)
- **Nova Scotia:** the notes of Thomas Brenton Smith from Queens County (1700–1950), which are genealogical notes about roughly seventeen hundred families extracted from local newspapers and other sources
- **Ontario:** an index and record images from Toronto Trust cemeteries (1826–1989)
- **Quebec:** notarial records (1800–1920) and guardianships (1639–1930)

- **Saskatchewan:** provincial records that include homesteads, voter lists, biographies, teacher registries, township registers, and military records (1879–1987); district court records (1891–1954); and probate estate files (1887–1931)

MEXICO

You'll discover a treasure trove of (mostly unindexed) Mexican records on FamilySearch.org, especially vital records from both civil registrations and Catholic Church records. In addition, there's a searchable national collection of nearly thirteen million 1930 census records and a browsable collection of a million miscellaneous record images from the state of San Luis Potosí (1570–1882), covering various notary, census, passport, land, and other records. See the whole list of collections for Mexico at **<www.familysearch.org/search/collection/location/1927078>**.

The largest collections include searchable nationwide baptisms (1560–1950) and marriages (1570–1950), Hidalgo Catholic Church records (1546–1971), and Distrito Federal (Mexico City) civil registration records (1832–2005) and Catholic Church records (1514–1970). Here are more record highlights for Mexico.

Church Records

Church records typically include baptism, marriage, and death records; you may also find confirmation records, parish censuses, and pre-marriage investigations. Because the Roman Catholic Church began keeping records of parishioners in the 1500s, church records may be some of the earliest records you come across. A mixture of searchable and unindexed collections is available for the following areas in Mexico:

- Aguascalientes (1620–1962)
- Baja California (1750–1984)
- Campeche (1638–1944)
- Chihuahua (1632–1958)
- Coahuila (1627–1978)
- Colima (1707–1969)
- *Distrito Federal*/Mexico City (1514–1970)
- Durango (1604–1985)

POWER-USER TIP

Try the IGI

Whether or not your family came from a country with dedicated collections on FamilySearch.org, remember to search for your ancestors in the International Genealogical Index (IGI) **<www.familysearch.org/search/collection/igi>**. Why? This resource indexes vital records from countries worldwide. The records come from user-submitted data and transcribed church records from the early 1500s to 1885. Just be sure to check for the original record or other sources to confirm the accuracy of the data you find before adding facts to your family tree. Learn more about the IGI in chapter 4.

- Guanajuato (1519–1984)
- Guerrero (1576–1979)
- Jalisco (1590–1979)
- Michoacán (1555–1996)
- Morelos (1598–1994)
- México (1567–1970)
- Nayarit (1596–1967)
- Nuevo León (1667–1981)
- Oaxaca (1559–1988)
- Puebla (1545–1977)
- Querétaro (1590–1970)
- San Luis Potosí (1586–1977)
- Sinaloa (1671–1968)
- Sonora (1657–1994)
- Tabasco (1803–1970)
- Tamaulipas (1703–1964)
- Tlaxcala (1576–1994)
- Veracruz (1590–1978)
- Yucatán (1543–1977)
- Zacatecas (1605–1980)

Civil Registrations

Civil registration of births, marriages, and deaths were first required in Mexico in 1859; however, some areas did not comply until about 1867. David A. Fryxell writes in the May/June 2015 *Family Tree Magazine*:

> [Mexican] civil registration records are packed with genealogical information. Birth records (*nacimientos*) usually contain the name of the child, gender, date and place of birth, and parents' names. Marriage records (*matrimonios*) typically include the names of the bride and groom; date and place of the marriage; the groom's and bride's ages, occupations, civil status, origins, nationalities, residences, and parents' names; and witnesses' names, ages, civil status, occupation, residence, and relationship to couple … Death records (*defunciones*) may give the name, age and gender of the deceased; place of birth; occupation and residence; date, time, place and cause of death; burial information; and informant's name and relationship to the deceased.

Many of the civil registration records for Mexico on FamilySearch.org have been added or updated since 2010. A mixture of searchable and unindexed civil registration collections is available for the following locations in Mexico:

- Aguascalientes (1859–1961)
- Baja California (1860–2004)
- Campeche (1860–1926)
- Chiapas (1861–1990)
- Chihuahua (1861–1997)
- Coahuila (1861–1998)
- Colima (1860–1997)
- *Distrito Federal*/Mexico City (1832–2005)
- Durango (1861–1995)
- Guanajuato (1862–1930)
- Guerrero (1860–1996)
- Hidalgo (1861–1967)
- Jalisco (1857–2000)
- Michoacán (1859–1940)
- Morelos (1861–1920)
- México (1861–1941)
- Nayarit (1868–2001)
- Nuevo León (1859–1962)
- Oaxaca (1861–2002)
- Puebla (1861–1930)
- Querétaro (1864–2005)
- Quintana Roo (1866–1902)
- San Luis Potosí (1859–2000)
- Sonora (1861–1995)
- Tamaulipas (1800–2002)
- Tlaxcala (1867–1950)
- Veracruz (1821–1949)
- Yucatán (1860–2005)
- Zacatecas (1860–2000)

POWER-USER TIP

Worldwide Records Collections

Some collections on Family-Search.org contain records from multiple countries, such as the BillionGraves Index, the Find A Grave Index, and the IGI. In addition, three searchable vital-records collections cover multiple countries worldwide, including countries not covered by other record collections, such as Angola, Bangladesh, Iran, Israel, Madagascar, and Malaysia.

AFRICA

Records from Ghana, Liberia, South Africa, and Zimbabwe are available on FamilySearch. org. The majority of African records date back to the 1800s, but some go back as far as 1660. Here's an overview of the records available for each country.

Ghana

The main resource of interest to genealogists is the unindexed collection of Accra marriages from 1863 to 2003. There's also a searchable collection of the 1984 Ghana census.

Liberia

A small collection (only 917 records) covers 1843 census records for the town of Monrovia.

South Africa

The most robust African record collections on FamilySearch.org are for South Africa. These collections cover church records (1660–2011), estate files for various towns and dates, marriage records for select provinces (1845–1955), parish registers (1801–2004), death records (1895–1972), and a variety of probate, slave, immigration, civil registration, and church records from the Western Cape Archives (1792–1992). About half of the collections are searchable.

Zimbabwe

You'll find two death record collections: searchable death notices for 1904 to 1976 and browsable death registers from 1890 to 1977.

ASIA

Most of FamilySearch.org's Asian records won't turn up when you use the site's search form to locate ancestors, because few of them are indexed. You'll need to browse through the images to find your ancestors. Here's an overview of available records for Asian countries.

China

Browse a collection of genealogies (1239–2014) that has more than thirteen million record images, plus cemetery records covering 1820 to 1983.

India

Searchable collections for this country include births and baptisms (1786–1947), deaths and burials (1719–1948), and marriages (1792–1948). For all other collections, you must browse the record images to find your ancestors. Those collections cover Protestant Church records (1854–2012), Hindu Pilgrimage records (1194–2014), land ownership pedigrees from Moga (1887–1958), Catholic priesthood records for the archdiocese of Goa (1724–1996), and more recent marriage records from select areas (1958–2013).

Indonesia

Record collections from this country—primarily naturalizations and court records—are relatively recent: Most date back only to the twentieth century. The naturalizations cover the years 1927 through 2013, and the court records cover 1925 to 2013. None of the Indonesia collections are currently searchable, but you can browse the record images.

Japan

The only searchable collection for Japan comprises passenger lists from 1893 to 1941. Browsable collections include census records (1661–1875), village records (709–1949), and genealogies (1700–1900). Village records may encompass censuses, financial records, tax records, and land records. The genealogies come from a collection at the National Archives of Japan in Tokyo, and some detail pedigrees back to medieval times.

Korea

You can browse a collection of Korean genealogies from 1500 to 2012, as well as a collection of civil-service examination records of officials and employees from South Korea (1392–1910). The exams allowed the employees and officials to qualify for promotions.

Philippines

Explore millions of searchable and browsable records: Searchable collections include births and baptisms (1642–1994), deaths and burials (1726–1957), marriages (1723–1957), Catholic parish registers for select archdioceses (1615–1982), and miscellaneous civil registrations (1888–1984). Unindexed collections include more civil registrations and church records dating back to the 1700s, as well as court records (1838–1936).

Sri Lanka

FamilySearch.org has a collection of Dutch Reformed Church records from the country's Colombo District (1667–1990). The records include baptisms, marriages, deaths, memberships, and other events. The records are unindexed, so you'll need to browse through the nearly thirty-four thousand record images.

AUSTRALIA AND NEW ZEALAND

FamilySearch.org's Australia and New Zealand collections include vital records, cemetery records, censuses, and probate records. Here are a few of the highlights.

Australia

The majority of the collections for Australia are searchable. These include nationwide births and baptisms (1792–1981), deaths and burials (1816–1980), and marriages (1810–1980). There's a browsable collection of cemetery inscriptions (1802–2005).

Location–specific records include a New South Wales census fragment (1841), a New South Wales index to bounty immigrants (1828–1842), Queensland cemetery records (1820–1900), New South Wales cemetery inscriptions (1800–1960), Maryborough public records (1847–1989), Tasmania civil registrations (1803–1933) and immigration office correspondence (1920–1943), a Victoria index to probate registers (1841–1989), and a New South Wales collection with miscellaneous cemetery, military, and church record transcriptions (1816–1982).

New Zealand

The largest New Zealand collection contains more than seven million searchable records from passenger lists (1839–1998). Other searchable collections include probate records (1843–1998), gravestones from twenty-four cemeteries in Central Otago (1861–2009), and an index to people associated with Albertland, an area north of Auckland (1862–1962).

SOUTH AMERICA

The majority of genealogical records for South American countries available on FamilySearch. org cover records from the Catholic Church, censuses, and civil registrations. Immigration, cemetery, and military records are also available for a few countries. The earliest records date back to the mid-1500s. About half of the collections are indexed and searchable, but the remaining collections must be browsed, image by image, to find your ancestors. Here's an overview of the South American records on FamilySearch.org.

Argentina

You won't be crying for Argentina when researching ancestors who lived in this country. The largest searchable collections of Argentine records contain national censuses (1869 and 1895) and baptisms (1645–1930). Additional vital-records collections exist for marriages (1722–1911). An 1855 census of the Capital Federal also is searchable. Collections of church records, including baptisms, confirmations, marriages, and deaths, cover the areas of Buenos Aires (1635–1981), the Capital Federal (1737–1977), Catamarca (1724–1971), Córdoba (1557–1974), Corrientes (1734–1977), Chaco (1882–1955), Chubut (1884–1974), Entre Ríos (1764–1983), Jujuy (1662–1975), La Pampa (1882–1976), La Rioja (1714–1970), Mendoza (1665–1975), Misiones (1874–1975), Neuquén (1883–1977), Río Negro (1880–1977), Salta (1634–1972), San Juan (1655–1975), Santa Cruz (1886–1964), Santa Fe (1634–1975), Santiago del Estero (1581–1961), Tierra del Fuego (1894–1950), and Tucumán (1727–1955).

Bolivia

You can search more than three million records of Bolivian baptisms (1560–1938), marriages (1630–1940), deaths (1750–1920), and various Catholic Church records (1566–1996).

Brazil

Several key searchable collections contain baptisms (1688–1935), marriages (1730–1955), deaths (1750–1890), and immigration cards from Rio de Janeiro (1900–1965). The other collections cover primarily Catholic Church records, civil registrations, and immigration records.

Collections of church records are available for Bahia, Ceará, Maranhão, Minas Gerais, Paraná, Pará, Paraíba, Pernambuco, Rio Grande do Norte, Rio Grande do Sul, Rio de Janeiro, Santa Catarina, Sergipe, and São Paulo. Date ranges vary by location, but typically begin in the 1600s and may contain records up to the present day. Immigration records include passenger lists from Bahia (1855–1964) and immigration cards and passenger lists from São Paulo starting in the 1880s to early 1980s.

In addition, there are some São Paulo burial records (1858–1977) and cemetery records from municipal cemeteries in Belo Horizonte (1897–2012). Civil registrations are available for six locations—Paraná, Paraíba, Pernambuco, Piauí, Rio de Janeiro, and Santa Catarina—and date coverage is typically from the mid-1800s to the present day.

POWER-USER TIP

Language of Brazil

Did you know the official language of Brazil is Portuguese, not Spanish? To become familiar with Portuguese genealogy terms used in official documents, see the Portuguese Genealogical Word List at <www.familysearch.org/learn/wiki/en/Portuguese_Genealogical_Word_List>.

Chile

If you have Chilean roots, FamilySearch.org gives you access to more than four million searchable records that cover baptisms (1585–1932), marriages (1579–1930), deaths (1700–1920), cemetery records (1821–2013), and civil registrations (1885–1903).

Colombia

Searchable Colombian collections include baptisms (1630–1950), marriages (1750–1960), deaths (1770–1930), Catholic Church records (1600–2012), and military records (1809–1958). An unindexed collection contains miscellaneous records from the Valle del Cauca (1549–1955), which may include censuses, wills and related records, and voter identification cards.

Ecuador

Collections of Ecuadoran baptisms (1680–1930), marriages (1680–1930), deaths (1800–1920), and Catholic Church records (1565–2011) are all searchable on FamilySearch.org.

Paraguay

You can search Paraguayan baptisms (1800–1930) and marriages (1800–1900) on Family-Search.org. Browse-only collections contain Catholic Church records (1754–1981), cemetery records for Asunción (1842–2011), and miscellaneous records (1509–1977), which may include information on wills, property, and employment.

Peru

The majority of Peruvian collections are searchable, but a few are available to browse only. Civil registrations cover the areas of Amazonas, Arequipa, Cajamarca, Callao, Cusco, Huánuco, Junín, La Libertad, Lambayeque, Lima, Puno, and Áncash. The date coverage for most of the civil registration records begins in the mid-to-late 1800s and extends to the 1990s or early 2000s. A municipal census collection encompasses enumerations from 1831, 1860, and 1866, with most records pertaining to Lima. A nationwide collection of Catholic Church records (1603–1902) is searchable, as well as nationwide collections of baptisms (1556–1930), marriages (1600–1940), and deaths (1750–1930).

Uruguay

Uruguay baptisms (1750–1900), marriages (1840–1900), and civil registrations (1879–1930) are all searchable on FamilySearch.org.

Venezuela

You can search collections of Venezuelan Catholic Church records (1577–1995) and civil registrations (1873–2003) on FamilySearch.org. In addition, you'll find two archdiocese-specific Catholic Church records collections: one for the Archdiocese of Mérida (1654–2013) and one for the Archdiocese of Valencia (1760, 1905–2013).

THE CARIBBEAN AND CENTRAL AMERICA

FamilySearch.org has more than seventy collections of records from the Caribbean and Central America. Most of these records cover vital statistics from civil registrations and church records.

The Caribbean

When researching Caribbean ancestors, start with the three FamilySearch.org searchable collections that cover multiple countries, including ones that don't have separate location-specific collections (such as Aruba). These regional collections include births and baptisms (1590–1928), marriages (1591–1905), and deaths and burials (1790–1906). Country-specific collections also cover vital records from civil registrations and church records. Some date as far back as 1590, but most date from the 1700s or 1800s. To see details on date coverage for the islands your ancestors are from, use the Historical Records collections list <www.familysearch.org/search/collection/list> and under the Place heading, click on Caribbean and Central America. Filter the list of collections further by selecting the specific country or island name. There are location-specific collections for the Bahamas, Barbados, the Dominican Republic, Grenada, Haiti, and Jamaica.

US Caribbean Islands

Two US territories—the U.S. Virgin Islands and Puerto Rico—are covered in records in the Caribbean and Central America collections. A collection for the U.S. Virgin Islands covers church records from 1765 to 2010. The Puerto Rico collections and contain Catholic Church records (1645–1969), civil registrations (1805–2001), and records of foreign residents during the time the country belonged to Spain (1815–1845).

Central America

FamilySearch.org has records for Costa Rica, El Salvador, Guatemala, Honduras, Nicaragua, and Panama. A Central American colonial records collection covers 1607 to 1902 and comprises primarily census records from El Salvador, Guatemala, Honduras, Nicaragua, and even Mexico. This collection is not searchable, so you'll need to browse through the record images to find your ancestors. Here are a few highlights of country-specific collections for Central America.

COSTA RICA

Searchable collections contain baptisms (1700–1915), marriages (1750–1920), deaths (1787–1900), civil registrations (1860–1975), and Catholic Church records (1595–1992).

EL SALVADOR

You can search El Salvador baptisms (1750–1940), marriages (1810–1930), and civil registrations (1704–1977). A collection of Catholic Church records (1655–1977) is available for browsing.

GUATEMALA

Baptisms (1730–1917), marriages (1750–1930), and deaths (1760–1880) are searchable. The remaining (unindexed) records are a variety of civil registration and church records from areas throughout Guatemala. In addition, there's one searchable 1877 census collection for Ciudad de Guatemala.

NICARAGUA

Research your family in searchable civil registrations from 1809 to 2013 and in browsable Catholic Church records from the Diocese of Managua.

PANAMA

Similar to other Central American countries, Panama has searchable baptisms (1750–1938), marriages (1800–1950), and deaths (1840–1930). There's also a browsable collection of Catholic Church records (1707–1973).

PACIFIC ISLANDS

FamilySearch.org has records for Guam (a US territory), Micronesia, and Samoa. For Guam, you can browse a variety of land, obituary, and census records from 1712 to 2000. Civil registration (1948–2009), court records (1951–2010), and land records (1971–2007) are available for the Pohnpei area of Micronesia (civil registrations are searchable). Samoan records include searchable baptisms (1863–1940, some from American Samoa) and burials (1895–1970).

GLOBAL RECORDS SEARCH STRATEGIES

Often, the biggest barrier to research in international records is understanding the language used in the records, the local record-keeping practices, and other cultural norms. For example, in certain cultures, women kept their maiden names after marriage. In addition, some countries' censuses list only heads of household.

For successful research in global genealogical records, start by first learning more about the genealogical records available for the country you're researching. Use the FamilySearch Wiki or heritage articles and toolkits at **<www.familytreemagazine.com/heritage>** to get started. Then employ the following strategies to search and browse records and hopefully pinpoint a record (or more) for your ancestors.

Know Naming Patterns

Naming patterns, including for surnames, varied by culture. For example, Spanish naming patterns used in Mexico commonly added a suffix (*–az, –ez, –iz, –oz,* or *–uz*) to the parent's name, so Hernandez would mean son of Hernando. Spanish surnames in Mexico also often used a preposition to connect the mother's name with the father's surname, such as De La Cruz. In addition, women in Mexico usually kept their maiden names when they married, so Maria López who married Juán Rodríguez, might become Maria López de Rodríguez. This information is vital when searching for records, since your ancestors could appear under a variety of different surnames. Search the FamilySearch Wiki by country name to find background about specific countries' naming patterns.

Learn the Language

Genealogical records were usually created in the local or national language. To be able to understand records as you search and find them, you'll need to know basics about the native tongue. For example, different alphabets may mean different alphabetization than you expect. Knowing key genealogical terms in the language of the records can help you scan through record images for important information. These four resources are valuable for deciphering non-English records:

- FamilySearch Genealogical Word Lists **<www.familysearch.org/learn/wiki/en/Category:Word_List>**
- *Genealogist's Instant Translation: At-a-Glance Glossaries for 22 Languages* **<www.shopfamilytree.com/genealogists-instant-translation-guide-at-a-glance-glossaries>**
- *Following the Paper Trail: A Multilingual Translation Guide* by Jonathan D. Shea and William F. Hoffman (Avotaynu)
- Google Translate **<translate.google.com>**

Use Ethnic Spellings

Keep in mind that foreign records use native spellings of names and locations, not the Americanized versions you may be familiar with. Use <www.behindthename.com> to learn various spellings of names. Consult maps and gazetteers to find place-name spellings.

Use Wildcards

As with any search, try wildcards if you have trouble finding records for your ancestors. An asterisk replaces multiple characters, and a question mark replaces a single character.

POWER-USER TIP

Remember Microfilm

Only a fraction of the world's records have been digitized, so if you don't see a collection for your ancestors' country, be sure to check the Family-Search Catalog for microfilmed records. If you find a relevant film, you can order a copy to view at a FamilySearch Center. See chapter 10 for instructions.

Remember to Browse Records

Many international records on FamilySearch.org are not yet indexed and searchable. That means you could miss out on some great ancestral discoveries if you don't check browse-only collections. To find a list of relevant collections to browse, visit **<www.familysearch. org/search/collection/list>**, and under the Place heading, select the region where your ancestors lived, then choose a country.

Keep in mind that you probably won't need to browse through every record. Note how the record images are organized and utilize any indexes within the record images to help you guess which image number corresponds to your ancestor's record. If records are in alphabetical order, you can skip around by guessing a starting number, then moving forward or back by five to ten images until you pinpoint their surname among other records.

KEYS TO SUCCESS

★ Know what records are available for the country you're researching. Check the country's listing in the FamilySearch Wiki, then browse the Historical Records collection list **<www. familysearch.org/search/collection/list>** to find records specific to that country.

★ Learn helpful genealogical terms in the language(s) of your ancestors' records. The genealogical word lists in the FamilySearch Wiki **<www.familysearch.org/learn/wiki/en/ Category:Word_List>** are a great place to start.

★ Browse unindexed collections to ensure you don't miss any potential ancestral finds. Many global records on FamilySearch.org aren't yet searchable. Be sure to utilize worldwide collections and the International Genealogical Index, too.

More Historical Records

In addition to the genealogical mainstays we've already talked about—vital, census, military, and immigration records—FamilySearch.org has an eclectic mix of records you won't find anywhere else. These exclusive collections come from churches, cemeteries, counties, townships, court records, and elsewhere. In this chapter, we'll explore some of the unique miscellaneous records on FamilySearch.org, along with strategies for searching for those records.

HOW TO FIND MORE HISTORICAL RECORDS

To see what additional records are on FamilySearch.org, go to **<www.familysearch.org/search/collection/list>**. In the menu on the left, go to the Collections heading and click Other or Miscellaneous. If you want to filter your search by location, select the location (such as the United States of America) under the Place heading.

Both the Other and Miscellaneous categories contain a variety of records, sometimes even on the same topics, such as county records or court records, so you'll want to look in both categories to be sure you don't miss a collection from your ancestor's location. The collections you find might have just a few hundred record images, or tens of thousands.

These tend to be unindexed collections that require browsing image by image, although a few searchable collections do exist.

In addition, collection titles in these sections can be vague. For example, there's one called Mississippi, State Archives, Various Records, 1820–1951. What are the "various records" this collection covers? To find out, you have to click on the collection title and read the brief description. In this case, the collection includes "narratives from former slaves, land records from the Office of the Secretary of State, lists of military veterans, military grave registrations, and naturalization records."

If the brief description doesn't give you the detail you want, click the Learn More link under the description. This will take you to a FamilySearch Wiki page that typically has a more thorough description of the collection with sample images of the record content, lists of the types of information included in the collection's records, and even some basic tips for searching or browsing the collection.

Now let's review examples of record types you might find in the Miscellaneous and Other sections of FamilySearch.org.

ADDITIONAL U.S. RECORDS

The Miscellaneous and Other categories of Historical Records on FamilySearch.org are great places to look when you can't find other collections containing certain records for your ancestors. Why? These categories are a sort of grab bag of sources and may surprise you by containing vital records, military records, or other records relevant to your ancestor's location and lifetime.

County and Municipal Records

Counties and townships or cities kept local records of their citizens. Not all states have collections of these records on FamilySearch.org, but if you do find records for the state, county, and/or town where your ancestors lived, you might just encounter genealogy gold. Many local court offices or archives contain vital records and land transactions. So if you haven't found a certain record for your ancestors in other collections, county and municipal collections may provide the research breakthrough you need.

The types of records contained in county record collections vary with each location and its record-keeping laws and practices. For example, two Montana counties have searchable collections of county records: Chouteau (1876–2011) and Pondera (1910–2012). The Chouteau County collection contains records from several repositories, including voter registers, school district records, church and cemetery records, newspaper clippings with vital-records information, probate records, naturalizations, deeds, and school census records. Meanwhile, the Pondera County collection has record images of birth, death, and land records from the county clerk's office, as well as some probate and naturalization records. See the variety in the collections labeled "county" records?

Municipality records are yet another hodgepodge. For example, the Ohio, Licking County, Hartford Township Records, 1881–1962 collection has burial records and cemetery deeds from Croton, Ohio. Other townships or cities FamilySearch.org adds in the future could have different records available.

Under the Other and Miscellaneous categories on FamilySearch.org, you'll find county records from the following states:

- **California:** San Francisco County (1824–1997)
- **Georgia:** Elbert County (1790–2002) and Fulton County (1827–1955)
- **Idaho:** five counties with records dating back to the 1880s
- **Montana:** four counties dating from as far back as the 1870s
- **North Carolina:** various counties in one collection covering 1883 to 1970
- **Ohio:** four counties dating back to the late 1860s
- **Oregon:** eleven counties, with records beginning in about the mid-1800s
- **South Carolina:** Darlington County (1798–1928)
- **Tennessee:** White County (1809–1975)
- **Texas:** four counties with records generally dating back to the mid-1800s
- **Utah:** two counties with records dating back to the mid-1800s
- **Washington:** a single collection covering various counties from 1803 to 2010
- **Wisconsin:** records for three counties dating back as far as 1825

Church Records

While you can typically find church records within FamilySearch.org's Birth, Marriage, and Death collections, check the Other or Miscellaneous categories, too. Collections categorized here may be denomination-specific, such as New Jersey, Calvary United Methodist Church Records, 1821–2003. Church records could contain baptism, marriage, or funeral information, but they also may include church membership lists or minutes of church meetings.

Cemetery Records

FamilySearch.org has various cemetery records, which may contain cemetery tombstone transcriptions, index cards of burial log books, or even a list of veterans buried in the cemetery. Transcriptions usually contain the name of the cemetery as well as information on the deceased such as his or her name, lot number, birth and death dates, and birth and death places. They may also contain the names of parents, spouses, or other relatives, as well as other important facts. Burial records at cemeteries may include the name of the person who owned the burial lot.

FamilySearch.org's miscellaneous collections include various cemetery records for a few locations in California, Indiana, and Ohio.

Freedmen's Bureau Records

The Freedmen's Bureau (officially named the Bureau of Refugees, Freedmen, and Abandoned Lands) kept records from 1865 to 1872. The bureau's purpose was to supervise relief and reconstruction efforts after the Civil War. Records created by the bureau are especially important for those researching African-American ancestors, as they can include names, ages, occupations, residences, former masters or plantations, relatives' names, and military service information. The records may include school records, hospital registers, censuses, marriage registers, land records, and even bank records. Field offices for the Freedmen's Bureau operated in sixteen states, primarily in the South. According to the FamilySearch Wiki, the field office records are typically the most useful records for genealogists.

The Other and Miscellaneous record categories contain Freedmen's Bureau Field Office collections from Alabama, Kentucky, North Carolina, and Texas, as well as a collection of Freedmen's Branch Records, which has records from multiple states' field offices.

Other Records

Collections in the Other and Miscellaneous categories aren't always small—some contain tens of thousands or millions of records. You may want to check out these particular collections with widespread coverage.

UNITED STATES PUBLIC RECORDS, 1970–2009

This searchable index **<www.familysearch.org/search/collection/2199956>** contains a whopping 875 million records. The data were compiled from a variety of publicly available records, such as telephone directories and property tax assessments. A person's name, address, birth date, and/or phone number may be included.

UNITED STATES NATIONAL REGISTER OF SCIENTIFIC AND TECHNICAL PERSONNEL FILES, 1954–1970

The 125 thousand records in this index <www.familysearch.org/search/collection/2126719> come from questionnaires sent to biology, chemistry, economics, geology, mathematics, psychology, meteorology, physics, anthropology, political science, and sociology professionals. Records may include the person's age, year of birth, marriage date and place, state of residence, and spouse's and parents' names.

UNITED STATES DECEASED PHYSICIAN FILE (AMA), 1864–1968

If your ancestor was a doctor, this browsable collection of record images <www.familysearch.org/search/collection/2061540> could prove useful in your research. The collection from the American Medical Association has more than seven hundred thousand images with biographical information on physicians. Records may list the physician's death date, the location where he practiced, school attended, cause of death, and professional affiliations. Although this collection is not searchable, when you click on the Browse Through 707,724 Images link, you go to an alphabetical surname index of the doctors included in the collection to help narrow your search.

UNITED STATES CONFEDERATE OFFICERS CARD INDEX, 1861–1865

Interestingly, this collection <www.familysearch.org/search/collection/2145147> does not appear in the Historical Records list of Military collections (at least it didn't as of this writing). If your ancestor fought for the Confederacy during the Civil War and you can't find him in other collections, this is a great place to look. The collection has more than two hundred thousand record images of Confederate officers. The images may contain information on the officer's company, dates of service, rank, and death information (if he was killed in action).

UTAH, PIONEERS AND PROMINENT MEN OF UTAH, 1847–1868

This searchable collection <www.familysearch.org/search/collection/2202712> contains nearly six thousand records that could be particularly useful if you're researching ancestors with LDS roots or who were early pioneers in Utah. The collection contains biographical sketches and photos of these prominent figures.

POWER-USER TIP

Better Image Browsing

I prefer to use Google Chrome when researching online, but I sometimes have trouble viewing record images on FamilySearch.org with that browser. If this happens to you, copy the URL from the browser's web address bar and paste it into a different browser (such as Internet Explorer or Firefox).

ADDITIONAL GLOBAL RECORDS

Millions of searchable and browsable international records reside in the Other and Miscellaneous categories on FamilySearch.org. The bulk of these collections for countries worldwide contain voting records, city records, naturalizations and passports, church records, and newspaper clippings. A few contain estate records, school records, employment records, obituaries, land records, civil registrations, and court records.

What's in Miscellaneous Collections?

The Other and Miscellaneous records on FamilySearch.org cover a wide range of records. Here's a brief overview of the types of records you may encounter.

Court Records

Courts documented their activities pretty thoroughly. If court records are among the collections you find, you may come across various record books, such as bond books, court minute books, court order books, and judgment books. You also might come across individual documents including affidavits made under oath by a witness or the subject of a court case, bastardy bonds in which fathers of illegitimate children agreed to pay support, complaints, depositions, injunctions, indictments, bail bonds, and confessions.

Coroner Inquests

Some county, court, or miscellaneous city records collections may contain records of coroner inquests. If a death was unusual or tragic, the coroner may have been contacted to examine the deceased and write a report. The reports could contain specifics about the cause of death, physical description of the deceased, funeral home information, and more.

Land Records

Various land records are among miscellaneous records on FamilySearch.org. You might encounter land grants or patents (original purchase of land from state or federal government), deeds (documents that transfer ownership from one person to another), or tract books (books that record multiple land transactions in a particular region).

Passports

Passports were documents that allowed a person to travel from one country to another, just like passports today. Each country had its own process for issuing passports (but some

To filter the Historical Records collections list **<www.familysearch.org/search/collection/list>** to show you relevant records for your ancestor search, first click on the appropriate region, then under the Place heading, select a country. Under the Collections heading, select Other or Miscellaneous. Let's take a closer look at the types of additional global records you might discover.

may not have bothered with them). If you do find a passport, it may contain the person's name, birth date and place, citizenship status, and arrival information. Information on a spouse or children may be included as well. Some countries may have records of actual passports, passport applications, or registers with a compilation of passport applications or other information.

Penitentiary Records

If you have any black sheep ancestors in your family line, you might end up tracing them to a prison or penitentiary. If you come across a collection with penitentiary records, the records may include the prisoner's name, age, physical description, habits, relatives' names, parents' place of birth, incarceration and release dates, and information on the courts where the person was charged.

School Censuses

School districts typically took a census each year to help the state determine the amount of funds to give each public school district. These records may contain children's and parents' names, the children's ages and/or birth dates, residence locations, races, and notations of any disabilities.

Voter Registers

In her book *Courthouse Research for Family Historians*, Christine Rose notes that "registered voters and election returns were intermingled among court minutes and sometimes in court orders." Because of this, voter information could show up among miscellaneous court records. It's also possible to find voters listed in specific registers or electoral rolls. Voting records could include information such as the person's name, date of birth, place of residence (perhaps even a street address), occupation, marital status, land ownership, and even naturalization status.

Voting Records

These records include electoral registers and voting lists and may include information on ancestors who were eligible to vote and/or who registered to vote. The records may contain an ancestor's name, date of registration, and residence (some may even have a street address). FamilySearch.org has electoral registers for places in England and Wales.

City Records

A plethora of city and municipal records are available for international cities, and these collection titles are often labeled as "miscellaneous city records" or "municipal records." The contents of the collections vary by city and/or country but may include city directories, civil registrations, church records, naturalizations, censuses (also called citizen rolls), passports, military records, voting records, hospital records, orphan records, tax records, land records, emigration records, cemetery inscriptions, funeral sermons, school records, guardianship and adoption records, employment or apprenticeship records, probate records, wills, family genealogical records, and business licenses, among others.

If you find a collection of these "miscellaneous" records for the time and place your ancestors lived in, it's definitely worth a look. The majority of the miscellaneous city records on FamilySearch.org cover areas in Germany, Austria, and Spain.

Naturalizations and Passports

Records of an ancestor's citizenship or passport for international travel may appear in FamilySearch.org's Other and Miscellaneous collections. For example, there's a collection of passports from Cantabria, Spain, from 1785 to 1863, with nearly twenty-five thousand record images and two collections of passport registers and application files from Portugal dating as far back as 1800. In addition, you'll find naturalization records from Indonesia (1960–2011). Some collections of "miscellaneous city records" may contain naturalizations or passports as well.

Church Records

Church records aren't limited to births/baptisms, marriages, and deaths. As such, you'll find some interesting collections in the Other and Miscellaneous categories—for example, a collection of priesthood records from India's Roman Catholic Archdiocese of Goa (1724–1996) with more than 630 thousand record images, and a collection of priest application files from Braga, Portugal (1596–1911). In addition, a collection of Catholic Church records from the district of Aveiro in Portugal covers baptism, marriage, and death records from 1550 to 1911.

Newspaper Clippings

It's not always easy to access foreign newspapers, but FamilySearch.org has collections of various newspaper clippings for countries worldwide. For example, a news clipping collection from Australia covers miscellaneous events (primarily births, marriages, and deaths).

SEARCH STRATEGIES

Many of the miscellaneous records on FamilySearch.org have not been indexed, so be prepared to spend time browsing record images. If you do find a searchable collection to peruse, consider yourself lucky.

Browse Efficiently

Although browsing collections can take some time, it's not a hopeless exercise. Plus, in most collections, options are available to help you narrow your search and focus your efforts and time. Before you begin browsing a collection, take a few minutes to check the record coverage dates and locations. Usually this information is in the collection's brief description and/or title, but you can sometimes find additional details if you click on the Learn More link from the collection landing page. Checking in advance will save you lots of time if you discover records don't cover the time period or town where your ancestor lived.

To browse efficiently, make use of any indexes provided or alphabetizing of records. Indexes may give a record image (in the original record group, not the online collection) where the record is located. This can help you make an educated guess about the online record image number. Alphabetized collections of record images also give you an advantage for guessing the right record image number. So instead of clicking image by image through a batch of three thousand record images, you can skip a few. For example, if a list is alphabetized and your ancestor's surname starts with the letter T, you can bet he won't be toward the front of the pack. Instead, he'll probably appear further back in the collection, say, around twenty-five hundred instead of 10. Once you get close, you can click the forward and back arrows to page through the records image by image, or you can enter a number in the Image box to skip forward two (or five, or ten) at a time.

Keep Life Events in Mind

If you come across a searchable collection, that's awesome. When you enter your search criteria, though, remember to include date ranges or locations for life events that would have been listed in the record you're searching.

More Free Websites for Key Genealogy Records

FamilySearch.org isn't the only website with free genealogy records and transcriptions. Be sure to check out these websites, too.

- **AfriGeneas <www.afrigeneas.com>**: This is an excellent site dedicated to African-American genealogy. It includes great information for beginners as well as databases for death records, library records, marriage records, and surnames.

- **BillionGraves <www.billiongraves.com>**: Search millions of geo-tagged headstone photos and transcriptions. You can contribute, too, by taking photos with your smartphone when you visit cemeteries.

- **Cyndi's List <www.cyndislist.com>**: If you're a genealogy beginner, this is a great place to start your research. The free site has tons of links to helpful websites (free and paid).

- **Ellis Island <www.libertyellisfoundation.org>**: Search for ancestors who arrived in New York from 1892 to 1957 in this database of more than fifty-one million passenger records. If your ancestors arrived in the 1800s before Ellis Island was opened, check the Castle Garden site **<www.castlegarden.org>**.

- **Find A Grave <www.findagrave.com>**: Search more than 120 million volunteer-contributed tombstone records and images on this site.

- **JewishGen <www.jewishgen.org>**: Researching Jewish roots? Tap into databases of Holocaust records, Yizkor books, given names, and more.

- **Mocavo <www.mocavo.com>**: Searching individual databases on this site is free. You can find a wide range of records including school yearbooks, church and local histories, newspapers, military records, court records, immigration and naturalization records, city and professional directories, and parish registers.

- **USGenWeb Project <usgenweb.org>**: Volunteers run USGenWeb sites for each US state. Depending on the state, you may find transcriptions of census records, vital records, obituaries, military records, and other genealogy records.

- **U.S. Bureau of Land Management General Land Office Records <www.glorecords.blm.gov>**: Look for land patents and deeds for your ancestors who became landowners in public land states.

- **WorldGenWeb Project <www.worldgenweb.org>**: This is the global counterpart to USGenWeb. You can find volunteer-transcribed genealogy records for the Caribbean, Asia, Africa, Central Europe, Eastern Europe, the United Kingdom and Ireland, the Mediterranean, Oceania, and South America.

For example, if you're searching a collection of miscellaneous records, such as the Manchester, England, miscellaneous records from 1700 to 1916 **<www.familysearch.org/ search/collection/2075052>**, read the FamilySearch Wiki entry with details about the collection first. You can access this by clicking on the Learn More link on the collection landing page. The Wiki entry usually will provide information on record content. In this case, the Manchester collection has apprenticeship, school admissions, workhouse, and prison registers. Each record type has different content, but most include at least a date of birth. Most do not include a death date.

So when you enter search criteria, you can narrow your results by adding a birth date range, but not a death date. Why? FamilySearch.org's system returns results that match all your criteria. If you enter both a birth and death date, but a record doesn't include both details, you may not get any results. Entering just the birth date range will help you find the most broad and relevant results.

Use Wildcards and Alternate Spellings

As always, start your searches broad, then narrow results. If your broad searches don't return results, keep searching. You can use wildcards (asterisk for more than one character; question mark for a single character) to help you find alternate spellings or misspellings of your ancestor's name. Try searching for nicknames your ancestors went by. Additionally, search for your ancestor's original ethnic name or spelling. For example, my great-grandfather Klaas went by Nick in the United States. When I search for him, I do searches on both first names. The website BehindtheName.com **<www.behindthename. com>** can help you find ethnic spellings of your ancestors' names.

KEYS TO SUCCESS

★ Review the list of Other and Miscellaneous collections **<familysearch.org/search/ collection/list>** by selecting the Other or Miscellaneous option under the Collections filter heading.

★ Get to know the collection's content—specifically record dates and locations—before you search it by viewing the collection description or the Learn More link on the collection landing page. Some collections may even have vital records or other important records that you can't find elsewhere online.

★ Be patient when browsing (and you will need to browse records, since many "miscellaneous" records are not searchable yet). Browsing records is time well spent when you locate a record with your ancestor's name in it. Check back regularly to see if any collections have been added for a particular location where your ancestors lived.

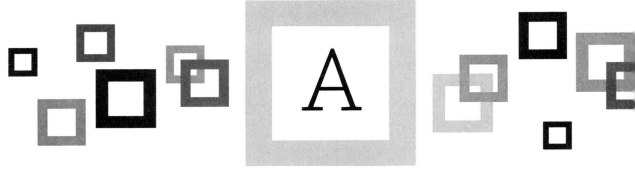

The FamilySearch Wiki

There's always something more to learn about the ancestors you're researching, as well as the places and time periods in which they lived. On FamilySearch.org, the Family History Research Wiki <**www.familysearch.org/learn/wiki**> provides an excellent resource to learn that information. With more than eighty-one thousand articles, the Wiki provides research advice and tips to help you move your research forward.

If you're new to genealogy, you can see basic how-to articles. If you want to know more about records available in a certain country or US state, you can delve deeper into the specifics of what's available and where, as well as what different types of information those records may contain.

HOW TO SEARCH THE WIKI

The Wiki allows you to search its articles by place or topic or to browse by country. If you have a specific topic in mind, such as California vital records, you can enter that into the search box on the Wiki's main page (image A). As you enter your search terms, the FamilySearch.org system suggests standardized queries you can choose if they match what you want to search, or you can continue typing your full search term and then hit Enter to search. The Wiki search box (unlike other search forms on FamilySearch.org),

lets you enter Boolean search operators to help focus your search. This means you can enter the words *and* or *or* between two terms, use quotation marks around words to find an exact phrase, or use a minus sign to exclude certain terms from the results.

A search results page (image **B**) will appear with a list of relevant articles. In addition, at the top of the search results page there are several link headings. Here's what you'll see when you click each heading in your search results.

- **Content Pages** shows the list of pages that have information on the topic you searched for.
- **Multimedia** shows a list of only images and PDF files or image lists related to the topic searched for.
- **Help and Project Pages** displays pages for volunteers to reference about certain Wiki projects they are helping with.
- **Everything** displays the broadest amount of search results.
- **Namespace** takes you to a new search results screen with even more result-filtering options.

From the search results list, click the link to the information to view the Wiki article.

Browsing the Wiki

If you're not sure exactly what you're searching for, you can browse the Wiki. To do so, click on the Browse by Country link (under the Getting Started box). This will take you to a list of countries. Click on the country of interest to you, such as Brazil, and you'll get a landing page for Brazil Genealogy information (image **C**). The main part of the page

B

Search results for "California Vital Records"

| California Vital Records | Search |

Content pages Multimedia Help and Project pages Everything Namespace Results 1 – 20 of 674 for **California Vi**

There is a page named "California Vital Records" on this wiki.

California Vital Records
...logy|**California**]] [[Image:Gotoarrow.png]] [[**California_Vital_Records**|Vital Records]]] '''Introduction to
Vital Records'''
27 KB (3,534 words) – 03:59, 6 February 2015

California Vital Records Index (FamilySearch Historical Records)
...rical **Records**|**California** Births and Christenings (FamilySearch Historical **Records**)]]
 ...lySearch
Historical **Records**|**California** Marriages (FamilySearch Historical **Records**)]]
482 B (52 words) – 15:54, 13 March 2012

California Archives and Libraries
...ited States|United States]] [[Image:Gotoarrow.png]] [[**California** Genealogy|**California**]]
[[Image:Gotoarrow.png]]] '''Archives and Libraries'''

 ...rovide services to help genealogists

C

Brazil Genealogy

Edit This Page

South America ▷ **Brazil**

Search Learning & How-To's

| Subject, Place or Keyword | Q |

BROWSE

by country   by topic

News and Events

Topics
- Archives and Libraries
- Biography
- Cemeteries
- Census
- Church Directories
- Church History
- Brazil Church Records
- Brazil Civil Registration
- Court Records
- Emigration and Immigration
- Encyclopedias and Dictionaries
- Gazetteers
- Genealogy
- Heraldry
- Historical Geography

Contents [hide]
1 Getting started with Brazil research
2 Jurisdictions, States
3 Research Tools
4 Websites
5 Featured Content
6 Did you know?
6.1 Help with the Brazil Wiki pages
6.2 Other Languages

–Boa viagem.jpg

Getting started with Brazil research

Do you want to access the FamilySearch Wiki in Portuguese? Click here! &

Welcome to the Brazil page of the research wiki! FamilySearch Wiki is a community website dedicated to helping people throughout the world learn how to find their ancestors.Through the Brazil page you will learn how to find, use, and analyze records for Brazil of genealogical value. The content on this page provides helps and tips for beginner, intermediate, and expert researchers alike. Here you will find helpful research tools and research guidance to aid you in your search for your ancestors. The Brazil page is a work in progress, your contributions and feedback are essential!

New to the Research Wiki?

In the FamilySearch Research Wiki, you can learn how to do genealogical research or share your knowledge with others.

Learn More

Getting Started

Wiki Home
Wiki Tools
About the Wiki
Resources for Individual Help
Browse by Country

D

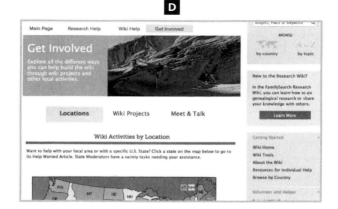

Main Page   Research Help   Wiki Help   Get Involved

Subject, Place or Keyword

BROWSE

by country   by topic

Get Involved
Explore all the different ways you can help build the wiki through wiki projects and other local activities.

| Locations | Wiki Projects | Meet & Talk |

Wiki Activities by Location

Want to help with your local area or with a specific U.S. State? Click a state on the map below to go to its Help Wanted Article. State Moderators have a variety tasks needing your assistance.

WA   MT   ND   MN   VT NH

New to the Research Wiki?

In the FamilySearch Research Wiki, you can learn how to do genealogical research or share your knowledge with others.

Learn More

Getting Started

Wiki Home
Wiki Tools
About the Wiki
Resources for Individual Help
Browse by Country

Volunteer and Helper

provides an overview about research in that location, including information on how jurisdictions in that location are organized so you'll know where to look for records. A list of
genealogy topics is located on the left. You can click on any of those topics to learn more
about those records and how to find them, such as Land and Property or Civil Registration. If a topic link is shown in red, it means there's no content available for that topic. If
the topic link is blue, it means there's a Wiki entry for that topic.

In addition to country pages, the Wiki also has pages on genealogy for each US state.
You can access a list of links to these pages from the United States Genealogy Wiki page
at **<www.familysearch.org/learn/wiki/en/United_States_Genealogy>**.

You also can browse the Wiki by topic, but it's a little trickier to find that option
since it's not on the main Wiki page. The browse-by-topic option is located in the upper
right corner of country genealogy pages. Or take a shortcut and go directly to **<www.
familysearch.org/learn/wiki/en/Category:Articles_by_topic>**. This list of links, however,
isn't quite as useful as the links to topics on the country genealogy pages.

HOW TO CONTRIBUTE TO THE WIKI

Just as you can create and contribute to Family Trees on FamilySearch.org, registered
users can volunteer to help with Wiki projects to add information and pages. Go to **<www.
familysearch.org/learn/wiki/en/Get_Involved>** to see an overview about volunteering
(image **D**). This page shows a US map and world map where you can find out which projects are going on in your local area or in a state or country of interest to you.

Under the Wiki Projects link (which takes you to **<www.familysearch.org/learn/wiki/
en/Get_Involved_in_Wiki_Projects>**), you can drill down to learn more about the projects
and find out ways you can help, such as editing an article, updating an article, expanding a
"stub," suggesting an article, creating a new article, being a moderator, and more. There's
also a list of all projects by topic, along with a column for experience level, so you know if
a project is for someone with beginner, intermediate, or other skill level. Under the Meet
and Talk link, you can see information about meetings for Wiki contributors where you
can learn about best practices and get tips for contributing to the Wiki.

FamilySearch Indexing Projects

H undreds of thousands of worldwide volunteers each year are the reason why so many records are indexed and available to search on FamilySearch.org. Anyone can volunteer to help index records. With nearly four hundred projects going on at a time, there's always a need for more volunteers. To get an overview about indexing on FamilySearch.org, visit **<www.familysearch.org/indexing>** (image **A**).

If you're unsure whether you want to do indexing, click the Test Drive icon on the main indexing page to get a glimpse of how indexing works. To get started as an indexer, you'll actually have to download a special indexing program at **<www.familysearch.org/indexing/get-started-indexer>**, register for a FamilySearch account (if you don't already have one), and then read the Indexing Basics resources to learn more about what you'll be expected to do.

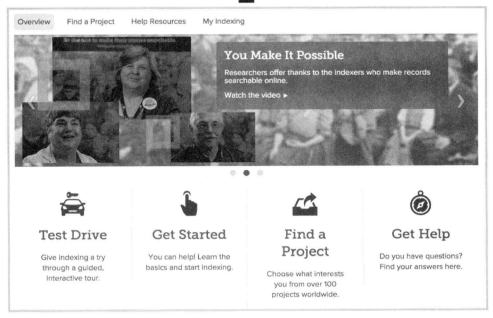

If you decide to become an indexer, you can then choose a project that interests you. Go to the Find an Indexing Project page **<www.familysearch.org/indexing/projects>**. You can then view projects in a list or by country. Each listing provides project details about the types of records being indexed, as well as additional information on basic guidelines and instructions for the particular indexing project.

There are many resources available on FamilySearch.org if you need help while indexing. For example, within the Indexing section is a nifty page of Handwriting Helps **<www.familysearch.org/indexing/help/handwriting>**, with tips to help decipher the handwriting in genealogy records (useful whether or not you're an indexer). The Handwriting Helps page has information for nine different languages.

And while it's important to try to be as accurate as possible as you transcribe and index records, know that batches of records are typically indexed by two indexers, and then they go through an arbitration process to reconcile any differences.

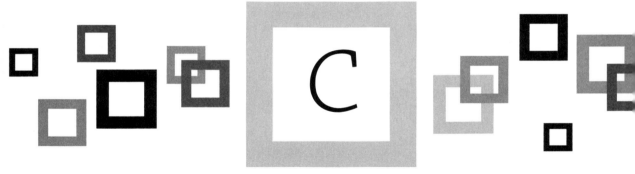

Research Worksheets

A s you uncover new ancestors and family tree details on FamilySearch.org, you'll want to track those family facts so you can make sense of what you've found—and so you don't waste time duplicating your own efforts. To supplement the worksheets and checklists within the individual chapters of this book, this section provides several forms to help you organize and review your work.

- **FamilySearch.org Research Tracking Worksheet:** Keep a record of the searches you conduct on FamilySearch.org.
- **Five-Generation Ancestor Chart:** Use this classic pedigree chart to record names and vital stats, and view your family tree at a glance.
- **Family Group Sheet:** Record information about one nuclear family—that is, two parents, their children, and their own parents.
- **Records Checklist:** Refer to this extensive rundown of genealogical records to ensure you've covered all your research bases.

You can download letter-size versions of these forms from **<www.familytreemagazine. com/free-forms>**.

FAMILYSEARCH.ORG RESEARCH TRACKING WORKSHEET

Ancestor(s) Searched For	Title (or URL) of Collection Searched or Browsed	Date Searched or Browsed	Search Terms Used (or Record Images Paged Through)	Notes About the Search or Findings	Saved Record to Source Box or Family Tree?

FIVE-GENERATION ANCESTOR CHART

Chart # _____
1 on this chart = _____ on chart # _____
see chart #

16

17
birth date and place
marriage date and place
death date and place

18

19
birth date and place
death date and place

20

21
birth date and place
marriage date and place
death date and place

22

23
birth date and place
death date and place

24

25
birth date and place
marriage date and place
death date and place

26

27
birth date and place
death date and place

28

29
birth date and place
marriage date and place
death date and place

30

31
birth date and place
death date and place

8
birth date and place
marriage date and place
death date and place

9

10
birth date and place
marriage date and place
death date and place

11
birth date and place
death date and place

12
birth date and place
marriage date and place
death date and place

13

14
birth date and place
marriage date and place
death date and place

15
birth date and place
death date and place

4
birth date and place
marriage date and place
death date and place

5
birth date and place
death date and place

6
birth date and place
marriage date and place
death date and place

7
birth date and place
death date and place

2
birth date and place
marriage date and place
death date and place

3
birth date and place
death date and place

1
birth date and place
marriage date and place
death date and place
spouse

FAMILY GROUP SHEET OF THE

_____ **FAMILY**

	Source #		Source #
Full Name of Husband		Birth Date and Place	
His Father		Marriage Date and Place	
His Mother with Maiden Name		Death Date and Place Burial	
Full Name of Wife			
Her Father		Birth Date and Place	
Her Mother with Maiden Name		Death Date and Place Burial	
Other Spouses		Marriage Date and Place	

Children of This Marriage	Birth Date and Place	Death Date, Place, and Burial	Marriage Date, Place, and Spouse

RECORDS CHECKLIST

Business and Employment Records

- ☐ apprentice and indenture records
- ☐ doctors' and midwives' journals
- ☐ insurance records
- ☐ merchants' account books
- ☐ professional licenses
- ☐ railroad, mining, and factory records
- ☐ records of professional organizations and associations

Cemetery and Funeral Home Records

- ☐ burial records
- ☐ grave-relocation records
- ☐ tombstone inscriptions

Censuses

- ☐ agriculture schedules (1850 to 1880)
- ☐ American Indian (special censuses)
- ☐ Civil War veterans schedules (1890)
- ☐ defective, dependent, and delinquent schedules (1880)
- ☐ federal population schedules (1790 to 1930)
- ☐ manufacturing/industry schedules (1810, 1820, 1850 to 1880)
- ☐ mortality schedules (1850 to 1880)
- ☐ school censuses
- ☐ slave schedules (1850, 1860)
- ☐ social statistics schedules (1850 to 1880)
- ☐ state and local censuses

Church Records

- ☐ baptism and christening records
- ☐ confirmation records
- ☐ congregational histories
- ☐ meeting minutes
- ☐ membership, admission, and removal records
- ☐ ministers' journals

Court Records

- ☐ adoption records
- ☐ bastardy cases
- ☐ civil records
- ☐ coroners' files
- ☐ criminal records
- ☐ custody papers
- ☐ estate inventories
- ☐ guardianship papers
- ☐ insanity/commitment orders
- ☐ licenses and permits
- ☐ marriage bonds, licenses, and certificates
- ☐ military discharges
- ☐ minute books
- ☐ name changes
- ☐ naturalizations
- ☐ property foreclosures
- ☐ voter registrations
- ☐ wills
- ☐ wolf-scalp bounties

Directories

- ☐ biographical
- ☐ city
- ☐ professional/occupational
- ☐ telephone

Home Sources

- ☐ baptism and confirmation certificates
- ☐ birth certificates and baby books
- ☐ checkbooks and bank statements
- ☐ death records and prayer cards
- ☐ diaries and journals
- ☐ family Bibles
- ☐ funeral/memorial cards
- ☐ heirlooms and artifacts
- ☐ letters and postcards
- ☐ marriage certificates and wedding albums

- ☐ medical records
- ☐ photographs
- ☐ recipe books
- ☐ report cards, yearbooks, and scrapbooks
- ☐ wills

Immigration Records
- ☐ alien registration cards
- ☐ citizenship papers
- ☐ passenger lists
- ☐ passports

Institutional Records
- ☐ almshouse
- ☐ hospital
- ☐ orphanage
- ☐ police
- ☐ prison
- ☐ school
- ☐ work-farm

Land and Property Records
- ☐ deeds
- ☐ grants and patents
- ☐ homestead records
- ☐ mortgages and leases
- ☐ plat maps
- ☐ surveys
- ☐ tax rolls
- ☐ warrants

Military Records
- ☐ Colonial wars
- ☐ Revolutionary War and frontier conflicts (War of 1812, Indian wars, and Mexican War)
- ☐ Civil War
- ☐ Spanish-American War
- ☐ World War I
- ☐ World War II
- ☐ Korean War

- ☐ Vietnam War
- ☐ draft records
- ☐ pension applications
- ☐ World War II records of relocations and internment camps for Japanese-Americans, German-Americans, and Italian-Americans

Newspapers
- ☐ birth announcements
- ☐ classified advertisements
- ☐ engagement, marriage, and anniversary announcements
- ☐ ethnic newspapers
- ☐ family reunion announcements
- ☐ gossip and advice columns
- ☐ legal notices
- ☐ local news
- ☐ obituaries
- ☐ runaway notices (slaves, indentured servants, wives)
- ☐ unclaimed-mail notices

Published Sources
- ☐ compiled genealogies
- ☐ genealogical periodicals
- ☐ local and county histories
- ☐ record abstracts and transcriptions

Vital Records
- ☐ birth
- ☐ death
- ☐ divorce/annulment
- ☐ marriage

INDEX

CREDITS

Thank you to FamilySearch and its Intellectual Property Office for giving permission to use screenshots of its website in this book. The following screenshots are published in this book with permission from FamilySearch and are © by Intellectual Reserve, Inc.

In addition, the Granite Mountain Vault photo (page 15) is published courtesy of The Church of Jesus Christ of Latter-day Saints.

ACKNOWLEDGEMENTS

When I started my career as a magazine editor and later became a freelance writer and editor, I never imagined I would one day write a book. I am truly blessed to have this opportunity, and there are many people I want to thank.

Thank you, Allison Dolan, for believing in me from the first day you hired me many years ago at *Family Tree Magazine* and for continuing to believe in me when you accepted my book proposal. I have learned so much from you over the years, and I have enjoyed working on this book. Thanks for editing this book and making me look good.

Thank you to the rest of the team at F+W, particularly *Family Tree Magazine* editors Diane Haddad and Tyler Moss. Diane and Tyler, thanks for the opportunities you've given me over the years to contribute to the magazine.

Thank you to the team at FamilySearch.org, especially Paul Nauta, Richard Kehrer, Susan Milliner, Lynn Turner, Ron Tanner, and Ron Saunders, for your cooperation and insights throughout the process of writing this book. I appreciate all the time and effort you spent to answer my questions and help ensure the accuracy and quality of information provided in the book, in spite of an ever-evolving website.

Thank you to Rick Crume, Sunny Jane Morton, and Clare Brown for allowing me to include your stories of success on FamilySearch.org.

And last but not least, thank you to my husband, Mike, who served as my sounding board and listened to me many nights talk about my progress on the book and exciting new things I learned during the process. Thanks also for your patience with me as I worked hard to meet my deadlines and for supporting me in all my career choices and opportunities.

ABOUT THE AUTHOR

Dana McCullough is a freelance writer and editor who frequently writes and edits content on genealogy and higher education topics. A former editor at *Family Tree Magazine*, Dana has written or edited content for twenty magazines and has contributed to the editing of eight books. Her writing has been published in *Family Tree Magazine, The Artist's Magazine, Family Circle, Brain Child, Better Homes and Gardens' Simply Creative Weddings, My College Guide, The Iowan, Wisconsin Woman*, and *Scrapbooks etc.*, among other national and regional consumer magazines.

Dana has a bachelor's degree in journalism from Iowa State University. When not working, Dana enjoys traveling and exploring new places, trying (and tweaking) new recipes, playing the piano, and of course, researching her family history—especially on FamilySearch.org.

You can find Dana at **<www.danamccullough.com>** or on Twitter @DanasCreative.

DEDICATION

To my late grandfather Harold Schmidt and grandmother Henrietta Gemignani Spanos. I am so grateful to have had you in my life and to have learned your stories of courage and bravery. You are my inspiration.

ISBN: 978-1-4403-4328-5

Other Family Tree Books are available from your local bookstore and online suppliers.
For more genealogy resources, visit **<shopfamilytree.com>**.

19 18 17 16 15   5 4 3 2 1

DISTRIBUTED IN CANADA BY FRASER DIRECT
100 Armstrong Avenue
Georgetown, Ontario, Canada L7G 5S4
Tel: (905) 877-4411

DISTRIBUTED IN THE U.K. AND EUROPE BY
F&W Media International, LTD
Brunel House, Forde Close,
Newton Abbot, TQ12 4PU, UK
Tel: (+44) 1626 323200,
Fax (+44) 1626 323319
E-mail: enquiries@fwmedia.com

DISTRIBUTED IN AUSTRALIA BY CAPRICORN LINK
P.O. Box 704, Windsor, NSW 2756 Australia
Tel: (02) 4577-3555

a content + ecommerce company

PUBLISHER AND COMMUNITY LEADER: Allison Dolan
EDITOR: Andrew Koch
DESIGNER: Julie Barnett
PRODUCTION COORDINATOR: Debbie Thomas

10/28/2015

929.1028 MCCULLOUGH
McCullough, Dana,
Unofficial guide to FamilySearch.org :
R2003201700 KIRKWD

Atlanta-Fulton Public Library